JAPANESE ACCOUNTING

JAPANESE ACCOUNTING

A Historical Approach

Kyojiro Someya

CLARENDON PRESS · OXFORD

This book has been printed digitally and produced in a standard specification in order to ensure its continuing availability

OXFORD
UNIVERSITY PRESS

Great Clarendon Street, Oxford OX2 6DP

Oxford University Press is a department of the University of Oxford.
It furthers the University's objective of excellence in research, scholarship,
and education by publishing worldwide in

Oxford New York

Auckland Cape Town Dar es Salaam Hong Kong Karachi
Kuala Lumpur Madrid Melbourne Mexico City Nairobi
New Delhi Shanghai Taipei Toronto
With offices in
Argentina Austria Brazil Chile Czech Republic France Greece
Guatemala Hungary Italy Japan South Korea Poland Portugal
Singapore Switzerland Thailand Turkey Ukraine Vietnam

Oxford is a registered trade mark of Oxford University Press
in the UK and in certain other countries

Published in the United States
by Oxford University Press Inc., New York

Reprinted 2011

ISBN 978-0-19-829045-2

Printed and bound in Great Britain by CPI Antony Rowe,
Chippenham and Eastbourne

PREFACE

In Japan several academic research organizations are concerned with accounting and related fields, including the Japan Accounting Association (JAA), the Japan Cost Accounting Association, the Japan Auditing Association, the Japanese Association for International Accounting Studies, and the Japanese Association of Accounting History. These organizations consist mainly of university faculty members responsible for teaching accounting, together with practising professional accountants and business financial executives. Founded in 1933, JAA is the largest of these organizations, with over 1,600 members as of 1994. Accounting research is very popular in Japan. Papers on the subject appear in the yearly reports of these organizations, as well as in the journals of various universities and publishers, and a large number of books on accounting are published every year. Unfortunately, almost all writing in the field is in Japanese, and hence inaccessible to readers of other countries.

The essays in the present volume trace the progress and investigations of one Japanese scholar of accounting over a forty-year period following the Second World War. The purpose of the book is to help people of other nations better to understand at least one direction taken by accounting research in Japan. It does this not by simply explaining the path taken in the modernization of Japan's accounting system, but rather by clearly defining the issues I have been concerned with. These illustrate the kind of problems the Japanese economy has had to overcome during the past fifty years, and the various responses to them made by Japanese scholars of accounting.

The Japanese economy suffered a devastating blow during the Second World War, followed by a high level of economic growth. Now, fifty years after the war, many people would like to understand how such a near miraculous recovery and spectacular growth were possible. Many factors were involved, to be sure, but it is generally recognized that accounting research and its practical application contributed greatly to the revitalization and expansion of industry. The control of rampant post-war inflation, the fostering of the stock exchange—crucial for the accumulation of industrial capital—and the rationalization of business management to enable increased productivity: no problem escaped the notice of accounting researchers.

The present book traces the footsteps of a single accounting researcher, but in doing so it illuminates, I believe, the focus of the majority of other accounting scholars participating in Japan's economic development in the last fifty years.

There are a number of individuals and organizations I wish to thank in connection with the preparation of this book, without whose help it could not have been completed.

The articles collected here span some forty years of my accounting research. One could not ask for a better environment than Waseda University, which has played a particularly important role in my research. I am also grateful to the editors of the journals in which the articles first appeared for permission to reprint them in this volume. They have been lightly edited to conform to the style of Oxford University Press books.

I should also like to express my warmest gratitude to Professor Paul Garner, Dean Emeritus of the University of Alabama, for his enthusiastic and unfailing support of international accounting research, and for his gracious assistance and advice during the preparation of manuscripts for publication abroad. My appreciation is also extended to Mr Dave Telke for translating what was not always the clearest of prose from Japanese into English.

Last, but by no means least, I should like to thank my wife for her patience in allowing me to devote myself to the preparation of this book.

K.S.

Tokyo
October 1994

CONTENTS

PART III. CASH FLOW ACCOUNTING

FIGURES

TABLES

1

The Course of my Accounting Research

It wasn't something I planned at the outset, but looking back over the course my accounting research has followed, I find that—almost inevitably—my research is deeply rooted in the economic development of Japan over the past half century, beginning with economic reconstruction in the post-war period and continuing through the surge in economic internationalization beginning in the latter half of the 1960s.

The close of the Second World War found the Japanese economy in ruins. Factories and other means of production had been virtually wiped out, the powerful pre-war industrial conglomerates known as Zaibatsu were dissolved, along with all their capital holdings, and inflation was rampant. It was these stark economic realities which gave direction to my early investigations, and in effect determined my three major research themes. My research in cash flow accounting theory originated as an attempt to deal with inflation, while my work on financial statement analysis stemmed from the urgent need of businesses to increase productivity. My investigations into financial accounting theories were closely bound to the fostering of the securities exchange as a means of amassing needed capital.

The mid 1960s brought a rapid increase in internationalization, not only of economics but of scholarship in general, and my attention was turned towards the areas of international accounting and accounting history.

CASH FLOW ACCOUNTING

Japan suffered severe inflation in the period following the Second World War. Because of the dire shortage of nearly everything there was never any worry about selling off goods acquired or items produced. One merely had to have merchandise or raw materials in stock for them to go up in value, and at the time such goods and products were sold, large profits were realized on the income statement. However, when the time came to restock merchandise or raw materials used in manufacture, they too had gone up in price, and one was forced to pay more than before for these items. On top of this there was always the need for new machinery and expanded facilities, and so forth, and coming up with the necessary funds was by no means an easy matter. Then there were wages to pay, operating expenses to be met, and taxes, all of which had to come from receipts on the sale of goods and products. For this reason businesses were always hard pressed for funds. In spite of the large profits recorded on the income statement, there never seemed to be any ready cash. Why was this so? This was the major problem facing me and the other accounting researchers of this period. In fact the problem was so grave that the suggestion was made that someone was employing some sort of bookkeeping trick and making off with the funds.

Whenever there is a shortage of cash, and wages and operating expenses cannot be met, business operations come to a halt. If loans and other debts cannot be repaid, a business is forced into bankruptcy. Scheduling income and outlay of cash and preventing such mishaps is an extremely important part of business operations. Yet according to modern accounting theory, with its shift in emphasis from cash basis to accrual basis accounting, cash flow accounting as such is viewed as a practical problem for business managers, not as a theoretical problem for research.

The idea that because there are profits there must exist a corresponding equivalent in cash is a common misconception among persons not acquainted with business accounting. To continue showing profits but still be plagued by a lack of cash means that a company is in fact operating below cost. This is a point I endeavoured to explain in a simple manner. But something also had to be done to correct the structural defects in the sort of business accounting which engendered such misconceptions. In this way then I came upon the realm of business accounting known as cash flow accounting, and suggested a system whereby a cash flow statement would be included together with the income statement and balance sheet as part of the financial report.

This then is the setting in which my theory of cash flow accounting and idea for a three-pillared financial statement were developed.

FINANCIAL STATEMENT ANALYSIS

At the close of the Second World War Japanese industry had been virtually wiped out and the economy was at a standstill. Nevertheless, amidst the ruins of war, the task of reconstruction was begun immediately. The first step was for the various industries to restore their productive capacity, and to this end it was expected that accounting would provide vital operating and managerial guidance. It was at this time that I began my research into methods for analysing the income statement and balance sheet that would indicate the operating performance and financial position of a business.

Banks analyse the income statement, balance sheet, and other financial statements for the purpose of evaluating the reliability of a company before making a loan, and investors do the same in selecting profitable investments. But more important is the role such analysis plays in guiding business operations. Applying everything from cost analysis to break-even analysis, I sought a way to improve operating performance. I read American and British accounting literature and attempted to introduce it to persons involved in business management. I expanded my area of research to include profit planning and financial planning.

I had the opportunity to study in the United States during 1957–8. Under an agreement between Waseda University and the University of Michigan I went to Ann Arbor, where I studied with Professor W. A. Paton, who was looked upon almost as a god by students of accounting in Japan. I also had a chance to exchange opinions and views with a number of other accounting professors, whom I knew previously only through the literature. I visited the Ford Motor plant and other companies and observed at first hand the techniques of business management employed by companies in the United States. This was at a time when travel abroad was not widely permitted by the Japanese government, and to receive such an opportunity was a valuable gift indeed.

After returning to Japan I broadened the scope of my research in financial statement analysis to include added value and differential cost analysis, and then turned my attention to the various problems involved in business planning employing the results of such analysis. The fruits of my research at this time included such ideas as capital budgeting, capital cost, and returns on capital investment. One research method I frequently made use of was to solicit questions and problems from persons involved in actual business management, and then to try to work out solutions.

FINANCIAL ACCOUNTING CONCEPTS

As to the fundamental concepts of financial accounting, my research on surplus was done in 1949 at the time of publication of 'Financial Accounting Standards for Business Enterprises' by the Economic Stabilization Board's Investigating Committee on Business Accounting Standards, and I delved into asset concepts in connection with my work on cash flow accounting. Such work, I believe, led the field in financial accounting research in Japan at this time. In addition I also widened my research to include the auditing of financial statements.

The fostering of the Securities Exchange as a place for amassing business capital played a vital role in Japan's economic reconstruction after the war. It is important that potential investors make investments only after thorough investigation of the company. Disclosure of financial information pertaining to a business is essential in allowing investors to decide what course of action to take. Great things were expected from accounting during this period. However, being the sort of person who tends to dispose of the easier problems first, I postponed my research into the area of financial accounting concepts until I had completed my investigations into cash flow accounting and financial statement analysis.

In the latter half of the 1960s rapid advances took place in economic internationalization. Not only was there an increase in imports and exports, but more and more businesses were inviting foreign investment, and more and more investors were seeking to invest abroad. There was also an increase in the number of multinational businesses. At this time I began turning my research efforts towards financial accounting from an international point of view. I called this area of research 'international accounting', and my investigations into this area began at a rather early date. This was facilitated by my affiliation with the Waseda University School of Commerce, which has always placed great emphasis on the international exchange of scholarship.

INTERNATIONAL ACCOUNTING

As business activities expand across national boundaries and more and more capital investments are made on an international scale, the chances for people to come in contact with financial information pertaining to foreign companies become more frequent. For this reason my investigation into international accounting consisted not only in studying the accounting literature of other countries but also in collecting annual financial reports from companies around the world, which I then analysed, compared, and classified. As a result I recognized three styles of financial reporting, which I labelled American-Canadian, British-Australian, and German-French.

In 1971 America left the gold standard, and Japan adopted a floating exchange rate. The resulting fluctuation in monetary units, which comprise the standard of measurement in accounting, created a host of new problems for Japanese scholars, who, since the close of the war, had experience in dealing only with a stable exchange rate. My response was to abandon the idea of using only the monetary unit of a single nation as the standard of measurement, and to adopt a system whereby companies having foreign branches or factories would allow the currencies of those nations to serve as standards of measurement as well. Financial statements would then be prepared combining accounting results based on the currencies of the various nations. I called this approach the foreign or multiple currency accounting standard.

The 1980s saw a great increase in international exchanges between accounting researchers, and a number of international conventions have been held, both in Japan and abroad. Many foreign researchers I met expressed an interest not only in the accounting system of Japan itself, but also in its historical development, and I felt an obligation to answer their enquiries. Moreover, having been elected to the Science Council of Japan in 1981, and having served as the president of the Japan Accounting Association in 1985, I had come into greater contact with scholars in other fields, and as a consequence had more reason to think about the nature of accounting science in comparison with other fields. Hence my research into the historical development of Japanese accounting. As part of my endeavours I compiled an index to articles on accounting appearing in technical journals during the Meiji (1868–1911), Taisho (1912–25), and Showa (1926–88) eras, and edited an anthology of essential writings in the field. At the same time I continued my investigation of the work of Luca Pacioli, said to be the author of the first text on the practice of bookkeeping.

Many scholars speak of Japanese accounting as having evolved from some ancient form into the structure in use today. To my mind, revolution plays every bit as important a role in the development of Japanese accounting as evolution. The first major revolution occurred when Western-style bookkeeping was adopted in the early days of Meiji, and the second major revolution came after the Second World War with the publication of 'Financial Accounting Standards For Business Enterprises'. If one traces the path of accounting research from the beginning of Meiji up to the present, one sees that even though all scholars use the common term 'accounting', the foundation upon which they build is not always the same. Consequently, what we today refer to as the field of accounting is in fact, in my opinion, not a single entity at all.

THE STEWARDSHIP ROLE OF ACCOUNTING

The older I grow, the more conscious I am of how little time is left for me to continue my research, and I prepare to bequeath the unsolved problems to scholars coming after me. After devoting some forty years to accounting research, I find myself once again coming round to the question of what exactly accounting means to me.

As I stated at the beginning, my accounting research is deeply rooted in the economic development of Japan over the past half century, and focuses most particularly, I believe, on the sort of accounting information that needs to be made known, whether in a society facing the perils of reconstruction, or in an industrial state entering the new age of internationalization. The significance of accounting, for me at any rate, lies in the information it presents to the user, information vital to the decision-making process.

The original, and common, meaning of accounting, however, is based on the principle of stewardship and the responsibilities this entails: someone is entrusted with someone else's money, and as part of his responsibility, he describes what amounts have been earned or paid out, and clearly states the balance.

In stock corporation businesses the responsibility of stewardship is towards the capital invested by the shareholders. Accounting functions to enable managers to report performance and financial position to shareholders, thereby fulfilling their obligation. The system for reporting such information is regulated by law. Under such a system shareholders are fully protected and cannot be held individually responsible for any liabilities or debts the company might incur. In a like manner, any interest creditors might have in the company may extend no further than the company's assets. In order to protect creditors it is stipulated that invested capital may not be paid back to shareholders as long as the company remains in operation, and that shareholder dividends may only be paid out of profits. Thus one of the major themes of stewardship-oriented stock corporation accounting is to compute the profit upon which shareholder dividends may be paid. Such a scheme has generally been accepted by accounting scholars up to now.

THE INFORMATION ROLE OF ACCOUNTING

At the same time, however, we see a recent trend towards expanding the definition of capital to include not only the original capital invested by shareholders but capital obtained from creditors and other sources. Even further, customers, clients, employees, the national government, and all other parties may share a profit/loss relationship with the company, consumers, the local populace, and even the environment itself. With such a broad definition given to the term 'capital', it is only natural that decision-making not be limited to the activities of investors or management. In this rapidly changing modern-day economic milieu we find even greater expectations placed on accounting to provide information vital to a whole range of decisions affecting society—indeed the entire planet—as a whole.

Although the system for disclosure of stewardship-related information is defined and regulated by law, the system for providing other relevant information has not yet reached that stage. The generally accepted method for supplying such information has been to append supplementary statements to the financial report. It is hard for me to imagine, however, that disclosure of information vital to the sort of economic decisions being made today can sufficiently be made in such a supplementary fashion.

Admittedly there exists an economic side and a legal side to the activities of society. While accounting research is obliged to pay due respect to the legal structure, I also believe, even more than before, that precedence must be given to economic realities over strictly legal formality. It is my dream that new laws and regulations will evolve, establishing a new financial reporting system that will enable accounting to fulfil its role as provider of vital economic information in the world today.

PART I.

JAPANESE ACCOUNTING HISTORY

2

Accounting 'Revolutions' in Japan

Accounting history is the study of the evolutionary process in accounting thought, practices, and institutions. The focal point of such study is the dynamic interaction between accounting and its environment. This consideration of the accounting history of Japan focuses on two significant events in the modern history of Japan that had revolutionary impacts on its accounting system.

The first of the two events, which took place in the latter half of the 1800s, involved the change from traditional diary-style bookkeeping methods to a modern system of accounting within a double-entry framework. The second revolutionary event, which occurred shortly after the Second World War, involved a virtually overnight change from Japan's traditional stewardship orientation to the investor orientation of financial reporting common in many parts of the world today. These two events are excellent examples of the fact that accounting cannot be understood in isolation, but that an analysis of accounting must include the economic, political, and diplomatic environments in which it is practised.

The function of accounting is, obviously, to provide information relevant to the decisions of managers, shareholders, creditors, and other parties interested in the process an enterprise uses to manage the capital of individuals or organizations. These parties cannot make relevant decisions without relevant information. Lack of relevant information on which decisions are based affects the development of the economy, which eventually causes the society to become incoherent. Economic development and accounting development go hand in hand, one stimulating and reinforcing the other. Such interaction was particularly strong with respect to the two revolutionary events discussed here.

Generally speaking, revolutions are discontinuities that have continuities in their undercurrent. Wells (1976) adopts the idea of revolution from Kuhn (1970) and identifies five steps in the process of moving from an old set of ideas to a new set: (1) the recognition of anomalies, (2) a period of insecurity, (3) the development of alternative sets of ideas, (4) the identification of schools of thought, and (5) the domination of the new practices or ideas. Wells elaborates on these points:

From *Accounting Historians Journal*, 16/1 (1989), 75–86.

> The first step is a precursor to the whole process; it initiates the period of crisis which follows. During that period, scientists become increasingly dissatisfied with the existing theoretical framework, and a search for alternatives begins. Therefore, the second and third steps are mutually interactive. As dissatisfaction grows, the search for alternatives gains impetus; as alternatives are discerned and discussed, the dissatisfaction is heightened. Schools of thought emerge, and one set of ideas gradually gains ascendency over the alternatives. (pp. 471–2)

This description may well hold true in describing accounting innovations as they took place in Europe and the United States, but in the case of modern Japan, changes in accounting thought and practice have not always occurred as evolutionary changes in response to changes in the internal environment. Since the latter half of the nineteenth century, Japan's economy, as well as its accounting methods, has been strongly influenced by powerful external forces, particularly from the United States and Europe. In this sense, Japan's two important accounting revolutions may best be characterized as imported innovations.

INTRODUCTION OF DOUBLE-ENTRY BOOKKEEPING

In any society and at any period in time, as wealth is obtained and economic activities are conducted, people need some accounting system to record what one has and how it is used. According to Nishikawa (1956) the earliest recorded mention of merchants' books dates to 1520. Ledgers dating from the early 1600s are among writing preserved today. Ogura (1978) reports that the comprehensive record of accounts kept by the Nakai family in 1745, the so-called 'Ledger of Good Fortune', although not explicitly employing a two-sided reckoning of debits and credits, did use a double-entry type of bookkeeping approach. Such an approach developed directly from the practices of merchants in Japan and shows no evidence of having been influenced by Western-style bookkeeping methods. This system existed until the middle of the 1800s, when the United States and the economic powers of Europe arrived at Japan's door in their search for raw material sources and markets for their products. At that time, Japan came under sudden and tremendous pressure to enter into trade agreements, and, as a result, found itself scurrying to borrow new industrial technology and economic institutions from the West. Western-style double-entry bookkeeping made its entry along with these other importations. Shimme (1937: 291) writes that the first use of the new Western-style bookkeeping was by the newly established Yokosuka Steel Plant at the very end of the Edo period in 1865.

Coming into power in 1868, the Meiji government put its entire energy into setting up political, economic, and social institutions based on American and European models. In the midst of such change, the transition from older bookkeeping methods to the Western-style approach was finally accomplished. Two important publications also helped to stimulate its eventual adoption.

In 1872, the year in which the National Bank Act was passed (with Japan's first stock-owned enterprise, the First National Bank, established the next year), the Ministry of Finance published *Bank Bookkeeping Methods*, which became the first work dealing with double-entry bookkeeping to appear in Japan. This work was a five-volume translation compiled from proposals by Alexander Allan Shand (1844–1930), a Scotsman who came to Japan at the invitation of the Ministry of Finance to teach bookkeeping methods for banks to the Japanese. In his introduction to *Bank Bookkeeping Methods* (1873), Yoshikawa, the compiler of this work, describes how this came about:

> From olden times there has existed no fixed method for keeping accounts in our country, each merchant keeping his own records as he saw fit. Because such books were haphazard and followed no established procedures, problems often arose and it was impossible to know what items were important and what items were not. The former Minister of Finance, Kaoru Inoue, was constantly concerned about this state of affairs while in office, and afterwards, at the time the National Bank was established, he said to me, 'This is the first bank to be established in our country. No one has any idea what methods to employ. If accounts are kept in such a haphazard fashion, then mistakes will be unavoidable and things will get out of control. I heard about an Englishman by the name of Shand, who is knowledgeable in the operation of banks. If this is true, then the best thing to do is have the Ministry invite him to help us set up our banks.' Thereupon I accepted his directive and requested Mr Shand to draw up a draft regarding bank account books and the formats to be used. Adding our own comments to places that were dealt with too simply and shaving down passages that were excessively wordy, we put them together, added an introduction, and succeeded in completing a statement regarding bookkeeping procedures and formats to be employed. (pp. 1–2)

The first time such bookkeeping methods were actually put to use was in December 1873, when the First National Bank closed its books for the first time and issued financial statements.

In most instances when established structures are replaced with something new, the new item is met with a certain amount of resistance, and the new process takes time to implement. In the case of double-entry accounting, however, it immediately received wholesale acceptance as part and parcel of the new banking system. It spread rapidly after its introduction.

The second important publication affecting the acceptance of the double-entry system was Fukuzawa's *Methods of Bookkeeping*. Part One appeared as two volumes in 1873. This work was, in fact, a translation of the American bookkeeping textbook by Bryant and Stratton. *Common School Bookkeeping* (1871). Part One of Fukuzawa's work contained the sections on single-entry methods. Part Two, dealing with double-entry bookkeeping methods, came out in 1874, again in two volumes. The publication of Part One of *Methods of Bookkeeping* predated *Bank Bookkeeping Methods* by six months, and for this reason *Methods of Bookkeeping* is often referred to as the first work in Japan dealing with the double-entry bookkeeping framework. Used as a textbook in elementary and junior high schools, this book played a vital role in the eventual acceptance of double-entry bookkeeping methods in Japan.

In this preface to *Methods of Bookkeeping*, in which he talks about his reasons for translating the original, Fukuzawa makes the following comment:

> In the bookkeeping methods of merchants I have seen or heard about, everything is in a state of confusion. An inventory of a single merchant's stores might take two months, and still not every item could be accounted for. This stands as proof that existing methods are no good, and yet I have yet to hear of anyone correcting the situation. Not only does this create inconveniences for the merchant himself, but for society as a whole. The present translation is only an introduction to Western bookkeeping methods, and although it will not change present methods and eliminate all inconveniences completely, still, familiarization with the bookkeeping fundamentals presented in Part One, followed by a deeper understanding to be obtained from Part Two, will surely eliminate some of the difficulties in public and private accounting throughout the land, to which this book, insignificant as it is, is better than nothing at all. (p. 2)

Bank Bookkeeping Methods and *Methods of Bookkeeping* were destined to remedy the deficiencies inherent in the bookkeeping practices followed in Japan at the time. After their publication, a rather long period of time passed before traditional bookkeeping methods were displaced altogether, but eventually merchants and businessmen gave up the old methods and adopted the Western double-entry approach. Truly, the introduction of double-entry bookkeeping stands as a major milestone in Japan's emergence as a modern capitalist nation.

INTRODUCTION OF INVESTOR-ORIENTED FINANCIAL REPORTING

Stock exchanges were opened in Tokyo and Osaka as early as 1878. In spite of this, however, the disclosure of investor-oriented financial information did not appear to be a matter of concern in Japan until the middle of the twentieth century. The reasons underlying this delay are as follows.

The Japanese Commercial Code was enacted in 1890, and the section dealing with companies went into effect in 1893. Undergoing a first amendment in 1899 and several subsequent revisions, this code remains in effect today. Even in its original form we can discover the primitive shape of those statutes pertaining to business accounting and other accounting matters currently in effect. The Commercial Code introduced into Japan a Continental style of financial reporting, whereby an 'inventory of assets' was prepared and submitted along with the balance sheet and income statement. The inventory of assets included liabilities as negative assets and itemized all movable and immovable properties, securities, and so on, with their assigned monetary values. The inventory's aim was to represent all assets belonging to the business, including liabilities, in a comprehensive manner. The function of the inventory of assets was not always clear because of its substantial overlap in content with the balance sheet. A commonly held view was that it was a prelude to the preparation of the balance sheet. There was also a view that regraded the inventory of assets as complementing the balance sheet by offering quantitative or interpretive details concerning assets and liabilities. Whatever the case, Japanese accounting thought at that time placed this inventory of assets at the central position among the various financial statements and placed greater emphasis on the balance sheet than on the income statement.

During the 1930s and early 1940s, standardization of the financial statements used to disseminate business financial information was urged. Such standardization was part of a government-sponsored programme of industrial rationalization aimed first at easing the depression, and later at unifying the military state in preparation for war. The Registered Public Accountant Act was passed in 1927, creating the job title of registered public accountant and signifying an attempt to improve the business accounting system. Nevertheless, the idea of the audit of financial statements performed by an independent, publicly certified professional was not fully developed because Japan's vital industries were the exclusive property of large, family-owned industrial conglomerates known as the Zaibatsu. Hence ideas such as the stock market being a place for industrial capital accumulation, or the function of accounting being to present financial information to investors, were totally irrelevant in Japan.

Littleton and Zimmerman comment in *Accounting Theory: Continuity and Change* (1962):

> Accounting actions for several generations gave evidence of a belief in the superior importance of the balance sheet. Interest was centered there because of a belief that this statement was at once a report on management's stewardship and a report on company solvency. American opinion in the last thirty years has tended to reverse this earlier emphasis, thus expressing the belief that the facts about company net earnings and the supporting detailed data of revenue and expense are of outstanding significance. Earning reports are considered to provide the key to the proper evaluation of management's effectiveness as well as a reliable clue (persistent earning power) to security values. (p. 258)

It would not be inaccurate to say that this evolutionary trend in America noted by Littleton and Zimmerman was all but absent from accounting thought, practices, and institutions in Japan until the mid-1940s. Not until

1945 and the close of the Second World War did the second great revolutionary change occur in Japanese accounting. This change was imposed at the direction of the Allied Command, which sought to build a democratic economy on the ruins of the dismembered Zaibatsu. In order to take away the controlling power of the Zaibatsu parent company over its various subsidiaries, all shares owned by the parent company and controlling families were forcibly turned over to the Holding Company Liquidating Committee, which sold the subsidiaries at current value to investors in the public sector. The purpose of dismembering Zaibatsu parent companies and turning over exclusively owned business shares to the public was to destroy, once and for all, the entire Zaibatsu empire, as well as to recruit investors from the public for the purpose of raising industrial capital.

The Securities and Exchange Act, patterned after the American system, was passed in 1947, amended the following year, and put into effect. In 1949 the stock exchange, which had been closed for many years, was re-opened. Amendments to the Commercial Code in 1948 and 1950 prohibited the instalment payment system for stocks and adopted instead a system of authorized shares that could be issued as the need arose. Likewise, non-par value shares were recognized. The results of such measures greatly affected the organizational and operational aspects of businesses.

Besides institutionalizing the disclosure of financial information directed towards the investor, the Securities and Exchange Act also stipulated that all business financial statements be audited as the primary tool for disseminating financial information. Thus, in one fell swoop, the idea of presenting accurate and useful information regarding current period earning power to the investor came to the foreground in Japanese accounting thought. In 1948 the Registered Public Accountants Act was replaced by the Certified Public Accountants Act. The first CPA examination was given in 1949. Also in that year, the Economic Stabilization Board's Investigation Committee on Business Accounting Systems published, as its interim report, 'Financial Accounting Standards for Business Enterprises', intended to serve as a standard in the preparation of financial statements. The preface to 'Accounting Standards' (ESB 1949) stated that '[such standards] represent a condensation of practices that are considered to be generally accepted as being fair and proper from among those developed in the practice of business accounting' (para. 2). Its content, however, reflected the newly imposed idea of depicting the earning power of a business by means of income in the current period, as well as the disclosure of such financial information as is useful to the investor in making investment decisions. 'Accounting Standards' thus assured that the new accounting revolution would find immediate and universal acceptance.

'Accounting Standards' continues to the present day with slight amendment. At the time of its drafting, Kurosawa, one of the members of the drafting committee, explained its nature as follows:

As for the financial statement standards presented here, in content they conform to the regulations of the Securities and Exchange Commission, and hence apply to financial statements intended primarily as financial reports to that commission. The concern of this investigatory committee did not end there, however. From a wider point of view, we recognized a need to consider those businesses not coming under the Securities and Exchange Act. Although the concrete features of such financial statements themselves will be prepared in accordance with these accounting standards, it is probable and necessary that different formats be prepared for different objectives in mind other than the Securities and Exchange Commission. In which event, it has been proposed as feasible for this committee in the future also to suggest revisions to, say, the Commercial Code or the tax laws. Be that as it may, it was necessary to distinguish between the ideals and realities of this question, or else these standards would never have assumed concrete shape. For this reason, then, our target was tentatively limited to matters coming under the Securities and Exchange Act. (1949: 32)

After four years of silence due to the war, the Japan Accounting Association held its Seventh Convention in May 1948. The round-table discussion on the theme 'Improvement and Unification of Financial Reports' addressed the problem of whether the goals and objectives of the balance sheet are in fact 'single' or 'multiple'. On this subject, the master of ceremonies, Iwata, expressed the following opinion:

. . . but what has to be considered here is *Who* is actually going to utilize the financial statements in question. The addressed parties may include long-term or short-term creditors, or shareholders, or the Government. Among these groups of creditors, banks are naturally by far the most important and most affected group. Banks, however, are not satisfied with financial statements and usually dig deeper than that. The Government, e.g. tax authorities, has the right to ransack account books, if it is not satisfied; general investors had the same rights but in actuality they could not or do not normally exercise their powers. For various reasons, such as being geographically remote or normally out of touch with the company in question, they are insufficiently influential or not given the opportunity to enter the premises to check the books. The weakest class of creditors and shareholders. i.e. general public investors, should, I think, be given the first priority in receiving protection. . . . In this light, I believe, corporate financial statements are now prepared and issued at each accounting period for the benefit of the public investors, including shareholders and corporate debenture holders. (1949: 65)

FACTORS THAT CONTRIBUTED TO JAPAN'S ACCOUNTING REVOLUTIONS

As we have seen, Japan experienced two revolutions in accounting, one in the latter part of the 1800s, and the second after the Second World War. The revolution in the latter part of the 1800s was a change in bookkeeping methods (i.e. the introduction of Western-style double-entry notation). Such methods, as clearly set forward in the first manuscript published by Pacioli in 1494, finally arrived in Japan after nearly 400 years. Double-entry bookkeeping subsequently served as the foundation upon which the modern capitalist economy of Japan could develop. The post-war accounting revolution changed the style of financial reporting and involved a shift in emphasis in all facets of accounting thought, practices, and institutions from stewardship-oriented accounting to accounting directed towards public investors. Through the implementation of this change, Japan was fully outfitted with the various structures making possible the disclosure of financial information, and the idea of making the so-called absentee investor the central figure among recipients of financial information became firmly implanted in Japanese accounting thought. In addition to contributing to the development of the stock market as a place for generating industrial capital, this shift in emphasis in financial reporting also served greatly to stimulate the then-exhausted Japanese economy.

Among the factors that contributed to these two accounting revolutions in Japan, two were common to both: (1) the fact that Japan's level of economic development lagged behind that of the West, and (2) the creation of new political, economic, and cultural entities by an external force. The first of these was the major cause of the revolutions; the second served as their trigger.

Because accounting develops in response to the needs of the environment or society, accounting revolutions come about as part of changes in the social economic structure. In 1873, at the time double-entry bookkeeping was adopted by the newly established First National Bank, Japan was just awakening from a long period of political, economic, and cultural isolation. Capitalist industrialization had not yet matured, and merchants and businessmen were using accounting methods that were largely unsatisfactory. In 1945, at the end of the war, when Japan began its economic recovery, the stock market did not function as a place for generating industrial capital, and thus the entire structure of business accounting was severely handicapped.

When nations of different levels of economic development come into contact, it is only natural that the nation lagging behind will begin an effort to reduce the difference between itself and the more advanced nations. The two accounting revolutions in Japan were the result of just such a catching-up process. At the same time, however, movements to revolutionize existing practices and institutions encounter a certain amount of resistance or a movement to preserve the status quo. Thus most changes and improvements that occur do not do so overnight but happen, in fact, gradually.

For this reason, it was necessary that some sort of external force trigger a revolutionary change in accounting practices so that institutions could keep pace with the change in accounting thought. In the latter part of the 1800s, this force appeared in the form of advanced capitalist nations that, having experienced the industrial revolution and possessing tremendous productive capabilities, came banging on Japan's door, demanding free-trade agreements. In order to remain an independent nation on an equal footing with these other capitalist giants, Japan was forced to undergo rather rapid political, economic, and cultural modernization. After the Second World War the Allied Command occupying Japan served as a force to trigger change. Without this outside force, it seems unlikely that Japan could have broken up the Zaibatsu conglomerates or adopted a policy of economic democracy in which industrial capital is widely dispersed throughout the public sector.

THE FUTURE OF ACCOUNTING IN JAPAN

Since the end of World War II, the Japanese economy has undergone tremendous development, but it is my opinion that the accounting structure in Japan has not kept pace with its own economic growth. For example, the practice of publishing interim financial statements as part of the financial reporting of a business was adopted only in 1977, and consolidated financial statements have only recently been required. As of yet, cash flow statements and value-added statements are not included among published financial statements. Although Japan ranks economically among the leading nations of the world, its financial reporting is inadequate. Will a third accounting revolution be required to close the gap? I do not think so, although an analysis of modern Japanese accounting history might tempt one to reach such a conclusion. The difference between Japan's two earlier revolutions and the present situation is that both revolutions were preceded by periods of Japanese isolation from the rest of the world. Today, such isolation is no longer possible. That is to say, advances in transportation and communication technology, together with an increasing tendency towards international co-operation, make it increasingly unlikely that individual nations will conduct economic activities independently and completely apart from worldwide economic activities. Differences in the level of economic development will eventually even out, and adjustments to new economic conditions will be gradual and more evolutionary.

Should any future revolution take place, it would doubtless be international in nature, occurring in response to specific technological innovations. Since the end of the 1960s, an international revolution in financial reporting, with economic income measurement giving ground to an informational approach, has been in progress. In Japan, there also has been much interest in this informational approach, but as yet there is little evidence that this approach soon will replace economic income measurement. A more likely scenario is one in which ever-increasing foreign investment in Japan and Japanese investment abroad will force a gradual but definite evolutionary change or adaptation upon the accounting structure in Japan. Future development of Japanese accounting will be of special interest to accounting historians as international investment patterns involving Japan become more complex.

REFERENCES

Economic Stabilization Board (ESB 1949), Investigation Committee on Business Accounting Systems, *Kigyo Kaikeigensoku* ('Financial Accounting Standards for Business Enterprise').

Fukuzawa, Y. (1873, 1874), *Choainoho (Methods of Bookkeeping)*, 2 vols. (Tokyo: Keiogijuku Shuppankyoku).

Iwata, I. (1949), 'Zaimushohyo no Kaizentoitu' ('Symposium on Improvement and Unification of Financial Statements'), *Kaikei*, 56: 185–216.

Kuhn, Thomas S. (1970), *The Structure of Scientific Revolutions*, 2nd enlarged edn. (Chicago: University of Chicago Press).

Kurosawa, K. (1949), 'Kigyo Kaikeigensoku to Zaimushohyo tono Kankei ni tuite' ('Symosium on Relationships between Financial Accounting Standards for Business Enterprises and Financial Statements'), *Kaikei*, 56: 261–84.

Littleton, A. C., and Zimmerman, V. K. (1962), *Accounting Theory: Continuity and Change* (Englewood Cliffs, NJ: Prentice-Hall).

Nishikawa, K. (1956), 'The Early History of Double-Entry Book-Keeping in Japan', in A. C. Littleton and B. S. Yamey (eds.), *Studies in the History of Accounting* (London: Sweet & Maxwell), 380–7.

Ogura, E. (1978), 'Wagakuni no Koyuu Kaikeiho no Hattatsu to Seiyoshiki Bokiho' ('Development of Japanese Bookkeeping and Western Bookkeeping'), in *Kindaikaikei 100 nen* ('Modern Accounting: 100 Years') (Tokyo: Moriyama Shoten), 40–53.

Shimme, S. (1937), 'Introduction to Double-Entry Bookkeeping in Japan', *Accounting Review*, 12: 290–5.

Wells, M. C. (1976), 'A Revolution in Accounting Thought', *Accounting Review*, 51: 471–82.

Yoshikawa, K. (1873), *Ginko Boki Seiho* ('Bank Bookkeeping Methods') (MOF).

3

Accounting and Financial Reporting in Japan

Accounting has been advancing within the framework of the nation. While accounting theories are exchanged internationally, accounting itself is actually bound by the political and legal conditions of each country. This fact has posed no special problem so long as economic activities of businesses are conducted only within the country. In recent years, however, such activities are expanding beyond the borders of the nation and into broader markets abroad.

Today, quite a few businesses are performing parts of their sales operations, investments and / or fund-raising activities in countries other than their own. The number of so-called multinational corporations, which conduct all their activities, including production, sales, and financial affairs, in more than one country, has been increasing rapidly.

Reflecting these tendencies, business accounting, which has made progress only within the framework of the country up to the present, is emerging from its traditional province into an international arena. In this environment, it will be very meaningful to study the accounting and financial reporting systems of other nations. I should like to talk here about Japan's accounting and financial reporting system.

FINANCIAL REPORTING SYSTEM

For investors, creditors, and other interested persons, when they make an investment, a loan, or engage in other similar activities, the most important thing they want to know is the financial condition of the company in which they plan to invest, etc. before making the final decision. For investors to have access to data concerning the financial condition of businesses, financial disclosure is obligatory for all publicly listed companies in every country. Also, as a check on the contents of financial data thus disclosed, an auditing system is prescribed by law.

In Japan, the obligations of corporations generally to disclose and have

From *Waseda Business and Economic Studies*, No. 16 (1980), 1–16.

audited financial information are stipulated by the Commercial Code. The Securities and Exchange Law endorses those obligations for larger companies whose stocks are publicly offered.

FINANCIAL REPORTING SYSTEM UNDER THE COMMERCIAL CODE

It was in 1899 that the Commercial Code of Japan was enacted. Since then, the Code has been revised many times, the last amendment being in 1974. The Commercial Code requires that directors of a corporation shall prepare and submit for approval to the general meeting of stockholders the following documents:

(1) Balance sheet
(2) Income statement
(3) Summary of operations
(4) Proposals concerning the apportionment of net income

These documents are called 'financial statements' for convenience, but the summary of operations is distinguished from others in that it takes the form of a written statement of the general economic environment, the activities of the company in question, and other information during the accounting term concerned.

The Commercial Code provides that the general meeting of stockholders shall be held within three months of the date of the accounts, and the notice of the general meeting is to be given to all stockholders at least two weeks before the meeting date. Since the notice is accompanied by the abovementioned financial statements and an auditor's report which is explained later, stockholders can know the financial situation of their company by about fourteen days before the general meeting is held.

Corporations are obligated to make available their financial statements and their schedules as well as an auditor's report at their head office for inspection by stockholders and creditors. These people can, at a fixed fee determined by the company, have all or part of these documents copied for their reference. After approval of the financial statements at the regular general meeting of stockholders, the balance sheet is published in the official gazette or in a leading daily newspaper. Thus the public can know the financial situation of each company.

The above is a summary of the system of financial disclosure of corporations in accordance with the Commercial Code of Japan. A problem in this system is that only the balance sheet is required to be released to the public in the case of a closed company. Companies are not required to disclose their income statement, which shows their performance. In the case of those corporations not publicly offered, no business results are publicized. For example, we cannot know the operational performance of IBM Japan, which has only one stockholder. That is why the newspapers made big news of IBM's results when they were made public in 1977. The data released included total sales, personnel expenses, and taxes paid. The question of foreign corporations releasing information may, however, be corrected in the near future.

In Japan, companies are allowed to adopt articles of association which determine the length of their fiscal term, as long as it does not exceed one year. Thus many major companies have adopted the six-month term system, and prepared their financial statements twice a year. At present, banks, and some others, still prepare accounts twice every year.

Behind this practice were the provisions of the Commercial Code which prohibited corporations from paying interim dividends to their stockholders. Under the Code, before the amendments of 1974, payment of dividends was not permitted until companies determined their profit by preparing a set of accounts. Thus, they were not able to pay dividends midway in their fiscal term; only year-end dividends were allowed. In order to pay dividends twice a year to stockholders—for example, in June and December—corporations had to divide a year into two fiscal terms, making the length of one such term six months, and had to prepare their accounts semi-annually.

But, by the amendments of the Code in 1974, the payment of interim dividends became lawful in Japan. Businesses no longer have to make the length of one fiscal term six months and to prepare their accounts twice a year so as to make two payments of dividends to their stockholders. After the amendments were made, therefore, almost all companies changed their financial system to the one-year term. But the amended Code does not obligate companies to prepare interim financial statements, which presents another important problem in the financial reporting system under the Commercial Code of Japan.

FINANCIAL REPORTING SYSTEM UNDER THE SECURITIES AND EXCHANGE LAW

To make an advantageous investment, investors need to know, as well as possible, the financial condition of the company before they make the final decision to invest or not. To help investors examine the financial status of a prospective company, the Securities and Exchange Law stipulates that corporations intending to solicit the subscription for newly issued securities or to solicit the sale or purchase offers for already issued securities in an amount of ¥ 100 million or more shall submit to the Minister of Finance at least forty days in advance a registration statement of the securities, Form 2 in the case of Japanese companies and Form 7 in the case of foreign companies. Those corporations soliciting such a subscription or the sale or purchase offers in an amount of ¥ 100 million or more, as well as those companies issuing securities listed on a stock exchange, are also requested to submit to the Ministry of Finance a report of securities, Form 3 in the case of Japanese companies and Form 8 in the case of foreign companies, within three months after the end of every fiscal term.

The registration statement of securities and the report of securities contain financial statements such as the balance sheet, the income statement, the distribution statement of net profit, and their schedules. We can know the financial situation of companies from these documents. The Commercial Code does not demand that companies prepare interim financial statements. But the Securities and Exchange Law provides that, when the length of the fiscal period is a year, those companies are obligated to submit to the Minister of Finance a mid-term report for the six months from the beginning of their fiscal year. Such a mid-term report includes interim financial statements.

As I said before, in the past, many major businesses in Japan adopted the six-month fiscal term system, thus submitting their report of securities every six months to the Minister of Finance. But the amendment of the Commercial Code in 1974 allowed companies to pay interim dividends, and major companies have changed their fiscal term from six months to one year. As a consequence, these companies now submit their report of securities only once a year. This causes a considerable inconvenience to investors in studying the financial condition of their companies. This is why from 1977 the Securities and Exchange Law obligated companies with a one-year fiscal term to submit the mid-term report.

Traditionally, in Japan, financial statements have been prepared only for each legal corporation, and no consolidated financial statements have been reported. But beginning in the year starting 1 April 1977, the submission of consolidated statements became mandatory as attachments to the registration statement of securities or to the report of securities.

The registration statement of securities, the report of securities, and the mid-term report including the consolidated financial statements are made available for inspection by the public at the Ministry of Finance. Statements and reports on the securities listed on the stock exchange are also available at each stock exchange for the same purpose. Copies of these statements and reports are sold at every government publication centre.

In Japan, it was not until after the War that the financial disclosure system of publicly offered companies was introduced. And it was in 1948 that the Securities and Exchange Law was enacted. During the pre-war years, the shares of many large companies were owned by a few giant financial cartels, and investment in corporate shares was made by only a limited number of people. After the war, such financial giants were dissolved and investment activities by the general public were promoted. This trend was called 'the democratization of securities'. The financial disclosure system under the Securities and Exchange Law is very important for the protection of investors. The present tendency is towards strengthening the system further.

AUDITING SYSTEM

Investors know the financial condition of prospective companies from the financial statements of such companies, and make decisions as to whether they continue or suspend their investment or whether they increase or decrease the amount of their investment. Therefore, if financial statements do not fairly present the results or financial position of the corporation, investors are in danger of making an erroneous decision. For this reason, it is very important to know how the auditing of publicly disclosed financial statements is carried out.

CERTIFIED PUBLIC ACCOUNTANTS

When we talk about the auditing system of companies in Japan, we need to begin with the system of certified public accountants.

After the war, the present CPA system was established. Before that, there were professional accountants called 'Keirishi' (registered public accountants). Keirishi were registered accountants in accordance with the Registered Public Accountant Law enacted in 1927, and as of 1948 there were over 25,000 Keirishi in Japan. But any university graduates who completed some accounting courses could register themselves as Keirishi without needing to take an examination, and thus the knowledge and skill in accounting and auditing of many Keirishi were inadequate. To improve such a situation, the Certified Public Accountant Law was enacted in 1948, and the new breed of professional accountants, CPA, who have a high level of expertise, was born. At the same time, the system of junior public accountants, who assist the work of the CPA, was initiated.

The certificate of CPA is given to those who have passed the CPA examination, consisting of three tests. The first test aims at judging whether an applicant has sufficient fundamental preparation for the second test. It includes a written test on the Japanese language, mathematics, and an essay. University graduates are exempted from this first test. The second test is given for the purpose of judging whether an examinee has sufficient professional expertise to serve as a junior public accountant. It is a written test on bookkeeping, financial statements, cost accounting, auditing, business management, economics, and the Commercial Code. The purpose of the third test is to judge whether a candidate has the high professional knowledge necessary to become a CPA. There are both written and oral examinations on such subjects as auditing, analysing and other aspects of financial affairs, and tax affairs. Applicants are also requested to write an essay. Those who take the third test must have completed one year of formal schooling and two years of practical internship after they have passed the second test.

From 1949 to 1978 the number of successful candidates for the second test totalled 6,785, or 7% of the total of 97,485 applicants. During the same period, 4,153 examinees out of 23,940 passed the third test; the success rate was 17.3%. As these figures show, it is very hard to succeed in the second and third tests. When the Certified Public Accountant Law was enacted in 1948, a special examination was given to former Keirishi, and those who passed that test were granted a CPA licence. Thus, as of March 1979, the total number of registered CPAs is 5,529. In addition to these, there are 35 foreign CPAs in Japan.

In 1966 the system of auditing firms was introduced. The principal jobs of a CPA are the auditing of financial documents, and under the new system, such jobs can be performed by a corporation jointly founded by CPAs. Such a corporation is called 'Kansa-hojin' (Auditing corporation). As of March 1979 there were fifty-one Kansa-hojin.

All CPAs and Kansa-hojin are members of the Japanese Institute of Certified Public Accountants.

AUDITING SYSTEM UNDER THE COMMERCIAL CODE

The Commercial Code stipulates that the directors of a corporation shall have their statutory auditor or auditors examine the financial documents to be submitted to the regular general stockholders' meeting. For this purpose, the directors of a company have to submit the financial documents to their statutory auditors not later than seven weeks before the date of the stockholders' meeting and have them audit the documents. They also must submit to their statutory auditors the schedules to such documents for auditing.

The statutory auditors examine the financial documents and submit an auditor's report to the directors within four weeks after receipt of them. I have already explained that the copy of such a statutory auditor's report is attached to the notice of the general stockholders' meeting. As for the schedules to financial documents, the statutory auditors must examine them and submit another auditor's report to the directors within two weeks after receipt of them. This report is made available, together with the auditor's report of the financial documents, at the head office one week before the general stockholders' meeting for inspection by stockholders and creditors.

This is the auditing system provided by the Commercial Code of Japan. The provisions of the Commercial Code on this system apply to all corporations regardless of their scale. For example, as of March 1980 the capital of the Tokyo Electric Power Company is 510 billion yen and the company's total assets amount to 5,667 billion yen. The capital of Nippon Steel Corporation totals 324 billion yen and the corporation's total assets are 3,335 billion yen. On the other hand, the capital of a company owned by one of my friends for which I serve as an auditor is only 50 million yen, and the company has total assets of only 700 million yen. And there are many businesses which are much smaller than this company.

The provisions of the Commercial Code apply to any company whether the scale is big or small. As a result, the auditing of a corporation under the Code has tended to be insufficient for larger corporations while it has been excessive for smaller ones.

The statutory auditors are appointed at a stockholders' meeting, but the qualifications of an auditor are not defined clearly. In some cases, those who lacked knowledge of accounting and auditing, or those who had no independence, were selected, and the auditing of financial documents was not always performed correctly. Cases have been found where corporate window-dressing escaped the notice of such statutory auditors.

To avoid these problems, the Law Concerning Special Rules of the Commercial Code as regards the Auditing of Corporations was enacted in 1974. This law stipulates special rules for the auditing of those companies with a capital of 500 million yen or more, and for the auditing of those corporations having a capital of 100 million yen or less. What is noteworthy about this law is the provision that those companies with a capital of 500 million yen or more shall have their financial documents examined not only by their appointed statutory auditors but also by Kaikei-kansanin. Kaikei-kansanin are selected by each company and must be either certified public accountants or Kansa-hojin.

In the case of these large companies, directors must supply their financial documents to their auditors and Kaikei-kansanin at least eight weeks before the date of the general stockholders' meeting. They also have to submit the schedules to the auditors and Kaikei-kansanin not later than four weeks prior to the stockholders' meeting. Both the statutory auditors and Kaikei-kansanin examine the financial documents and submit their own auditor's report to the directors, and the statutory auditors can entrust Kaikei-kansanin with the auditing of accounting affairs.

AUDITING SYSTEM UNDER THE SECURITIES AND EXCHANGE LAW

As mentioned before, it was only six years ago that the auditing by Kaikei-kansanin, that is, professional auditors as well as statutory auditors appointed by stockholders, became obligatory in the case of those companies having capital of 500 million yen or more. As interim exceptions, the provisions apply to those corporations with a capital of 1 billion yen or more. However, most of these large companies had already been audited by CPAs or Kansa-hojin in accordance with the provisions of the Securities and Exchange Law.

Article 193–2 of the Securities and Exchange Law, which was enacted in 1949, stipulates as follows:

> The balance sheet, income statement and other documents related to the accounting of financial affairs stipulated by the ordinance of the Ministry of Finance, which shall be submitted in accordance with the provisions of this law by those companies that issue securities listed on a stock exchange or others which are stipulated by the cabinet order, shall be subjected to an audit by a certified public accountant or accountants who have no special interest with said companies or others.

This provision was the first one in Japan which obligated corporations to have their financial statements examined by professional auditors. Under this provision, the financial statements contained in the registration statement of securities and the report of securities accompany the auditor's report by certified public accountants or Kansa-hojin. Thus in Japan the auditing system of financial statements under the Securities and Exchange Law was born thirty years ago. Since then, the auditing system has progressed well and in the 1977–8 fiscal year those companies which had their financial statements audited in accordance with the Securities and Exchange Law totalled about 2,100.

GENERALLY ACCEPTED AUDITING STANDARDS

The auditing standards approved and adopted by the Business Accounting Deliberation Council of the Ministry of Finance in 1956 consist of general standards, standards of fieldwork, and standards of reporting. The standards are similar to those approved and adopted by the AICPA. The Council also published standard auditing procedures. Indispensable procedures of auditing included the confirmation of accounts receivable and the observation of inventories. In 1977 the auditing standards for interim financial statements were approved and adopted.

The examinations of financial statements by certified public accountants or Kansa-hojin are generally reliable. But in the past thirty years there have been some defects. One recent case of this was the window-dressing by Fuji Sash Industries and Fuji Sash Sales that occurred in May 1978. These two sister companies overstated their income by 43 billion yen, of which 33.4 billion was by Fuji Sash Industries and 9.6 billion yen by Fuji Sash Sales. The amount was the highest ever in Japan. You will understand the significance of the overstatement when you realize that the capital of Fuji Sash Industries was only 4.8 billion yen and the capital of Fuji Sash Sales only 1 billion yen.

This window-dressing was not found until the companies went bankrupt. It was natural that the question arose as to why the public accountants for these companies failed to discover such a giant amount of overestimation. As a result, the accountants were suspended from serving as CPAs. What was worse, however, was the fact that this event contributed substantially to a decline in trust among the public in certified public accountants in general. The Japanese Institute of Certified Public Accountants has since made continued efforts to reinforce systematic auditing and the independence of certified public accountants to prevent a recurrence of a Fuji Sash type incident.

ACCOUNTING SYSTEM: FINANCIAL ACCOUNTING STANDARDS FOR BUSINESS ENTERPRISES (FASBE)

In Japan, financial statements are deemed to have been prepared fairly if they have been prepared in accordance with the 'Financial Accounting Standards for Business Enterprises'.

Accounting has a function of measuring the economic activities of a corporation and communicating the result to the managers, investors, creditors, and other interested parties of the Corporation. In particular, to those people other than the managers of a company, information transmitted by accounting is the sole means of judging the performance and financial condition of the company. Therefore, the measurement and communication by accounting need to be conducted in accordance with generally accepted principles.

Accounting is the language that communicates the economic activities of a business. Unless both the preparers and the users use the same language, no information will be communicated correctly. In accounting, therefore, all people concerned must have the same understanding of the methods of measurement and the communication of a company's assets, liabilities, capital, income, expenses, and others. If the man who prepares financial statements employs his own definitions and his own measurement method for assets, etc. in the preparation of financial statements, and makes such statements by his own method, what will happen? The readers of such financial statements will not be able to know the economic activities of a corporation correctly. They may even misunderstand the company's activities and financial condition.

If financial statements are to be used in a correct manner, they need to be prepared according to those principles that are accepted by a wide range of people, that is, generally accepted accounting principles. In Japan, such accounting principles were codified in 1949 under the name of 'Financial Accounting Standards for Business Enterprises', which were published as an interim report of the Business Accounting System Measure and Survey Committee of the Economic Stabilization Board.

The Financial Accounting Standards for Business Enterprises are composed of three parts: general considerations, income statement, and balance sheet. FASBE resembles considerably 'A Statement of Accounting Principles' written by T. H. Sanders, H. R. Hatfield, and U. Moore, and published by the AIA in 1938. It was partly amended in 1954 by the Business Accounting Deliberation Council of the Ministry of Finance, and 'Notes to FASBE' were issued with regard to those matters on which there were doubts about the accounting processes and for which there were different interpretations. Several times amendments were made thereafter on the FASBE and they now play a leading role in setting the standards for preparing fiancial statements. In addition, the Standards for Cost Accounting were stipulated in 1962 as the standards for the definition and enforcement of cost accounting by corporations.

For the same purpose, the Principles for Consolidated Financial Statements, and Notes to them, were provided in 1975 as the standards for preparing consolidated financial statements. The Accounting Standards for Interim Financial Statements were stipulated in 1977 as the standards for making interim financial statements.

LAWS CONCERNING ACCOUNTING STANDARDS

FASBE and other standards approved and adopted by the Business Accounting Deliberation Council are important standards for drafting financial statements. Though they are not laws, every company has to follow these standards. However, some businesses do not observe such standards unless they are forced to do so by law. Thus, a considerable portion of FASBE and other standards are contained in the provisions of the Commercial Code. Also, the methods of drafting financial statements prepared in accordance with the provisions of the Commercial Code are stipulated by the 'Regulations Concerning the Balance Sheet, Income Statement, and Schedules of Corporations' which were promulgated in 1963.

The terms, format, and method of preparation for use in the balance sheet, income statement, statement of profit distribution or of loss disposal, and schedules, which are part of the documents concerning financial accounting to be submitted to the Minister of Finance under the Securities and Exchange Law, are provided by the 'Regulations Concerning the Terms, Format, and Method of Preparation for Use in the Financial Statements, etc.' The current version of the Regulations was also introduced in 1963.

Also, of those documents concerning financial accounting which are similarly submitted to the Minister of Finance in accordance with the Securities and Exchange Law, the terms, format, and method of preparation for use in consolidated financial statements are defined by the 'Regulations Concerning the Terms, Form, and Method of Preparation for Use in Consolidated Financial Statements', which was enacted in 1976. As for the terms, format, and method of preparation for use in interim financial statements, the 'Regulations Concerning the Terms, Format, and Method of Preparation for Use in Interim Financial Statements' was enacted in 1977.

INTERNATIONAL ACCOUNTING STANDARDS

Every nation has its own reporting system for measuring the economic activities of companies and for communicating them in the form of income statement, balance sheet, etc. to the interested persons. While the basic principles for preparing financial statements in each country are essentially the same, some differences do exist from nation to nation. Such differences in the standards for making financial statements will, however tiny they may be, present an obstacle to the correct understanding of the financial statements prepared by foreign corporations.

To settle such problems, organizations of public accountants all over the world jointly established the International Accounting Standards Committee in 1973. The role of the Committee is to prepare international accounting standards and to eliminate existing differences in accounting standards. As of March 1979 the Committee established eleven standards and three exposure drafts.

In Japan, therefore, an important theme is how to introduce these international standards into the accounting process. In adopting such standards, adjustments to the provisions of Japanese laws, in particular adjustment to the provisions of the Commercial Code, are essential. At present, the Japanese Institute of Certified Public Accountants is studying what differences really exist between international and Japanese standards.

This is not related to such differences in accounting standards, but here I should point out the fact that there are important differences in the method of expressing net worth in a balance sheet between the United States and Japan. In Japan, the amount of term-end dividends to shareholders is not determined until the proposal for it is approved at the regular general shareholders' meeting. Thus, such an amount is not deducted from the net worth and included in the net worth in the balance sheet as of the end of the term in question. By way of contrast, in the balance sheet of American companies, the amount of term-end dividends is expressed as liabilities upon declaration by the board of directors, and is excluded from net worth.

ACCOUNTING AND INFLATION

In every nation, people are suffering from the rapid pace of inflation. This is the same both in the United States and in Japan.

Since accounting employs currency units for measurement, it has a very weak resistance to inflation. In today's accounting, the principle is that assets are valued in the balance sheet at their acquired cost. Thus, the same assets may be recorded at different values depending on the time when they were acquired. When inflation advances rapidly, the values of the assets recorded on the balance sheet are often significantly different from their real values. For example, the land purchased a long time ago is entered at a very low cost.

Therefore, we cannot know the current values of the assets of a company from its balance sheet. The balance sheet cannot be said to show information on the financial condition of a company sufficiently. Similarly, as such expenses as depreciation are calculated on the basis of acquired cost in the income statement, the statement does not represent correctly the expenses incurred in the economic activities of a company. We cannot say that income statements show information on the business performance of a company fairly.

We think that we should take some appropriate measures in accounting to avoid these distortions in financial statements caused by inflation. In Japan in the 1950s a special law was enacted to enable revisions of the balance sheet values of corporate assets according to the fluctuations of commodity prices. But since then no further action has been taken to deal with the effect of inflation on the accounting process.

TAX SYSTEM: INCOME TAX

Companies have the legal obligation to pay a certain amount of income tax, depending on their income. In computing the amount of income tax, companies have to base their calculation on their income for the fiscal term in question. The method of computing the amount of taxable income is stipulated by the Income Tax Law for individually operated businesses, and by the Corporate Income Tax Law for corporations. The calculation of taxable income is performed in essentially the same manner as that for the computation of income in business accounting.

However, because of taxation techniques, or tax policies, tax laws often have stipulations that disallow deductions for part of expenses included in business accounting, or that permit a special method of computation which cannot be approved in business accounting. Therefore, the amount of taxable income is determined by making adjustments to the income calculated in business accounting. Some adjustments for determining taxable income can be made on a tax return, but a certain accounting process is also needed and this often has a grave influence on business accounting.

The tax rate is now 10% for an income of 600,000 yen or less of an individually operated business. The rate is progressive, and becomes 75% for an income of 80 million yen or more of such a business. In the case of a corporation, the rate is 28% for an income of 7 million yen or less, and 40% for an income of over 7 million yen.

LOCAL TAX

In addition to the national tax, companies have to pay the local tax to the prefecture and the city, town, or village where they are located. Principal taxes paid to the prefecture are inhabitant tax and business tax, while those paid to the city, town, or village are inhabitant tax and real estate tax. The amount of these taxes varies from area to area and also depends on the size of income. But in the case of a corporation, the total amount of these taxes will exceed 20% of the total income of such a corporation.

SUMMARY

I have been talking about the accounting system and the reporting system in Japan. These systems are essentially the same as those of other nations. However, compared with the accounting and reporting system of other countries, the Japanese system seems to be bound more strongly by the Commercial Code and other laws.

Companies are slow to obey FASBE and other standards for preparing financial statements unless such standards are made mandatory by the force of law. Thus there was a period in Japan when accountants made every effort to incorporate in detail the contents of FASBE into the provisions of the Commercial Code. But laws, including the Commercial Code, have their own position. Therefore, when the standards for drafting financial statements are included in the provisions of laws, accounting procedures become very inflexible and stiff.

Accounting has a function of measuring the economic activities of a company, and communicating information which the persons interested in the company need in order to make various decisions. But this function does not work well if it is restricted by the provisions of laws. Adjustments to the international accounting standards will also become harder to make. From these experiences, Japanese accountants now think that it is not very desirable to incorporate in detail FASBE into the stipulations of law.

4

Accounting Principles and Users of Financial Information

In July 1949 the Investigation Committee on Business Accounting Systems of the Economic Stabilization Board of Japan submitted an interim report, 'Business Accounting Principles', and a report, 'Working Rules for Preparing Financial Statements', which stipulated the standard formats and methods of preparation of financial statements based upon the principles outlined in the interim report. Regarding the purpose of 'Business Accounting Principles', the foreword of the report states:

> Since business accounting systems in Japan, as compared with those in the Western countries, have much room for improvement and lack uniformity, it is presently difficult to understand financial conditions and results of business activities of business enterprises. In order to realize the sound development of business enterprises in our country and to promote the benefits of the whole society, any difficulty should be removed as quickly as possible. Further, for the rational solution of the current problems such as the induction of foreign capital, rationalization of business enterprises, justification of taxation, democratization of investment in securities, and proper industrial financing, which are essential to the reconstruction of Japanese economy, the improvement and unification of the business accounting system are urgent problems to be undertaken. Therefore, Business Accounting Principles are to be established aiming at the establishment and maintenance of the standards of business accounting, and consequently offering a scientific basis for the democratic and sound development of the national economy of Japan.

Later, the investigation was taken over by the Business Accounting Deliberation Council, and in 1952 'Business Accounting Principles' was partly modified, resulting in the publication of a supplementary paper entitled 'Notes on Business Accounting Principles' which dealt with various issues regarding accounting methods.

As the Japanese Commercial Code was revised, in 1963, 1974, and 1981, 'Business Accounting Principles' and related notes were subjected to significant revisions.

More than thirty years have passed since the publication of 'Business

From *Waseda Business and Economic Studies*, No. 19 (1983), 1–13.

Accounting Principles' in 1949, and the social and economic business environment has changed greatly, creating a need for an increasingly large and diversified pool of information regarding business activities. In this context, business accounting has come to assume an increasingly important role as an essential source of information serving the multifarious needs of business activities. The question arises now as to what kind of information needs are to be serviced by business accounting.

IMFORMATIONAL FUNCTIONS OF ACCOUNTING

The developmental stages of accounting have a pattern common to all societies, irrespective of the country, tradition, or culture (Dubois and Someya 1977). Accounting, a practice which has existed in human societies from time immemorial, can be defined as a human attempt to measure the results of individual or organizational economic activities and transmit relevant information to those interested in these activities. Obviously, humans have needed accounting, and particularly the recording functions which it ably provides, to aid the fallibility of human memory. If accounting were limited only to its recording function, however, it would not have found such extensive applications in society at large. The wide-ranging acceptance and utilization of accounting today is due to the versatile functions, far surpassing the function as a mere memory tool, it performs.

The individual person naturally wants to know about the results, good or bad, of any action taken. One anxiously seeks the best option out of many choices so as to attain optimum results. The same thing can be said about the economic activities performed by organizations. Accounting aptly fulfils this need for both individuals and organizations by clearly indicating whether the economic actions that have been taken are successful and, if not, where problems exist. Accounting, in short, provides an ideal decision-making aid for all organizations. In other words, accounting has become an indispensable tool for every person and every organization in modern society because it can provide vital information.

The information function performed by accounting, however, began to assume an entirely new role with the advent and development of limited liability companies, where ownership and management are separated. In enterprises where individuals invest in and manage the business for themselves, the owners of the enterprise are at once the managers of the entity. Ownership and management are inseparable. With a typical joint-stock company, which operates with capital funds collected from a large number of investors, the situation is entirely different. Most investors provide money but do not participate in the management. The management of the enterprise is entrusted to a small number of directors chosen irrespective of whether or not they are investors in the company. Here, the owners of the company and the managers who run it are different persons, that is, ownership and management are completely separated.

The management is entrusted with capital by the shareholders, operates the enterprise, and distributes to the shareholders the profit earned from the operation. There have thus appeared what are called 'absentee investors', since most investors only invest and do not participate in the running of the company. These investors buy shares to earn dividends, on the one hand, and out of expectation of the possible rise of share prices, on the other. They will retain the shares if they consider the investment profitable, or will sell them if it becomes unattractive. They can relinquish their position as shareholders at any time. Since most shareholders invest, but do not participate in management, they depend solely upon the management's report in evaluating the enterprise's economic activities and financial status.

For the convenience of such 'absentee investors', the management of the enterprise submits reports; this is the very area where accounting plays a most important role in imparting pertinent information concerning the enterprise's economic activities and financial status. The dividend to be paid to the shareholders is determined by the profit measured by accounting. The decision of shareholders to continue or discontinue their investment (or of prospective investors to buy or not to buy) will hinge upon the information supplied by accounting reports on the enterprise's financial positions and business activities.

It was at this stage that the necessity for accounting principles was first brought into the limelight. For information to be correctly communicated, common understanding of the words or codes used between the sender and receiver of information is required. Likewise, for the correct utilization of accounting information on enterprises by the receivers a common understanding of the method of measurement must be established between the senders, the management of the enterprise, and the receivers, the current or future shareholders.

ACCOUNTING METHODS FOR THE PROTECTION OF INVESTORS

In the 1930s the problem of accounting principles was widely discussed in the United States. It is said that a report made by the 'Committee on Cooperation with the Securities Exchange' of the American Institute of Accountants headed by Chairman George O. May became the cornerstone for later research activities on accounting principles (Storey 1964). That report was based on correspondence between the Committee of the Institute and the Committee for Public Offering of Shares of the New

York Stock Exchange. The main items of the proposition are described in a letter sent by the Committee of the Institute to the Committee of the New York Stock Exchange.

Reacting to the harsh experience of the catastrophic losses incurred by a great number of people through the fall of stock prices starting in 1929, Congress enacted the Securities Act in May 1933 for the purpose of protecting investors. The Securities Exchange Act was enacted the following year, and subsequently the Securities and Exchange Commission was founded. One of the representative writings on accounting principles in those days was a book entitled *A Statement of Accounting Principles* by Thomas H. Sanders, Henry R. Hatfield, and Underhill Moore, published by the American Institute of Accountants in 1938. A letter, written to T. H. Sanders by Huskins and Sells Foundation, Inc., to whom the drafting of this report was entrusted, states (Sanders *et al.* 1938: pp. xii–xiii):

> The stock exchanges in their efforts to promote greater publicity of corporate financial information, the Federal government in its administration of the securities act of 1933, as amended, designed to afford adequate disclosure with respect to new issues of securities, and through the securities exchange act to insure the same information to the holders of and prospective investors in listed securities, have raised sharply the question as to what are accepted principles of accounting. Notwithstanding the difficulties involved, accountants who certify to financial statements filed with the Securities and Exchange Commission have been required by the regulations of that commission to express an opinion concerning such financial statements and the practices of the registrant in the light of accepted principles of accounting.
>
> Accounting practices at present are based, in a large measure, upon the ethics and opinions of reputable accountants, and to some extent upon the accounting provisions of the various laws, but wide variations of opinion often exist among equally reputable practitioners. There is no unified body of opinion, nor is there any official tribunal for the final determination of technical differences of opinion.
>
> . . .
>
> Therefore, it would seem most appropriate and opportune that a committee composed of eminent accountants and lawyers should be appointed to formulate a code of accounting principles which would be useful in the clarification and improvement of corporate accounting and of financial reports issued to the public . . .

As is evident from this statement, the main aim of formulating accounting principles in the 1930s in the United States was to provide corporate financial information for the benefit of present and future shareholders. Further evidence of this trend is too abundant to enumerate here.

Let us now examine who actually were the parties to whom Japan's 1949 enactment of 'Business Accounting Principles' was addressed. In the foreword of that report under the title of 'A Statement of Business Accounting Principles', a very wide range of intended objectives was mentioned, but it can certainly be conceived that Japan's 'Business Accounting Principles' also aimed, in actuality, at establishing some kind of rules for presenting financial information for the benefit of present and future shareholders. When the giant financial combines called Zaibatsu were dissolved, a great number of their shares were sold to the general public, and this necessarily required the corporations to present data on their financial status. The Securities and Exchange Law as well as an auditing system for corporate financial statements by certified public accountants were successively enacted, testimony to the government's desire to ensure both protection for investors and healthy development of the securities market. It is also clear that the aim of enacting 'Business Accounting Principles' included provision of a basis for auditing of corporate financial statements by certified public accountants.

K. Kurosawa, the drafter of 'Business Accounting Principles', replied to a question by K. Sato in the course of a conference devoted to investigation of measures to be taken for setting up the business accounting principles, in the following manner (ESB 1949):

> For the present, we are considering the rules regarding financial statements with particular reference to those pertaining to the Securities and Exchange Committee. Therefore, our considerations presently deal with financial statements centring on financial reports to be submitted to the Securities and Exchange Commission, although this investigative group's concern is not limited to this question only. As you have said, there is also a need to consider those enterprises which are not regulated by the Securities and Exchange Law. Although the concrete formats for financial statements for these enterprises need not be prepared in compliance with these Accounting Principles, we envisage a possibility or even a need for separate formats looked at from different angles, although incorporating the basic principles. If this is going to happen, ideally the commercial code or tax laws should be revised. In the mean time, we must reconcile this ideal and reality to arrive at the solution of our present problems. Therefore, we are now limiting our target to the area of the Securities and Exchange Law.

CHANGE OF SOCIAL ENVIRONMENT AND ACCOUNTING PRINCIPLES

Basically, there is no difference in the conditions requiring the establishment of 'Business Accounting Principles' in 1949 and today. The fact that financial statements are especially important for general investors who have limited access to and ability in understanding corporate financial statements has not changed at all.

In other words, the importance of providing appropriate financial information to present and future public shareholders is no less great today than in the past.

It should be noted, however, that the environment surrounding corporate operations in general has changed materially during the past thirty odd years. Capital composition, for example, has substantially changed. Today, the level of dependence on borrowed capital is rapidly increasing, substantially reducing the ratio of shareholders' equity. Other conspicuous changes include: (1) A trend towards the increase of corporate income tax, reflecting the Government's increased budget for social welfare in line with the national target of a welfare state; (2) structural changes in Japanese society and industries which have induced the constantly increasing influx of the agricultural population into big cities with the resultant increase in blue-collar workers earning income from large industries; (3) increasingly stronger claims for higher wages by such wage-earners to safeguard their living standards which are continually threatened by the ever rising domestic and world-wide inflation; (4) consumers' grave concern over the increasing cost of manufactured goods reflecting utility and other price increases; (5) industrial hazards such as air pollution, deteriorating water quality, and noise, which have created growing regional concern over the operation of enterprises; (6) the *raison d'être* of various industries being disputed *vis-à-vis* societal objectives. Therefore the requirements for entrepreneurial information are constantly becoming more varied and complex.

The concept of 'Business Accounting Principles', moreover, has been reflected in the accounting rules of the Japanese Commercial Code, and in the assessment of taxable income. It does more than merely provide information to the shareholders. Kurosawa's ideal, mentioned in his speech at the Investigation Conference on the Business Accounting Systems concerning accounting principles, has been gradually implemented. If we focus our attention on providing information to shareholders, creditors, and management levels, however, we could certainly prepare information which could be commonly used effectively for different classes of users, without strictly delineating the aim of each class of users, because the decision models, used by these users, are more or less the same. The report *Objectives of Financial Statements*, issued in 1973 by a study group of the American Institute of Certified Public Accountants, touches upon this very point in the following manner (p. 18):

> Classifying users as investors, creditors, and managers is helpful in discussing their principal activities. While users may differ, their economic decisions are similar. Each user measures sacrifices and benefits in terms of the actual or prospective disbursement or receipt of cash. Further, the distinction between an investment and a credit decision often is not sharp.

R. J. Chambers (1979: 90) also states:

At no point has it been necessary to consider the idiosyncratic features of decision-makers, the users of the information. It should be apparent that any party interested in the financial affairs of an enterprise is interested in its solvency, its debt-dependence, its asset composition and its rate of return. All four are expressive of aspects of its performance, and any one or more of them may be suggestive of its trading and financing prospects. Accountants cannot know how the assessments of users will take account of the specific features of a given enterprise. They can have no idea of 'degrees of relevance' of information to particular users, or of the rate of exchange at which some relevance may be 'traded off' for some reliability (or any other characteristic) by any user. . . . In the light of that ineluctable ignorance, the only course to adopt is to ensure the 'representational faithfulness' of the indicators of solvency, debt-dependence, asset compositon and rate of return—for between them, those indicators embrace every element of periodical financial statements.

The information necessary for financial decisions on industrial problems, if they are concerned only with economic matters such as wage negotiations, could be drawn also from the same information sources as utilized by other users. A problem surfaces, however, when we want to define exactly what information is required of corporate economic activities *vis-à-vis* societal objectives: the current economic and social system requires that economic activities pursued for profit be in harmony with societal needs. The interaction and harmony of these two needs are most important considerations; accounting principles must also support both needs.

Enterprises could perhaps increase profits and lower cost by not going to the expense of installing the requisite pollution-prevention equipment at the expense of air or water pollution and the destruction of the natural environment, and reflect the result in their financial statements. The social costs incurred by such entrepreneurial conduct are not clearly identified, however. The pollution-prevention laws make it obligatory now for enterprises to equip facilities with pollution-prevention devices so as to bear part of the social cost. A number of companies nowadays make a positive contribution by giving funds to hospitals and other social facilities, or by employing handicapped people. I am not in a position to define the contents of the requisite information on corporate economic activities in relation to social needs, but consider the inclusion of such social needs in the area of business accounting principles to be an important future subject. From this viewpoint, the report entitled *A Statement of Basic Accounting Theory* issued in 1966 by the American Accounting Association states (p. 19):

It is not necessary to know in detail the needs of all the diverse users of accounting information to prepare relevant reports for them, for certain classes of information are relevant to many decisions. As more is learned about external users, however, and as their decision models are refined and become better known, accounting theory and practice will change.

CONCLUSION

G. R. Byrne (1937: 368), in his prize-winning treatise in commemoration of the fiftieth anniversary of the American Institute of Accountants, writes that the confusion which exists in the interpretation of accounting principles

> results in large part because there is no clear distinction, in the minds of many, between that body of fundamental truths underlying the philosophy of accounts which are properly thought of as *principles*, and the larger body of accouning rules, practices and conventions which derive from principles, but which of themselves are not principles

and stresses the importance of making a strict distinction. May (1937: 423), in his comments on Byrne's treatise, writes:

> This phrase ('accepted principles of accounting consistently maintained') first appeared in the form of a certificate suggested by the Institute's special committee on cooperation with stock exchanges, of which I was chairman, and I recall the discussion and searching of dictionaries which took place before the perhaps rather magniloquent word 'principle' was adopted in preference to the humbler 'rule'.

He adds that the definition given in the Oxford Dictionary, 'a general law or rule adopted or professed as a guide to action; a settled ground or basis of conduct or practice', as regards the term 'principle', is the most appropriate one when talking about accounting.

In 1970 the Accounting Principles Board of the American Institute of Certified Public Accountants, in its statement No. 4, entitled *Basic Concepts and Accounting Principles Underlying the Financial Statements of Business Enterprises*, commented on accounting principles as follows:

> 138. Generally accepted accounting principles therefore is a technical term in financial accounting. Generally accepted accounting principles encompass the conventions, rules, and procedures necessary to define accepted accounting practice at a particular time. The standard of 'generally accepted accounting principles' includes not only broad guidelines of general application, but also detailed practices and procedures.
>
> 139. Generally accepted accounting principles are conventional—that is, they become generally accepted by agreement (often tacit agreement) rather than by formal derivation from a set of postulates or basic concepts. The principles have developed on the basis of experience, reason, custom, usage, and, to a significant extent, practical necessity.

Similar thoughts concerning the concept of accounting principles were also clearly expressed in Japan in the 1949 interim report of the Investigation Committee on Business Accounting Systems. K. Kurosawa (1950: 131), in response to various commentaries regarding 'Business Accounting Principles', stated:

> Public announcement of the Accounting Principles and Rules for Financial Statements was prepared as a major attempt to solve the contradictions existing among the Japanese Commercial Code, Tax Laws, and accounting practices. The Accounting Principles, as announced then, were not in any way mere summaries of the basic theory of accounting, which are only conceptual and not suitable as institutional rules, as sometimes erroneously interpreted by some scholars of accounting.

Thus inasmuch as the accounting principles are institutionalized rules, which corporations must abide by, financial statements should be prepared in accordance with these rules and should contain useful information to enable the users of the statements to make effective decisions. In any event, there is no denying that accounting principles should be used as the basis of corporate accounting.

In recent years, however, a fresh need has arisen in the financial reporting environment, which necessitates incorporation of information regarding the possible effects of price fluctuations on the corporations' operations as a result of the sharp price fluctuations which are taking place domestically and internationally these days. This situation is giving rise to a new trend to try to expand the scope of information beyond the boundaries of the conventional format of financial statements (FASB 1978, Burton 1981). In spite of these changes occurring in the financial environment, there seems to be little change in the concept and method of preparing financial statements, that is, the basis of preparation of financial information is centred, as it always has been, around investors and creditors only, without regard to the specific needs of other users.

At this time, when significant changes have taken place in the world economic environment, it is necessary to expand the range of users for which financial information is prepared. Under the circumstances, it appears quite useful and important for us to consider providing pertinent information for new types of users, as they become identifiable, after careful research and study of such intractable aspects as mentioned below:

(1) What type of users are identifiable as new users of corporate financial information? What are the patterns of decision-making of these new users?
(2) Do the traditional general-purpose financial statements satisfy the needs of such new users?
(3) Will contradictions arise between the new information requirements and the basic freedom-of-trade principle which forms the nucleus

of our current social and economic system? If contradictions are liable to occur, how can we reconcile them?

These problems have to be solved if the Accounting Principles are to find a new sphere of development.

REFERENCES

American Accounting Association (1966), Committee to Prepare a Statement of Basic Accounting Theory, *A Statement of Basic Accounting Theory.*

American Institute of Certified Public Accountants (1970), Accounting Principles Board, 'Basic Concepts and Accounting Principles Underlying Financial Statements of Business Enterprises', *Statement of Accounting Principles Board, No. 4* (New York: AICPA).

American Institute of Certified Public Accountants (1973), *Objectives of Financial Statements* (Report of the Study Group on the Objectives of Financial Statements) (New York: AICPA).

Burton, J. G. (1981), 'Emerging Trends in Financial Reporting—An Analysis of the Changes taking Place in the Reporting Environment', *Journal of Accountancy,* 152/1: 54–66.

Byrne, G. R. (1937), 'To what Extent can the Practice of Accounting be Reduced to Rules and Standards?', *Journal of Accountancy,* 64/5: 364–79.

Chambers, R. J. (1979), 'Usefulness—The Vanishing Premise in Accounting Standards Setting', *Abacus,* 15/2: 71–92.

Dubois, D. A., and Someya, K. (1977), 'Accounting Development in Japan: The "Convergence" Theory', *Accountant* (5 May), 500–2.

Economic Stabilization Board (1949), Investigation Committee on Business Accounting Systems, 'Kigyo Kaikeigensoku to Zaimushohyo tono Kankei ni tsuite' ('Symposium on Relationships between Business Accounting Principles and Financial Statements'), *Kaikei,* 56/3: 261–84.

Financial Accounting Standards Board (1978), 'Objectives of Financial Reporting by Business Enterprises', *Financial Accounting Concepts Statement No. 1.*

Japan Accounting Association (1949), 'Zaimushohyo no Kaizentoitsu' ('Symposium on Improvement and Unification of Financial Statements'), *Kaikei,* 56/2: 185–216.

Kurosawa, K. (1950), 'Keidanren no Kaikeigensoku no Kaisei ni kansuru Iken ni tsuite' ('A Comment on Opinions of Federation of Economic Organization on Revision of Accounting Principles'), *Kaikei,* 58/3: 387–90.

May, G. O. (1937), 'Principles of Accounting', *Journal of Accountancy,* 64/6: 423–5.

Sanders, T. H., Hatfield, H. R., and Moore, U. (1938), *A Statement of Accounting Principles* (New York: American Institute of Accountants).

Storey, R. K. (1964), *The Search for Accounting Principles: Today's Problems in Perspective* (New York: AICPA).

5

Views from Abroad: Japan

In considering recent developments in business accounting in Japan, one must review the various statute revisions that have had a great effect on business accounting.

The source of authority for financial reporting practices employed by Japanese businesses is the Commercial Code (the Code) and the Securities and Exchange Act (the Act). Basically, the Code requires that company directors prepare a balance sheet, an income statement, and a business and financial summary along with proposals for appropriation of earnings or disposition of deficits for each fiscal period. These are to be presented and approved at a general shareholders' meeting. The Code also requires company directors to publish the balance sheet publicly, either in the Official Gazette or in a daily newspaper. The Act requires that companies whose stock is listed at the Securities Exchange and all other major companies submit, at the end of every business year, a securities report to the Minister of Finance. This report includes a balance sheet, an income statement, and an appropriation of earnings or disposition of deficits statement with supporting schedules and itemized listings. The securities report then goes on file for public reference at the Ministry of Finance; additional copies are to be on file at the company's main and major branch offices. Recently, the system of financial reporting for businesses set forth in the Code and the Act has undergone a series of important revisions.

MAJOR REVISIONS TO THE AUTHORITATIVE LITERATURE

The 1981 Revisions of the Code and Act

In 1981 certain sections of the Code and the Act were revised. These revisions included measures (1) enabling shareholders to propose items to be included on the agenda of the general shareholders' meeting, (2) prohibiting the bribing of shareholders who otherwise would insist on raising troublesome issues, (3) raising the minimum par value of newly

This chapter was first published in *Journal of Accounting, Auditing and Finance*, NS 1/2 (1986), 161–5, and is reproduced by kind permission of the *Journal of Accounting, Auditing and Finance*, an imprint of Greenwood Publishing Group Inc., Westport, CT.

formed companies' capital stock from ¥500 to ¥50,000 per share, and (4) permitting the issuance of bonds with stock purchase warrants. The scope of these revisions was far-reaching, and their effect on business accounting practices was profound.

The reserve allowance regulation of the Code permitted inclusion of allowances for other than legal liabilities on the balance sheet. Prior to amendment, the definition of reserve allowances was not clearly stated, admitting, among other things, the possibility of allowances as an appropriation of retained earnings. The 1981 revision limited inclusion of reserve allowances under liabilities to 'those amounts comprising expenses or losses for that year'. This made it impossible to include allowances as appropriation of retained earnings (though these are legal) among the liabilities.

The 1982 Revisions of Financial Accounting Standards

The Business Accounting Deliberations Council (BADC), the organ responsible for setting accounting standards in Japan, revised its 'Financial Accounting Standards for Business Enterprises' in 1982. In these revisions, both allowances for estimated liability and allowances made for valuation of assets were treated as allowance items pertaining to the computation of specific expenses or losses in the future, thus merging their identity. Moreover, in order that accumulation of depreciation should not be included as part of these reserve allowances, the term *allowance for depreciation,* which had been used until that time, was changed to *accumulated depreciation.* In reporting allowances for unexpected losses, an amendment requires a disclosure that 'no provision is made for allowances against contingencies having a low probability of occurring'. Clearly, this indicates the tendency to recognize such reserve allowances.

Auditing Large Businesses

The Act requires that the balance sheet, income statement, and other documents pertaining to financial computation that must be submitted to the Minister of Finance must be attested to by a CPA or an auditing corporation having no special interest whatsoever in the company. The Code, on the other hand, requires only that financial statements and other information required to be presented at the general shareholders' meeting be audited by a statutory auditor, but it does not require this statutory auditor to be a CPA or an auditing corporation. In order to improve the auditing of larger businesses coming under the Code's auditing provisions, a 1974 law, especially directed towards businesses with capital of over 500 million yen (hereafter referred to as 'large businesses') and companies with capital of less than 100 million yen, required that the balance sheets, income statements, business and financial summaries, and other appended schedules and listings be audited by an independent auditor (Kaikei Kansanin) as well as by a statutory auditor, and that this independent auditor must be either a CPA or an auditing corporation.

The 1981 revisions of the Code and the Act included companies with total liabilities of more than 20 billion yen in the category of large businesses, even though their capitals may be less than 500 million yen. Moreover, the revisions required large businesses to make public their income statements as well as balance sheets by publication in either the Official Gazette or in a daily newspaper.

Ministry of Justice Regulations

Ministry of Justice regulations were revised in 1982 to conform with the 1981 revisions of the Code and the Act. These regulations decide the form of the balance sheet, income statement, and other statements required by the Code. They now stipulate disclosure in the notes to the financial statements of (1) the methods used for evaluating assets, (2) computation of fixed-assets depreciation, (3) significant reserve allowances, (4) other significant accounting policies pertaining to balance sheet and income statement preparation, and (5) earnings per share, etc., for the period. Moreover, large businesses are required to include in their business and financial summaries all subsequent events, that is, significant events affecting the financial position of the company occurring after the date of the balance sheet.

Further, in 1982 the BADC amended its 'Financial Accounting Standards for Business Enterprises' by adding sections on disclosure of significant accounting policies and disclosure of significant subsequent events. Examples of these disclosures were given earlier.

RECENT DEVELOPMENTS

Consolidated Financial Statements

Prior to 1976 business financial statements required to be made public were prepared for each individual legally defined company, and consolidated financial statements were not used. In 1976, however, the Ministry of Finance regulations were revised and, starting with the fiscal period beginning April 1977, companies were required to include consolidated financial statements among the documents attached to the securities report submitted to the Minister of Finance.

In 1975 the BADC published its 'Financial Accounting Standards for Consolidated Financial Statements', which sets the standard for the preparation of such statements. The section of these standards dealing with capital investments in unconsolidated subsidiaries and affiliated companies, however, was not effective until the fiscal period beginning April 1983; thereafter, amounts computed by the equity method were included in the balance sheet.

The introduction of consolidated financial reporting is an attempt to bring Japanese business accounting practices more in harmony with international standards. As of now, such reports are required only of major companies; accordingly, Japan has taken only the initial step at this time towards eventual realization of its goals.

Fiscal Periods

In the past many major businesses in Japan operated on the basis of six-month fiscal periods because, under the Code, dividend payments to shareholders were not permitted without an accurate computation of net income. Companies wishing to pay dividends twice a year were consequently forced to close their books every six months. With revision of the Code in 1974, however, interim dividend payments were permitted and, consequently, most companies have now switched to one-year fiscal periods. Businesses that operate on one-year fiscal periods are required by the Act to submit semi-annual reports to the Minister of Finance.

Interim Statements

In 1977 the BADC issued 'Standards for Interim Financial Statements', which deals with the preparation of interim financial statements to be included in the semi-annual report. Until 1977 interim statements were generally prepared on a stand-alone basis; that is, the first six months of the business year were conceived of as an independent accounting period. The 1977 standards, however, were based on the assumption that interim statements should be prepared as an integral part of the fiscal year's statements and are thus of value in predicting income for the entire business year. These standards for interim financial statements were effective for interim periods beginning in April 1977.

The Code does not yet require that consolidated and interim financial statements be included in the report presented to shareholders. These statements, however, have found their way into the system for disclosing financial information under the Act. One can expect further investigation into the conceptual aspects of consolidated and interim reporting as these statements come increasingly into use.

Foreign Currency Translation

With the introduction of consolidated financial reports, a need arose for foreign currency translation standards. In 1979 the BADC published

'Standard Accounting Procedures for Foreign Currency Transactions', which summarized accounting and reporting standards for foreign currency transactions, etc.

Since 1968 the BADC has issued procedural standards regarding foreign currency transactions in response to specific changes in the foreign exchange environment, including such things as the devaluation of the British pound, the lifted limits on the range of exchange fluctuation, the fixing of a standard foreign exchange market, and the shift towards floating exchange rates. But because these procedural standards were limited to the specific instances for which they were intended, there was a need to devise a more general and comprehensive set of accounting standards applying to foreign currency transactions and financial statements.

The standards adopted in 1979 employed a monetary–non-monetary method compounded by a current–non-current method for the translation of foreign currency transactions and monetary items on the foreign currency financial statements for the main offices and foreign branches, the temporal method for the translation of non-monetary items such as inventory and tangible fixed assets of foreign branches and, also, a partially amended temporal method for the translation of foreign currency financial statement items of overseas subsidiaries.

Auditing Small Business

One recent major accounting concern has been auditing of small businesses. The total number of companies issuing stock in Japan is something over one million. Of these, approximately 20,000 have a capital of over 100 million yen, while nearly 800,000 companies are in existence with capitals of less than 10 million yen. In spite of these large numbers, only 5,000 companies are currently required to be audited by an independent auditor.

In 1984 the Ministry of Justice made a general inquiry into the feasibility of compelling companies not currently audited by independent auditors and not open to public inspection to submit to limited 'audit' by an auditing authority (CPA, Auditing Corporation, Junior Accountant, or Registered Tax Accountant) to see if their books contain any omissions or false items, and to see if the figures on their balance sheet, income statement, and appended schedules and itemized listings agree with their books. This matter currently is still under discussion. Should this type of restricted auditing be established? Should auditing authority in such cases be extended to other than CPAs and auditing corporations?

Recent Literature

Among articles recently appearing in leading Japanese journals in the field of accounting are such titles as 'Effects of Factory Automation on

Cost Management', 'Effectiveness of the Decision Support System in Response to Demands of Management Accounting Information', and 'Auditing in an EDP Environment'. The 1985 Japanese Accounting Association Convention had as its main theme 'Problems Involved in the Rapid Growth of Accounting Information Needs', at which these newly emerging problems were discussed from a variety of different angles.

International Accounting

Japan has always had a keen interest in the accounting concepts and practices of other countries, and this interest has reached a new intensity over the past few years. Among the topics under current investigation are the FASB Statements of accounting standards and concepts, the IASC Statements of international accounting standards, and the EEC directives concerning company law, all of which deal with the various requirements and practices of financial reporting in other countries and harmonization of accounting standards on an international level. The Japanese Association for International Accounting Studies was established in 1984 and serves as a focal point for people interested in comparative research into accounting practices around the world, as well as for people involved in preparing financial reports destined for other countries.

History

In contrast to the challenges of these newly developing areas of accounting, a good deal of research is going into the historical development of accounting, as well as into that eternal problem, the philosophical basis of accounting.

The Japanese Accounting Association (JAA) was founded in 1937, and 1987 was its fiftieth anniversary. A volume was published tracing its fifty-year history. In 1987 the thirteenth World Congress of Accountants was held in Tokyo, as well as the sixth International Conference on Accounting Education in Kyoto. The Japanese Institute of Certified Public Accountants was in charge of the former and the JAA in charge of the latter.

6

The Coming of Age of Accounting in Japan

I

In so far as people can own and control wealth and engage in economic activity, there will always be a need for adequate and proper accounting. This is as true in the East as it is in the West. Around the sixteenth century, Japanese merchants, for example, employed their own unique brand of bookkeeping known as the 'daifukucho', or 'ledger of good fortune'. However, with the introduction of Western bookkeeping methods in the 1800s, this uniquely Japanese style of account-keeping was gradually replaced, and it eventually disappeared altogether.

The year 1873 is generally regarded by accounting historians as the starting-point in the modernization of Japanese business accounting. In June of that year the first volume of Yukichi Fukuzawa's *Choai no ho* ('Methods of Bookkeeping') was published, and in December a translation of *Bank Bookkeeping* by the Scotsman Alexander Allan Shand appeared. Also, 31 December of that year marked the end of the First National Bank's first fiscal period, and Japan's very first financial report was prepared according to Shand's bookkeeping methods. It should be noted that in 1973 the Japan Accounting Association (JAA) celebrated the centennial of modern accounting in Japan with series of lectures and other events.

Fukuzawa's *Choai no ho* was in fact a translation of H. B. Bryant and H. D. Stratton, *Common School Bookkeeping* (New York, 1871). In the following years there appeared several other translations and Japanese works based upon European and American bookkeeping texts. It was in this manner that Western bookkeeping methods were introduced into Japan and they gained rapid acceptance. Japanese authors quickly entered the field. Several bookkeeping textbooks appeared, including those by Nobuhisa Ohhara (Ohhara Bookkeeping School), Zensaku Sano (Tokyo Commercial High School, later upgraded to Tokyo Commercial College),

From *Information Bulletin of the Union of National Economic Associations in Japan*, No. 6 (1986), 1–6.

Sekigoro Higashi (Kobe Commercial High School), and Ryozo Yoshida (Waseda University, who later moved to Tokyo Commercial College). Some ran through several editions before 1910.

Japan's first commercial code was enacted in 1890, and the section which dealt with companies became effective in 1893. Although it was revised in 1899, this code is the predecessor of the commercial laws in effect today; and in those regulations the original pattern for current existing regulations pertaining to commercial books, company accounting, and other matters relating to financial accounting can be seen. It was a continental system of financial reporting, centring around the inventory and the balance sheet, which was introduced and which dominated the accounting scene in Japan. In explaining what items ought to be included on the inventory and the balance sheet, and how they are to be priced or evaluated, the pronouncements of Keijiro Okano (Tokyo Imperial University, the predecessor of the present Tokyo University), Joji Matsumoto (also, Tokyo Imperial University), and other professors of law were influential.

Ryozo Yoshida's *Kaikei-gaku* ('Study of Accounts') was published in 1910, and was the first book to use the term 'Kaikei-gaku'. Other authors used terms such as 'Keiri-gaku' ('Study of General Rules of Accounting') and 'Keisan-gaku' ('Study of Computation'). In the *Kokumin Keizai Zasshi* ('Journal of Economics and Business Administration') for 1915 Seijiro Kano (Tokyo Commercial High School) asserted that 'Keiri' was in fact the most appropriate translation of the word 'accounting', and the ensuing argument between him and Shigeo Nakamura (Meiji University) is well known. The matter was effectively settled in 1913 when the Kobe Society of Accounting used the word 'Kaikei' in its title, and so did the Japan Society of Accounting (JSA) founded in 1917 by Naotaro Shimono, Sekigoro Higashi, Ryozo Yoshida, and Shigeo Nakamura. There could be no further argument when the JSA began publishing its periodical under the title of Kaikei (i.e. 'Accounting'). In 1929 the Third International Congress on Accounting was held in New York with Sekigoro Higashi, Naotaro Shimono, and Seitaro Suyama (Osaka Commercial College) as the first Japanese to be delegates at this important international gathering. Their presence reflects not only an increased interest in works on auditing, cost accounting, and financial analysis but also the research which was beginning into balance sheet value theory and Schmalenbach's concept of a dynamic balance sheet.

II

The financial statements of any business enable decisions concerning business operations, capital investments, loans, etc. to be made. Financial statements serve as essential reference sources in grasping the overall operating results and immediate financial position of any business entity. As people come to realize their importance, the setting of standards for financial reporting becomes a fundamental concern for accounting research.

In 1930 the Ministry of Commerce and Industry created a Special Department for the Rationalization of Industry, and within it set up a Committee on Financial Management. Japan, like other nations, naturally was feeling the effects of worldwide depression, and industry was depressed. Rationalization as a means of relieving the depression was the first order of concern for the Ministry, and financial statement standardization was urged to assist in the process. The Committee on Financial Management, after four years of deliberation, proposed a draft standard for the balance sheet, the inventory, and the income statement. After soliciting opinions from relevant governmental departments, various economic organizations in the private sector, major banks and businesses, scholars and other concerned parties, the committee decided on its Standard Procedures for Financial Statements (SPFS) in 1934.

SPFS set the general standards that businesses were to follow in the preparation of their financial reports. Because of its enlightened nature, and because it was explained and discussed in many textbooks on accounting, the SPFS contributed much to later developments and progress in the field of accounting. Several of the important scholars of the day, including Ryozo Yoshida, Tetsuzo Ohta (Tokyo Commercial College, the predecessor of the present Hitotsubashi University), and Sekigoro Highashi had been involved in its preparation, and it became and remained customary for scholars from the accounting field to be included in the decision-making process concerning the various standards pertaining to business accounting.

Yasubei Hasegawa's (Waseda University) *Studies in Budgetary Control* was published in 1930, followed by Eiichi Furukawa's (Yamaguchi Commercial High School, who later moved to Hitotsubashi University) *Budgetary Control* in 1933 and Rintaro Aoki's (Kansei Gakuin University) *Management Accounting* in 1936. In 1937 the Japan Accounting Association (JAA) was founded by Ryozo Yoshida, Tetsuzo Ohta, Kinzo Sambe (Keio University), Gen Murase (Tokyo Commercial College), Seiichi Okada, Yoshio Watanabe (Higashi–Watanabe Accounting Firm), Yasubei Hasegawa, and Kiyoshi Kurosawa (Yokohama Commercial High School, the predecessor of the present Yokohama National University). The Japan Society of Accounting (JSA), founded in 1917, supported approximately 1,000 members at this time. Most of its members were either owners or managers of businesses, or worked in accounting departments or as professional accountants. Accounting scholars were a small minority in the Society. JAA as distinct from JSA was intended for accountants in the academic world.

Although the war in the Pacific did not start until December 1941, Japan's economy had been on a war-time basis from the mid-1930s. Both people and materials were mobilized for the war effort. The National Comprehensive Conscription Act was enacted in 1938; based upon this, various regulations were passed and put into effect. The army and the navy demanded that military suppliers employ acceptable standards of cost accounting, and submit reports on production, product cost, and finance. They themselves also conducted official inspections of finished goods and of all relevant books. The army and the navy introduced their own set of rules, which were mandatory for those companies with which they were involved. All their cost sheets, balance sheets, and income statements had to be submitted for inspection. Later these complex rules were examined by the Committee for Unification of Various Financial Rules established within the Cabinet Planning Board, and in 1941 this committee presented its Uniform Rules for Manufacturing Industry Cost Accounting (RMICA). In the same year, separate drafts for the balance sheet, the inventory, and the income statement procedures were announced for industrial firms. If the Ministry of Commerce and Industry's intervention to rationalize accounting procedures in 1934 is considered as Stage I, then the Cabinet Planning Board's plans for standardization of the financial statements in 1941 must be taken as Stage II. Stage II failed to produce any finalized procedural standards for the various financial statements, but through actual application of RMICA in various factories, certainly this period saw a rapid development of cost accounting systems, as well as enormous advances in cost accounting research.

III

With the end of the war in 1945 Japan's economy was completely shattered. But as in any age, scholarship itself will remain and go on; by 1946 some universities had resumed publication of their official journals and bulletins, which carried papers on accountancy. Annual meetings of JAA, discontinued during the war, resumed again in 1948.

As is well known, for several years following the war Japan was under American occupation. The American occupational forces insisted on breaking up the Zaibatsu, or large family-owned industrial conglomerates, and most companies released their common stock to the public. In 1948 the Securities and Exchange Act (SEA) was passed, modelled after the American Securities Act of 1933 and Securities Exchange Act of 1934. A Certified Public Accountants Law was passed in the same year, and in 1949 the first CPA examination was given. In this way CPA auditing according to clause 193 of the SEA got underway in 1951. But before this, in 1949, the Investigation Committee on Business Accounting of the

Economic Stabilization Board published as a tentative statement its Principles of Business Accounting—otherwise known as financial Accounting Standards for Business Enterprises—together with Standard Procedures for Financial Statements (SPFS). Again in 1950, Auditing Standards and Standard Auditing Procedures were published. Principles and Auditing Standards were written into the laws by the Ministry of Finance and other related government organs.

Accounting scholars, including such talented individuals as Michisuke Ueno (Tokyo University), Tetsuzo Ohta, Kiyoshi Kurosawa, Iwao Iwata (Hitotsubashi University), and Koichi Sato (Waseda University), played a substantial part in preparing the Principles and Auditing Standards which soon became the standard text. Because the Principles introduced ideas such as surplus and a current operating performance concept of income, with which Japanese accountants were not familiar, there followed a rapid blossoming of research into these areas.

The Commercial Code was amended in 1950, and in addition to introducing authorized capital stock for stock companies, it also recognized the issuing of non-par value stock. In 1962 the definition of deferred assets was expanded and a clause concerning allowances was introduced. A Ministry of Justice statute was put into effect in 1963, setting the method in which items are to be listed on the balance sheet and income statement of stock companies. Some amendments were made in both Statutes and the Principles of Business Accounting to bring consistency to the whole system.

In post-war Japan the production of goods could not keep pace with demand and inflation was rampant. An Asset Revaluation Law was passed in 1950, which carried out its work in a series of three steps. Inflation accounting, where assets are valued at replacement or current cost, emerged as a major topic of accounting research. Business rationalization was an important concern in getting the national economy back on its feet, and the Investigation Committee on Rationalization of Industry of the Ministry of International Trade and Industry published its Guideline for Internal Control of Businesses in 1951. Profit planning aimed at the realization of business goals, profit management by product, market or other segments, cost management, and other challenges of management accounting joined the ranks as important topics in accounting research. Cost accounting, financial analysis, budgetary control, and other areas of research were gradually incorporated into the concept of management accounting.

IV

The system for financial reporting for businesses in Japan is backed by the Commercial Code and the Securities and Exchange Act, but in order to improve the system of financial disclosure, including its auditing, these laws undergo revision from time to time. Recent research in accounting has been partially carried out with a view towards possible application in such statute revisions.

The Commercial Code now stipulates that the balance sheet and income statement submitted by company directors at the general shareholders' meeting be audited by a statutory auditor, but does not stipulate that this auditor be a certified public accountant. Because of this, a law making special provision for the auditing requirement of the Commercial Code was enacted in 1974 for the purpose of strengthening the auditing of large companies. According to this law the balance sheets and income statements of companies having a capital stock of 500 million yen or over, or with total liabilities of 20,000 million yen or over, must be audited by a kaikei kansanin (CPA) in addition to the audit by the statutory auditor. In 1982 the Ministry of Justice regulation determining the form of balance sheet and income statement of stock companies was revised to require disclosure of (1) significant accounting policies pertaining to the preparation of these statements, and (2) significant subsequent events, that is to say, important facts relating to the financial situation of the company arising after the end of the fiscal term. The auditing system of the Commercial Code and the system for financial disclosure are therefore two important areas of concern in recent accounting research.

It was for a long time customary in Japan for business financial statements to be prepared individually for each entity or business as defined by law, and no such thing as consolidated financial statements existed. However, with revision of the Ministry of Finance law in 1976, taking effect in 1977, it is now required that consolidated financial statements be included among the documents attached to the securities report filed with the Minister of Finance as stipulated in the Securities and Exchange Act. Again, in the past, many major businesses in Japan operated on the basis of a six-month fiscal period. The reason for this was that the Commercial Code did not allow dividend payments to shareholders without first ascertaining net income after closing the accounts. With the 1974 revision of the Commercial Code, however, interim dividend payments became permissible, and subsequently virtually all businesses now operate on a one-year fiscal basis. The SEA requires that companies operating on one-year fiscal terms submit semi-annual reports to the Minister of Finance, and hence the role of the interim financial statements included in such reports has come to be of prime importance. Disclosure procedures for consolidated and interim financial statements eventually made their appearance in the financial disclosure system of the SEA, and further research in these areas is now indicated.

Japan has traditionally taken a keen interest in the accounting theory and practices of other countries, and in recent years such interest has gathered momentum. A number of research projects are underway pertaining to United States FASB accounting standards and concepts, IASC International Accounting Standards, the United Nations Commission on Transnational Companies, EC directives concerning company law, and other such regulations and practices in financial reporting that have been developed abroad, as well as research into the probable harmonization of accounting standards on an international level. In October 1987 the Thirteenth World Congress of Accountants was held in Tokyo, and the Sixth International Conference on Accounting Education was held in the same month in Kyoto. The Japanese Institute of Certified Public Accountant was a host for the former, while JAA was a host for the latter. By playing host to such prestigious international gatherings, accounting research in Japan took on an even greater international flavour.

7

International Conferences on Accounting Education

BACKGROUND

International conferences on accounting have a long history. Any article on the International Conferences on Accounting Education (ICAE) must therefore make references to an earlier series, the International Congresses on Accounting (ICA). Until the ICAE got under way in 1962 as a meeting place for accounting educators from all over the world, some of the various objectives of the ICAE were partially performed by the ICA.

The first international conference was held in St. Louis (USA) in 1904. It was one of the events associated with the World's Fair held in St. Louis the same year, and was hosted by the then-named American Federation of Public Accountants. Invitations were sent only to accounting organizations in English-speaking nations, with 91 persons attending, including two from England and three from Canada. Following an interval of twenty odd years a second international congress was held in Amsterdam in 1926. This time there were three sponsoring groups, including the Netherlands Institute of Accountants, with 381 persons in attendance from 17 nations.

The first conference was entitled Congress of Accountants, while the second was called the International Accountants' Congress. From the third conference on the title International Congress on Accounting was used. Both the first and second conferences were designated as conventions for 'accountants', and in both cases the organizations hosting them were public accountant groups. At the same time, however, invitations to the second congress were also sent to Columbia University and to New York University in the United States, and representatives from these schools were sent. It is noteworthy that university professors were prominent among the delegates presenting papers.

The nature of these congresses became rather clearly defined at the 3rd ICA. Held in New York in 1929, the 3rd ICA was jointly sponsored by

From *Waseda Business and Economic Studies*, No. 22 (1986), 1–7.

the American Institute of Accountants together with four other groups, one of which was the American Association of University Instructors in Accounting, the forerunner of the present-day academic group, the American Accounting Association; Robert H. Montgomery of Columbia University (and also a very prominent certified public accountant) was chosen as congress chairman. A large number of the papers presented at this congress were prepared by university professors.

Seitaro Suyama (Osaka Commercial College), in his book, *International Congress on Accounting* (Daido-shoin, 1931), published after his return from the third conference, defined the significance of the ICA as follows (p. 1):

> An International Congress on Accounting for the purpose of allowing accounting scholars, accountants, and other accounting professionals a chance to present research reports, hold discussions, and get to know one another better has been held three times now. Each conference has seen an increase in the number of participating nations and a proliferation of topics. A glance at the topics taken up will give a good idea of where the big accounting concerns lie relevant to the time, and a survey of which countries the various speakers come from will give a good picture of accounting interest around the world.

Japanese participation at the ICA dates therefore from the third congress, and in addition to Seitaro Suyama quoted above, Sekigoro Higashi (Japan Society of Registered Accountants) and Naotaro Shimono (Tokyo Commercial College) were also in attendance. At this convention Naotaro Shimono presented a paper entitled 'The Nature and Form of the Balance Sheet'.

The 4th ICA was held in London in 1933, followed by the 5th ICA in Berlin in 1938. Only one person representing the Japan Society of Registered Accountants attended each of these: Kotaro Fujimoto (Tokyo Commercial College) on overseas tour in London was present at the 4th congress, and Ryoichi Obayashi (Tokyo Commercial College), studying in Germany at the time, was at the 5th. Unlike today, attendance at such international gatherings required a long sea voyage, which took much time and money.

After an interruption due to the war, the 6th ICA was held again in London in 1952. Hosted by seven accounting associations in England, 36 countries including England participated and attendance was 2,510, or 3,264, counting guests. This congress was attended by Katsuji Yamashita (Kobe University) from Japan. Beginning with the 7th congress, held in Amsterdam in 1957, the International Congress of Accounting came to be called the International Congress of Accountants (ICA). Following this the 8th ICA was held in New York (1962), the 9th in Paris (1967), the 10th in Sydney (1972), the 11th in Munich (1977), the 12th in Mexico City (1982), the 13th in Tokyo (1987), called the 13th World Congress of Accountants, all the way down to the 14th World Congress of Accountants which was held in Washington, DC, in October 1992.

INTERNATIONAL EDUCATION CONFERENCES

The 1st International Conference on Accounting Education (ICAE), proposed and sponsored by the Accounting Department of the College of Commerce and Business Administration at the University of Illinois as an opportunity for the exchange of teaching techniques and research on an international level, regarding the various problems relating to accounting education, was held in Urbana, Illinois in 1962. Hosted by the university and held on campus, it ran for three days beginning on 1 October, and immediately followed the 8th ICA held in New York. From this time on the ICAE has been held every five years at about the same month as the ICA, in London (1967), Sydney (1972), Berlin (1977), and Monterey, Mexico (1982). Since 1962, then, the ICAE and ICA have been conducted separately, the ICAE addressing itself mainly to teachers of accounting and the ICA to accounting professionals. For the sake of those persons interested in attending both conferences, however, the practice has been to hold them in the same or a neighbouring country, one right on the heels of the other.

The ICAE customarily takes place over three days. Besides a general meeting, there is the main body of the convention consisting of the presentation of papers, following which lecturers and people in attendance divide into smaller groups for more personal discussion.

The 1st ICAE was attended by 101 people plus guests from 13 countries including the United States: 59 delegates from 29 universities together with another 16 people from the business world, or a total of 75 in all, came from the USA, and 26 other people attended from other countries. Canada, Australia, New Zealand, England, Scotland, and Mexico each had three representatives, Ghana and Japan each had two, while Argentina, West Germany, Holland, and Korea each had one. Representing Japan were Ichiro Katano (Hitotsubashi University) and Toru Takezaki (CPA).

The first topic for general discussion at this conference was 'The Nature of Accounting Education', with two reports, 'The Purpose of Accounting Education' (A. C. Littleton), and 'The Scope of Accounting Education' (G. L. Groeneveld), followed by several papers and discussions on the theme 'Approaches to Accounting Education', including 'Approaches to Accounting Education in England' (R. B. T. Castle), 'Education of the Public Accountant in Mexico' (A. E. Charles), 'Some Views on Methods of Accounting Education in Japan' (Ichiro Katano), and 'Accounting Education in Germany' (E. Knorr).

The second topic for general discussion was 'the University and Accounting Research', with two reports, 'The Nature of Accounting Research' (M. Moonitz) and 'International Exchange of Accounting Research' (E. L. Kohler), followed by several papers and discussions on the unifying theme 'Opportunities for Research in Accounting', including 'Behavioral Sciences and Accounting Research' (N. M. Bedford), 'Mathematical Applications' (R. V. Mattessich), 'National Income Accounting' (J. E. Smyth), and 'The Development of Concepts and Principles' (R. K. Yorston).

The 2nd ICAE was held 30 August–1 September 1967 in London immediately prior to the 9th ICA in Paris. Approximately 120 people attended this conference, with Toshio Iino (Hitotsubashi University) and two others representing Japan. At the 2nd ICAE, lectures presented included 'What the Executive Expects of the Public Accountant' (F. S. Capon) and 'Present State of Accounting Education in the United Kingdom' (W. T. Baxter); reports included 'A Curriculum for International Accounting' (G. G. Mueller), 'Some Thoughts on the Epistemology of Accounting' (R. Mattessich), 'Post-Graduate Education in Accounting' (L. W. Snudden), 'Changing Emphasis in Accounting' (B. E. Burke), 'Accounting Education in America' (R. I. Dickey), 'Examinations in Accounting' (V. K. Zimmerman), 'Accountancy Education in the Computer Age' (E. Knorr), and 'Accounting Education for Managers in the Computer Age' (J. Y. D. Tse). Under the unifying theme 'The Professional Accountant and Education', the challenges reported on included 'Accounting Vocational Education in the Netherlands' (G. L. Groeneveld), 'Relationship Between the Practicing Accountant and Education' (S. Bray), and 'Education for the Mature Professional' (R. W. Estes), with such areas as 'Holding Companies and Consolidations—One Classroom Technique' (L. Kritzinger), 'Accounting Education in France' (J. Nataf), and 'Training of the Certified Public Accountant in Japan' (Toru Takezaki), being discussed under the unifying theme 'Approach to Accounting Education'.

The 3rd ICAE was held in Sydney, 21–3 October 1972, immediately following the 10th ICA. Delegates to this convention numbered over 200, representing 17 nations. From Japan Kiyoshi Kurosawa (Dokkyo University) along with eight others attended. Papers presented and discussed at this convention included 'The Two Roles of a University—Inquiry and Teaching' (W. J. Vatter), 'The Role of the Academic as a Critic' (K. F. Byrd), 'What is Empirical Research' (G. J. Staubus), 'The Use of Empirical Material in Teaching Accounting' (J. R. Small), 'An Appraisal of Professional and Individual Research' (G. G. Mueller), and 'The Structure of Accounting Theory' (R. J. Chambers).

The 4th ICAE was held 5–7 October 1977 in West Berlin, immediately before the 11th ICA in Munich. 230 persons attended representing 40 nations, and the Japanese delegates included Kenkichi Matsuo (Meiji University) and others. This conference had as its comprehensive theme

'Accounting Education for Practical Use in a Single World', with three major topics brought up for discussion. The first was 'The Development and State of Conventional Accounting Education Systems' (L. Perridon); the second was 'New Demands on Systems of Accounting Education' (M. Damerval); and the third was 'Recent Demands Made of Accounting Education by Accounting and Auditing', divided into the subtopics 'Inflation Accounting' (R. J. Chambers), 'Forecast Auditing' (J. R. Small), and 'Social Accounting' (R. L. Brummet).

The 5th ICAE was held 14–16 October 1982 in Monterey, following the 12th Congress in Mexico City. 160 delegates from 25 countries attended. A lecture entitled 'Accounting Education—Its Importance and Necessary Conditions (From the Point of View of Economic Development)' (A. J. H. Enthoven) was followed by three papers, 'Accounting Education at the Undergraduate Level' (D. N. Ramirez and R. M. Quintanilla), 'Accounting Education at the Graduate Level' (H. Mann), and 'Continuing Professional Education' (K. W. Kubin) which then served as focal points for group discussion.

The 6th International Conference was held 7–10 October 1987 in Kyoto, Japan, immediately before the 13th Congress in Tokyo. The International Association on Accounting Education and Research (IAAER) was founded on 17 August 1984, and, in co-operation with the Japan Accounting Association (JAA), sponsored the 6th International Conference on Accounting Education. 542 delegates and 105 guests from 38 countries attended. This conference had as its comprehensive theme 'Accounting Education and Research to Promote International Understanding'. Three speeches, entitled 'Mutual Understanding and Mutual Respect Worldwide Among Accounting Educators and Research Scholars' (S. Nakajima), 'Emergence of Accounting as a World Discipline' (G. G. Mueller), and 'International Harmonization of Accounting and Reporting from a European Point of View' (A. Zünd), were followed by presentation of 80 technical papers and a panel discussion entitled 'International Exchange of Accounting Education and Research—The Past, Present and Future'.

This brings us to the 7th International Conference on Accounting Education which was held in Arlington, Virginia, in 1992. The American Accounting Association was primary sponsor along with the IAAER. The theme for the conference was 'Internationalization of Accounting Education'.

A SUMMARY WITH CONCLUSIONS

The International Conference on Accounting Education has never been merely a forum for discussing accounting course curriculum and teaching methods. Rather, it is a place where persons engaged in the teaching of accounting at the university level can meet together in a friendly atmosphere and discuss the various challenges relating to accounting education and research on a broader international level. For this reason, it is often referred to as the International Conference of Accounting Educators.

Ever since the 1st International Conference on Accounting Education in 1962, the custom has been to hold these conferences in the same or a neighbouring country as the International Congresses of Accountants, either just before or just after the Congresses. Indeed, one of the original reasons for having the international education conferences at all was that the accountants' congresses gave accounting educators from all countries an opportunity to hold an international convention of their own. Therefore, until the present time, whenever the decision is made as to the time and place of the next congress, it has essentially meant that the time and location for the next education conference has been set as well.

Noteworthy is that most of the education conferences to and including the 5th were hosted either by one or several universities, rather than by an independent organization like the JAA, which hosted the 6th Conference along with the IAAER. Also, the 7th Conference was hosted by the American Accounting Association, again with the IAAER.

Accounting is by its very nature an international discipline and practice with no boundaries to its impact. Accounting researchers and people making their careers in accounting in America and Europe began holding international conferences at the beginning of this century. These international conferences made great contributions to the development and progress of accounting theory and practice in the various nations of the world. We should appreciate the things the people of these host nations did to contribute to the development of accounting as a science, and as a practising art.

Japan naturally has had its share of delegates at these international congresses. A great many of the delegates have been sponsored by the government organ representing scientists and scholars in Japan, namely the Science Council of Japan, at the suggestion of the Japan Accounting Association. The impact of attendance at these conferences has undeniably played a big role in the rapid development of the theory and practice of accounting in Japan. In spite of this fact, not before 1987 did our country have the pleasure and honour of hosting both of the international congresses on accounting.

Currently the international exchange of ideas and information in all the sciences has reached fever pitch. In the case of accounting, however, Japan's international exchange has tended to be uni-directional: much coming in, little going out. From the time international conferences on accounting got underway at the beginning of this century, with the exception of Mexico and Australia, the host nation had always been either America or a European country. 1987 marked the Japan Accounting

Association's fiftieth year since its founding, and there can have been no more appropriate way to celebrate its golden anniversary than to have hosted the 6th International Conference on Accounting Education here in Japan.

8

The Slip Accounting System: Traditional Bookkeeping Procedures in Japan

An accounting system which uses slips for journalizing purposes or slips bound, account by account, as substitutes for accounting records, and therefore requires neither journal nor ledger, is called 'slip accounting' or 'slip bookkeeping'. Slips were introduced into Japan early in the Meiji era (1868–1911) by the Scotsman Alexander Allan Shand, who designed a bookkeeping system for the National Bank of Japan. Since that time, this method has been employed not only by Japanese banks, but also by nearly all Japanese business firms. While accounting systems in Europe and the United States primarily use accounting books, those in Japan depend largely upon slips. This is a singular characteristic of Japanese accounting.

GENERAL POINTS

The 'slip' constitutes the basic bookkeeping document. It describes briefly the details of a transaction and becomes a means of recording, calculating, and communicating the effects of the transaction. Receipts for cash or goods issued by the recipients of the cash or goods are considered objective and verifiable evidence. These slips can be prepared inside and outside business firms to prove the occurrence of transactions. Yet only slips prepared *within* the business are accepted as a part of the firm's accounting system.

To serve as objective and verifiable evidence, slips must bear the signatures of the person in charge. Receipts and other papers vary from company to company in size and method of entry. Therefore, it is inconvenient in many cases to use such documents as the main records of one company. Moreover, some transactions are not supported by vouchers from the other party. For these reasons, it is now customary for each company to prepare slips in certain forms for all its transactions and to use them as the primary accounting records.

From *International Journal of Accounting*, 7/1 (1971), 99–114.

One of the primary purposes of an accounting system is to record all transactions in the accounts. A slip prepared for each transaction facilitates the journalizing of the transaction because the slip indicates the accounts to be debited and credited. Such a slip is called the accounting slip or journalizing slip.

The following types of slip are generally used today: general, cash-receipts, cash-payments, purchases, and sales. Their use depends upon the particular accounting system adopted by the firm. There are several kinds of accounting systems which use slips: (1) the one-slip system which uses a general slip only; (2) the three-slip system, using cash-receipts, cash-payments, and general slips; and (3) the five-slip system, using cash-receipts, cash-payments, purchases, sales, and general slips.

The fundamental method of recording a transaction is to prepare an accounting slip on the basis of a voucher, journalize it, and post it into the ledger. It is possible, however, to omit the use of the journal and post the transaction directly from the slip to the accounts in the ledger as the slip may serve as the journal. Since slips can be easily classified and totalled by account, it is possible to prepare daily summaries of slips and post the total of all slips affecting the same account. Furthermore, since slips permit duplication, it is possible to use them as the ledger by filing the duplicate slips by account.

THE SINGLE-SLIP SYSTEM

Direct Posting from Slips to Ledger Accounts

Under the single-slip system, general slips are prepared for all transactions. Each general slip shows the account titles and amounts to be debited and credited. Fig. 8.1 shows an example of a slip for a cash sale transaction.

Since entries on general slips do not differ from an ordinary journal entry, the general slips when filed together form a journal, thereby eliminating the use of a journal. Fig. 8.2, an illustrative series of Tokyo Shoten's transactions on 1 April 197– on general slips, may be explained as follows:

1. Cash sales ¥10,000
2. Cash received on accounts receivable: Kitakyushu Shoten, ¥50,000; Nagoya Shoten, ¥30,000
3. Goods in the amount of ¥50,000 are sold to Yokohama Shoten; ¥10,000 is paid in cash, balance on account
4. A loan of ¥50,000 is obtained from the Japan Commercial and Industrial Bank
5. Payments made on accounts payable due: Osaka Shoten, ¥40,000; Kyoto Shoten, ¥20,000

GENERAL SLIP
1 April 197–
No. 1

Amount	*Debit*	*Description*	*Credit*	*Amount*
10,000	cash	sales for cash	sales	10,000
10,000		Total		10,000

Fig. 8.1. Slip for a cash sale transaction

GENERAL SLIP	
Cash 10,000	Sales 10,000

GENERAL SLIP	
Cash 80,000	Accounts receivable 80,000

GENERAL SLIP	
Cash 10,000 Accounts receivable 40,000	Sales 50,000

GENERAL SLIP	
Cash 50,000	Loan payable 50,000

GENERAL SLIP	
Accounts payable 60,000	Cash 60,000

GENERAL SLIP	
Purchases 30,000	Cash 30,000

GENERAL SLIP	
Operating expenses 20,000	Cash 20,000

GENERAL SLIP	
Purchases 120,000	Accounts payable 120,000

GENERAL SLIP	
Accounts receivable 110,000	Sales 110,000

GENERAL SLIP	
Notes receivable 70,000	Accounts receivable 70,000

GENERAL SLIP	
Accounts payable 50,000	Notes payable 50,000

Fig. 8.2. Tokyo Shoten's transactions on 1 April 197—

6. Cash purchases ¥30,000
7. Operating expenses of ¥20,000 are paid in cash
8. Goods purchases on account from Osaka Shoten, ¥50,000; Kyoto Shoten, ¥40,000; Kobe Shoten, ¥30,000
9. Goods sold on account to Kitakyushu Shoten, ¥50,000; Nagoya Shoten, ¥60,000
10. Promissory notes received on accounts receivable due: Nagoya Shoten, ¥40,000; Yokohama Shoten, ¥30,000
11. Promissory notes are drawn up on accounts payable due: Kyoto Shoten, ¥30,000; Kobe Shoten, ¥20,000

Under the single-slip system, the general slip is called the journalizing slip or the accounting slip. In this article, however, it is called the general slip for the purpose of comparison with the multiple-slip systems.

Preparing Daily Reports and Posting Totals to Ledger Accounts

The amounts on the general slips could be posted to the ledger accounts directly. Since the slips can be classified in any way, it seems advisable to total them by the individual accounts and to post totals only, thereby reducing the number of postings required. This will also decrease the number of errors made in the posting process.

Two methods of posting the total amounts to the ledger accounts can be used: (1) the totals may be entered in a two-column journal and posted to their respective accounts; or (2) a daily report may be prepared and used to post the amounts to their respective accounts. A daily report is a summary which gives the total debits and total credits for each account each day. A daily report prepared from the general slips prepared for the 1 April transactions of Tokyo Shoten is illustrated in Fig. 8.3. The P/R column shows the number of each account in accordance with a chart of accounts.

Trial-Balance Form Ledger

A daily report prepared from general slips can be expanded further by adding to or subtracting from the balances of the accounts of the preceding day the debit and credit amounts of the accounts indicated in the daily report. When a balance column is provided in the daily report and the balances of the accounts for each day are entered therein, the daily report can be used as a ledger. This type of ledger is called a tabular ledger. By totaling the debit and credit balances of the accounts on this type of ledger, a trial balance can be prepared to test the accuracy of the

DAILY REPORT 1 April 197–						
Debit	*P/R*	*No. of slips*	*Account*	*No. of slips*	*P/R*	*Credit*
150,000	1	4	Cash	3	1	110,000
70,000	2	1	Notes receivable			
150,000	3	2	Accounts receivable	2	3	150,000
			Notes payable	1	11	50,000
110,000	12	2	Accounts payable	1	12	120,000
			Loan payable	1	13	50,000
			Sales	3	31	170,000
150,000	41	2	Purchases			
20,000	42	1	Operating expenses			
650,000						650,000

Fig. 8.3. Daily report for transactions of Tokyo Shoten, 1 April 197—

postings. Because this type of ledger fulfils the function of the trial balance, it is called the trial-balance ledger (see Fig. 8.4).

Multiple Copies of Slips

When the general slips for each day are classified and totalled account by account and the totals are posted to the respective ledger accounts, the ledger accounts become too condensed to show any details. Therefore, it is advisable to prepare for each general slip as many copies as there are accounts to which the entries in the slip should be posted. In this way, the original slips are filed in the chronological order of transactions while the duplicate copies are filed by account. The account on each slip should be circled. See Fig. 8.5, which shows goods in the amount of ¥50,000 sold to Yokohama Shoten. Ten thousand yen is received in cash. The balance is on account.

LEDGER 1 April 197–								31 March 197–
Account no.	*Account*	*No. of slips*	*Debit*	*No. of slips*	*Credit*	*Dr./Cr.*	*Balance*	*Balance*
1	Cash	4	150,000	3	110,000	Dr.	90,000	50,000
2	Notes receivable	1	70,000			"	150,000	80,000
3	Accounts receivable	2	150,000	2	150,000	"	200,000	200,000
4	Inventories					"	100,000	100,000
5	Fixtures					"	50,000	50,000
41	Purchases	2	150,000			"	150,000	
42	Operating expenses	1	20,000			"	20,000	
	Total of debit items					Dr.	760,000	480,000
11	Notes payable			1	50,000	Cr.	150,000	100,000
12	Accounts payable	2	110,000	1	120,000	"	160,000	150,000
13	Loan payable			1	50,000	"	80,000	30,000
21	Capital stock					"	200,000	200,000
31	Sales			3	170,000	"	170,000	
	Total of credit items					Cr.	760,000	480,000
	Today's total		650,000		650,000			

Fig. 8.4. Trial-balance ledger

Single-Account Slip

By preparing each slip with as many copies as the number of accounts affected, these copies can conveniently be filed by individual accounts. This method has one disadvantage, however. The number of copies needed varies from transaction to transaction. Therefore it seems advisable to enter only one account in the debit and credit column of each general slip.

When using single-account general slips, the slip for each transaction is best prepared in triplicate so that the first copy can be filed in the chronological transaction order, the second used as a debit slip, and the

GENERAL SLIP 1 April 197–			
Debit	*Amount*	*Credit*	*Amount*
Cash	10,000	Sales	50,000
Accounts receivable	40,000		
Total	50,000	Total	50,000

GENERAL SLIP 1 April 197–			
Debit	*Amount*	*Credit*	*Amount*
Cash	10,000	Sales	50,000
Accounts receivable	40,000		
Total	50,000	Total	50,000

GENERAL SLIP 1 April 197–			
Debit	*Amount*	*Credit*	*Amount*
Cash	10,000	Sales	50,000
Accounts receivable	40,000		
Total	50,000	Total	50,000

Fig. 8.5. Multiple copies of slips

third as a credit slip. (See example in Fig. 8.6.) When single-account general slips are used, the ruled lines on the debit slip and those on the credit slip are usually printed in different colours for easier classification. The slips are filed chronologically.

When using single-account general slips, transactions involving more

GENERAL SLIP 1 April 197–			
Debit	*Cash*	*Credit*	*Sales*
Description			
Total			10,000

(for chronological file)

GENERAL SLIP 1 April 197–			
Debit	*Cash*	*Credit*	*Sales*
Description			
Total			10,000

(for debiting)

GENERAL SLIP 1 April 197–			
Debit	*Cash*	*Credit*	*Sales*
Description			
Total			10,000

(for crediting)

Fig. 8.6. Single account general slips

than one account in the debit and/or the credit column should be divided so that the transactions can be journalized in such a way that only one account will appear in the debit and credit columns. For example, of Tokyo Shoten's transactions on 1 April, the one described as 'goods in the amount of ¥50,000 are sold, ¥10,000 are received in cash, and the balance is on account' can be divided as shown under Method 1 or Method 2.

CASH-RECEIPTS SLIP 1 April 197–	
Account credited	*Sales*
Description	
Total	10,000

Fig. 8.7. Cash-receipts slip

Under Method 1, the transaction is journalized as a charge sale of ¥50,000, of which ¥10,000 are received immediately in cash. Under Method 2, the transaction is journalized as if there were two transactions—a cash and a charge sale:

Method 1

1. Accounts receivable	50,000	Sales	50,000
2. Cash	10,000	Accounts receivable	10,000

Method 2

1. Cash	10,000	10,000 Sales	10,000
2. Accounts receivable	40,000	40,000 Sales	40,000

THE THREE-SLIP SYSTEM

Introduction of Special Slips

Under the three-slip system, the cash-receipts and the cash-payments slips are used in addition to the general slip. Separate cash-receipts slips and cash-payments slips are needed because in most business firms cash transactions are more frequent than any other transactions. Special cash-transaction slips allow an easy distinction of cash transactions from other transactions. Furthermore, entries in slips can also be simplified.

The cash-receipts slip is normally ruled with red lines. Since a cash-receipt transaction is automatically a debit to the cash account, only the account title to be credited is stated in the account title column as in Fig. 8.7.

The cash-payments slip, also called the disbursements slip, is normally ruled with blue lines. Since a cash-payment transaction is always a credit to cash, only the account title to be debited is stated in the account title column as in Fig. 8.8.

CASH-PAYMENTS SLIP 1 April 197–	
Account debited	*Accounts payable*
Description	
Total	40,000

Fig. 8.8. Cash-payments slip

Daily Reports on Cash Receipts and Cash Payments

The amount to be posted to debit the cash account is the total of all amounts entered in cash-receipts slips. The amount to be posted to credit the accounts other than the cash account can be found by totalling the amounts entered in cash-receipts slips account by account. If a daily summary of cash-receipts slips is prepared by classifying and totalling the cash-receipts slips for the day account by account, the totals entered in the summary are posted to debit the cash account and credit the other accounts. This daily summary of cash-receipts slips is called the daily report of cash receipts. (See Fig. 8.9.)

When goods are sold to Yokohama Shoten and ¥10,000 of the sales price of ¥50,000 is received in cash and the balance recorded on account, the posting to debit the accounts receivable account and to credit the sales account is made from the daily report prepared from general slips. Therefore, the title of the account affected, entered on the cash-receipts slip, should be 'miscellaneous'. Since no posting is made from the daily report of cash receipts to the accounts receivable and sales accounts, a check mark is placed in the P/R column of the daily report of cash receipts to indicate that there is no need for posting.

The amount to be posted to credit the cash account is the total of all amounts entered in cash-payments slips. The amounts to be posted to debit other accounts can be determined by totalling the amounts entered on the cash-payments slips for each account. If a daily summary of cash-payments slips is prepared by classifying and totalling the slips for the day, account by account, the total amount of the summary report is posted to credit the cash account and the total amount of each account to debit the other related accounts in the ledger. The daily summary of cash-payments slips is called the daily report of cash payments or disbursements.

CASH RECEIPTS SLIP	
Sales	10,000

CASH RECEIPTS SLIP	
Accounts receivable	80,000

CASH RECEIPTS SLIP	
Miscellaneous	10,000

CASH RECEIPTS SLIP	
Loan payable	50,000

DAILY REPORT OF CASH RECEIPTS 1 April 197–

Account	*No. of slips*	*P/R*	*Amount*
Accounts receivable	1	3	80,000
Loan payable	1	13	50,000
Sales	1	31	10,000
Miscellaneous	1	2	10,000
Cash	4	1	150,000

Fig. 8.9. Daily report of cash receipts

Daily Report of Other Transactions

With cash-receipts slips being used for cash receipts and cash-payments slips for cash payments, all other transactions are recorded on general slips. The method of entry is identical with that used for the general slips under the single-slip system. Each general slip should show the account title and amount to be debited and the account title and amount to be credited.

To post the entries of the general slips to the ledger accounts, daily totals for each account are obtained by classifying and totalling the general slips account by account. The daily report based on general slips summarizes the general slips and shows the daily total for each account.

For posting from the daily report based on general slips to the ledger accounts, the amounts shown for each account on the debit and credit sides of the report should be posted to the corresponding ledger accounts. Because the posting to the cash account is made from the totals of the daily report on cash receipts and the daily report on cash payments, a check mark is placed in the P/R column of the daily report based on general slips to show that there is no need for posting. (See Fig. 8.10.)

Combined Daily Report

When the three slips, cash-receipts, cash-payments, and general, are used, these slips are classified and totalled to prepare three daily reports: the

GENERAL SLIP	
Cash 10,000	Sales 50,000
Accounts receivable 40,000	

GENERAL SLIP	
Purchases 120,000	Accounts payable 120,000

GENERAL SLIP	
Accounts receivable 110,000	Sales 110,000

GENERAL SLIP	
Notes receivable 70,000	Accounts receivable 70,000

GENERAL SLIP	
Accounts payable 50,000	Notes payable 50,000

DAILY REPORT
OF
OTHER TRANSACTIONS
1 April 197–

Debit	*P/R*	*No. of slips*	*Account*	*No. of slips*	*P/R*	*Credit*
70,000	2	1	Notes receivable			
150,000	3	2	Accounts receivable	1	3	70,000
			Notes payable	1	11	50,000
50,000	12	1	Accounts payable	1	12	120,000
			Sales	2	31	160,000
120,000	41	1	Purchases			
10,000	2	1	Cash			
40,000						400,000

Fig. 8.10. Daily report of other transactions

daily report of cash receipts, the daily report of cash payments, and the daily report based on general slips. For combined posting a combined daily report may be prepared by totalling for each account the amounts entered in the three daily reports instead of directly posting the amounts shown in them to the ledger accounts. The daily totals entered in the combined daily report can then be posted to the ledger accounts.

Therefore, the balances in the accounts at the end of the day can be determined by adding to or subtracting the debit and credit amounts of the accounts shown in the combined daily report from the balances of the previous day. By providing a balance column in the combined report and entering the balances at the end of each day in this column, the combined daily report can be used as a trial-balance form ledger.

The daily report shown in Fig. 8.11 is a combination of the daily report of cash receipts, the daily report of cash payments, the daily report based on general slips, and the combined daily report. It illustrates the relationship between the first three daily reports and the combined daily report. The report has a balance column and, therefore, can serve as a trial-balance ledger. The amounts in the balance column are determined by adding to or subtracting from the balances of 31 March. For this reason, the amounts marked 'unclassified' represent a transaction included in two daily reports which are offset by each other to avoid double posting.

FIVE-SLIP SYSTEM

Two more slips—purchases and sales slips—are added to the cash-receipts, cash-payments, and general slips when purchases and sales are as frequent as cash receipts and payments. By using specialized slips for purchases and sales transactions, such transactions are easily distinguished from other transactions. The purchases slip is prepared on the basis of the purchase invoice but the sales slip is generally a duplicate copy of the sales invoice. This is the five-slip system.

Purchase transactions are journalized on purchases slips and are summarized in the daily report of purchases which is posted to debit the purchases account and to credit the accounts payable account. Sales transactions are journalized in sales slips and are totalled in the daily report of sales which is posted to debit the accounts receivable account and to credit the sales account.

CONCLUSIONS

Various methods of employing slips to record transactions in accounts have been presented. The advantages and disadvantages of these three-slip accounting systems may be indicated.

The single-slip system is easy to operate as it uses only one type of slip as the accounting slip. Copies produced by duplication can be filed by account to serve as substitutes for ledger accounts. On the other hand, some transactions cannot be described adequately on slips because the same form of slip is used for all transactions, and slips cannot easily be prepared by clerks other than accounting clerks because a knowledge of the debit and credit accounts is necessary.

The three-slip system is easy to operate. Cash-receipts slips and cash-payments slips are easily prepared if the clerk can singly distinguish cash receipts from cash payments, even though he does not know

(31 March 197–)

DAILY REPORT
1 April 197–

Acct. no.	Account	Daily report of cash receipts		Daily report of cash payments		Daily report of other transactions		Total		Balance	
		Dr.	Cr.	Dr.	Cr.	Dr.	Cr.	Dr.	Cr.	Dr.	Cr.
1	Cash	150,000			110,000	xxx	xxx	150,000	110,000	90,000	
2	Notes receivable					70,000		70,000		150,000	
3	Accounts receivable		80,000			150,000	70,000	150,000	150,000	200,000	
4	Inventories									100,000	
5	Fixtures									50,000	
11	Notes payable						50,000		50,000		150,000
12	Accounts payable			60,000		50,000	120,000	110,000	120,000		160,000
13	Loan payable		50,000						50,000		80,000
21	Capital stock										200,000
31	Sales		10,000				160,000		170,000		170,000
41	Purchases			30,000		120,000		150,000		150,000	
42	Operating expenses			20,000				20,000		20,000	
	Unclassified		10,000			10,000		xxx	xxx	xxx	xxx
		150,000	150,000	110,000	110,000	400,000	400,000	650,000	650,000	760,000	760,000

Fig. 8.11. Combined daily report

double-entry principles. On the other hand, the system does not completely remove the shortcomings of the single-slip system as purchases and sales must be entered on general slips as do other miscellaneous transactions.

The five-slip system is better in several ways. The most suitable form for each type of transaction can be developed for the slips used for cash receipts, cash payments, purchases, and sales. The different types of slips can be prepared easily by all personnel, not just accountants. On the other hand, the system is difficult to operate as it requires many types of slips, and because the slips differ in size and form, they cannot be substituted for ledger accounts by binding them.

Each of the three methods has its advantages and disadvantages. The single-slip system is most suitable for those small businesses in which the owners themselves oversee sales, purchases, cash receipts and payments, and accounting. In other cases, the accountant should prepare accounting slips on the basis of slips originally prepared for individual transactions by the different persons in charge of the transactions. In view of its advantages, particularly that of preparing slips largely for cash receipts and payments, the three-slip system is suitable for financial businesses which have few transactions other than cash receipts and payments. The five-slip system is considered suitable for business firms in which a considerable degree of division of labour exists in the fields of sales, purchases, cash receipts and payments, and accounting.

The slip system has many elements similar to modern punch-card and other systems based on unit posting devices. The system has been widely used in Japan with manual methods of recording for a much longer time than modern punch-card accounting.

PART II.

PROBLEMS IN FINANCIAL ACCOUNTING THEORY

9

The Development of Financial Accounting

THE FUNCTIONS OF FINANCIAL ACCOUNTING

Financial accounting, as is suggested by the word 'financial', is accounting connected with the capital-raising activities of business enterprises. The capital needed for the various activities of a business enterprise is obtained from its investors and creditors, and these people are keenly interested in how effectively the enterprise uses the capital and how the capital is maintained. Financial accounting provides this information for them on the capital invested in the enterprise. These functions of financial accounting are very important for smooth capital-raising operations. If financial accounting is inadequate the investors and creditors cannot find out how effectively the capital invested in the enterprise is used, or whether that capital is maintained. As a result, they will hesitate to invest in the enterprise, thereby making it difficult for the enterprise to raise the necessary capital.

Therefore financial accounting plays a particularly important role in incorporated business enterprises, in which ownership is separated from management—viz. the capital is contributed by a large number of people who do not take part in management—rather than in enterprises managed by people who have supplied the capital. In the case of corporations, the capital is supplied by a large number of stockholders but the management is entrusted to the directors elected by the stockholders. Business today is so complicated that it is not always easy to manage an enterprise. For this reason, people with excellent managerial ability are elected to the management, whether they are stockholders or not, and the stockholders entrust this management with the operation and control of the capital. This makes financial accounting remarkably important to the management as an aid to controlling the capital received in trust from the stockholders, periodically determining income available for dividends to the stockholders, and providing the stockholders and creditors with

From *Waseda Business and Economic Studies*, No. 7 (1971), 23–33.

information on the business operations of the enterprise, which they need for making decisions on investments and loans. For the majority of stockholders who do not directly participate in the management of the enterprise, the amount of income available for dividends determined by financial accounting is the only information available on the legality of the amount of dividends paid by the enterprise. Besides, information furnished by financial accounting about the business operations of the enterprise can be said to provide the main basis for judgement on the profitability and security of the investment in the enterprise.

However, there are difficulties in designing a form of financial accounting which will satisfactorily perform both of its two principal functions: (1) determination of income available for dividends and (2) supplying information on the business operations of the enterprise. For example, suppose that a firm holds some land, the value of which has risen. This would be regarded as a gain in an economic sense. But the existing law prevents this gain from being brought into account as profit available for dividends. Thus, since the determination of income available for dividends is of a predominantly legal nature, information on the business operations of the enterprise cannot be fully supplied in terms of concepts related to the determination of income available for dividends. Conversely, the concepts employed for information on the business operations of the enterprise cannot be directly related to the determination of income legally available for dividends.

Therefore, financial accounting can perform both its functions satisfactorily only when the concepts relating to the determination of income available for dividends accord with those relating to the measurement of the business operations of the enterprise. In ordinary cases, satisfactory performance of one of the functions leads to unsatisfactory performance of the other. Financial accounting has continued to wrestle with the problem of how to ensure the satisfactory performance of both functions.

LEGAL CAPITAL AND PAID-IN CAPITAL

The separation, in financial accounting, of the function of determining income available for dividends and that of supplying information on the business operations of the enterprise first occurred when corporations adopted the practice of issuing par value stock at a premium or refraining from crediting to the capital stock account a portion of the amount contributed by purchasers of no-par stock. In financial accounting, it is important to make clear the amount of capital received by the management in trust from the investors. The management must control this capital in such a way that there is no improper distribution of it. Therefore, it is a major task of financial accounting to distinguish clearly between the capital held by the management in trust from the investors and the income resulting from its operation.

The income of an enterprise is the increase in its net assets which could be distributed as dividends without any impairment of the invested capital. The capital is not maintained if the distribution of the corporate assets exceeds the amount of income. But if the amount of income is not properly determined and the distinction between capital and income is not maintained, no one knows whether capital is maintained. The distinction between capital and income is overwhelmingly important as a matter of maintenance of the capital received by the management in trust from the investors.

In the case of corporations, stock is issued for the capital paid in by the stockholders. When par value stock is issued, the capital of the corporation is the par value multiplied by the number of shares of capital stock issued and outstanding. When no-par stock is issued, the capital is the issue price per share multiplied by the number of shares of capital stock issued and oustanding. Such amount of capital represents the total amount of the capital received by the management in trust from the stockholders. In the case of corporations whose stockholders have only a limited liability, it denotes the net worth which the corporation should maintain for the protection of the creditors. When the net worth exceeds the amount of capital, a profit accrues. The amount of such profit represents in legal terms the total amount available for dividends and signifies in economic terms a result of the use of the capital.

However, the practice of issuing par value stock at a premium—namely, above par—or of not crediting to the capital stock account a portion of the amount contributed by purchasers of no-par stock, has complicated the question: 'What is the capital received by the management in trust from the stockholders?' Economically, it is indisputable that the excess over par or stated value is a part of the stockholders' investment. In this sense, the capital received by the management in trust from the stockholders, including the excess over par or stated value, is certainly the capital contributed by the stockholders. Legally, however, the capital of a corporation is the par value multiplied by the number of shares of capital stock issued and outstanding in the case of par value stock, or the stated value multiplied by the number of capital stock issued and outstanding in the case of no-par stock. Therefore we have two different concepts of capital: legal capital and paid-in capital.

Thus the excess over par or stated value received from a sale of capital stock legally belongs to the category of income, but economically falls into that of capital. This means that the amount of capital to be maintained, and therefore the amount of income, varies according to whether the accountability of the management is viewed in legal or economic terms. Financial accounting combines the legal and economic classifications of capital and income to produce the concept of capital surplus, which is placed between capital stock, which is of the nature of capital in both legal and economic terms, and earned surplus, which is of the nature of income in both legal and economic terms.

Accounting classification	*Legal classification*	*Economic classification*
Capital stock	Capital	Capital
Capital surplus	Income	Capital
Earned surplus	Income	Income

From this viewpoint, the profit from a consolidation or merger of corporations and the profit from the retirement of capital stock are both considered as a capital surplus. If the acquisition of Company B by Company A, for example, is considered to mean that the stockholders of the former acquire the shares issued by the latter for the former's net worth, the profit from the acquisition, i.e. the excess of Company B's net worth over Company A's capital stock increased by the acquisition, is undoubtedly a capital paid in by the stockholders, although it is not legally recognized as such. (Of course, this does not apply to the formal merger of two or more corporations which are considered substantially to constitute a single economic entity.) In the case of the retirement of capital stock, a procedure to reduce the amount of legal capital, the profit from the retirement, i.e. the excess of the amount originally received on the issue of the stock over that paid back to the stockholders, is considered economically to retain the nature of the stockholders' paid-in capital, although it legally loses the nature of capital. The profit from a consolidation or merger and that from the retirement of capital stock are both legally included in the category of income, but economically they fall into the category of capital.

The introduction of the concept of capital surplus into financial accounting reflects an effort to realize, within the framework of the very formal legal distinction between capital and income, the economic fact that the capital received by the management in trust from the stockholders is the total amount of capital paid in by the stockholders. Income available for dividends is produced when the net worth exceeds the amount of legal capital. However, it is certain that par value stock premiums and other surpluses, which, as pointed out here, are not legally recognized as capital, constitute the stockholders' investment, and not the income resulting from the use of the capital. The profitability of capital cannot be measured in terms of legal concepts of capital.

The capital surplus concept has been introduced into financial accounting in an attempt to ensure the satisfactory performance of the two functions: determination of income available for dividends, and the supply of information on the business operations of the enterprise. Today, the economic distinction between capital and income is respected to a considerable extent even in the legal determination of income available for dividends:

par value stock premiums and other items mentioned above are now excluded from income available for dividends.

NOMINAL CAPITAL AND INVESTMENT PURCHASING POWER

The separation, in financial accounting, of the function of determining income available for dividends and that of supplying information on the business operations of the enterprise also resulted from the fluctuation of the purchasing power of money as the yardstick in financial accounting.

Financial accounting is concerned with the capital-raising activities of business enterprises; it accounts for the capital received by the management in trust from the investors and creditors. Therefore financial accounting traces the flow of such capital from the time of its arrival in the enterprise until it finally leaves the enterprise. Once brought into the enterprise, capital should not be lost without reason. Whether contributed by the stockholders or loaned from a bank, capital is generally raised in the form of money. It is spent on goods and services and then recovered in monetary form. Capital in monetary form is called monetary assets, and the capital invested in goods or services and not yet recovered in monetary form is called non-monetary assets. To trace the movement of capital invested in a business enterprise, it is necessary to bring to light the types of assets into which the capital brought into the enterprise goes. In this sense, the debit side of the balance sheet can be said to indicate the forms of assets in which the management has invested the capital received in trust from the stockholders and creditors.

It should be noted here that the price of non-monetary assets stated on the balance sheet does not represent the value of such assets, but the amount of capital invested in such assets. For example, a transaction involving the purchase of a tract of land and the payment of ¥10,000,000 in cash for it means, in financial accounting, the investment of a capital of ¥10,000,000 in that tract of land rather than the acquistion of ¥10,000,000 worth of land. Therefore, value of the land is indicated as ¥10,000,000 on the balance sheet irrespective of the subsequent fluctuation of its actual price. It means that a capital of ¥10,000,000 is invested in the land. For the same reason, goodwill is stated on the balance sheet only when it has been acquired by purchase. Goodwill without any cost is not shown on the balance sheet because financial accounting is concerned with the indication of the amount of capital invested in goodwill rather than the value of goodwill.

Capital invested in goods and services is recovered in the form of revenue, i.e. the prices of goods and services sold. The accounting period in which the capital invested in goods and services is recovered in the form of revenue is determined by the time at which trading transactions occur which are connected with the said goods and services. That amount of capital invested in goods and services which should be recovered as the revenue for a certain accounting period is called the expenses for that period. When revenue and expenses are equal, capital has been recovered without any excess or shortage. When revenue exceeds expenses, the capital invested in business operations has been recovered, and there accrues a surplus or profit. When revenue falls short of expenses, the capital invested in business operations has not been fully recovered, thereby causing a loss of capital. Income determination which compares revenue and expenses for each accounting period is nothing but accounting for capital maintenance.

Here problems are raised by the concept of capital held in trust and controlled by the management. Is it enough for the management just to maintain the nominal amount of the capital held in trust? Or does it have the responsibility of maintaining the real purchasing power of entrusted capital when there are fluctuations in the purchasing power of money? It is true that in the case of capital borrowed from a creditor, it is enough for the management to repay him the nominal amount stipulated in the loan agreement. However, can the management fully perform its trust responsibility to the permanent investors in the enterprise, merely by maintaining the nominal amount of capital held in trust?

If so, income available for dividends will appear when capital recovered by business operations exceeds the nominal amount of capital received in trust from the investors. The law evidently takes this position. However, when the purchasing power of money is lowered by inflation, the management cannot maintain the entrusted capital in real terms by maintaining the nominal amount of that capital. From an economic viewpoint, the management can be said to perform its trust responsibility only when it maintains the purchasing power of the capital received in trust from the investors. In this case, the income of the enterprise is calculated on the assumption that the purchasing power of capital should be maintained.

In financial accounting, which uses money as the unit of measurement, the decline of the purchasing power of money causes a separation of the legal and economic concepts of capital received by the management in trust from the investors. Legally, such capital is a nominal amount of money, but economically it should be the real purchasing power of money. In financial accounting to date, the amount of capital received by the management in trust from the investors has never been determined in terms of purchasing power, although it occasionally occurred that the amount of capital invested in fixed assets, etc. was adjusted to a change in the purchasing power of money. For this reason, financial accounting is not considered to be satisfactorily performing the function of supplying information on the business operations of enterprises, even though it can determine income legally available for dividends.

ACCOUNTING FOR CAPITAL MAINTENANCE AND ACCOUNTING FOR DECISION-MAKING

In the present article, I have taken the position that financial accounting is concerned with the capital-raising activities of business enterprises and that it accounts for capital which the management receives in trust from investors and creditors. Pointing out that there are two quantitative concepts of such capital—legal capital and paid-in capital—and two qualitative concepts, nominal capital and investment purchasing power, I have considered these concepts in relation to the two principal functions of financial accounting: determination of income available for dividends and the supply of information on the business operations of enterprises.

Certainly, legal capital and nominal capital are concepts related to the determination of income available for dividends, as paid-in capital and investment purchasing power are concepts related to the measurement of the business operations of enterprises. If either of these sets of concepts is adopted at the expense of the other, financial accounting cannot satisfactorily perform both its functions. For this reason, financial accounting has solved the problem of the separation of legal capital and paid-in capital by introducing the concept of capital surplus so that both concepts of capital can be compatible. Today, the law too recognizes the economic concept of paid-in capital, permitting the exclusion of the greater part of capital surplus from income available for dividends. Thus the difficulties caused by the separation of legal capital and paid-in capital have been almost completely obviated.

With regard to the separation of nominal capital and investment purchasing power, however, financial accounting still rejects the concept of investment purchasing power in favour of nominal capital. This is clearly oriented to the determination of income available for dividends, and not to the measurement of the business operations of enterprises. Herein lies the weakness of the informative function of financial accounting. However, such weakness is not likely to be eliminated even by introducing the concept of investment purchasing power into financial accounting, for financial accounting concerns itself with the capital-raising activities of business enterprises and accounts for capital which the management receives in trust from investors and creditors. As long as financial accounting is accounting for capital held in trust by the management, it cannot go either legally or economically beyond accounting for capital maintenance; it has to give precedence to the function of determining income legally or economically available for dividends.

In recent years, the information function of financial accounting has come to be considered so important that arguments have been advanced for the appraisal of assets at the current cost and even the recognition of goodwill without cost. There is no doubt that acquisition cost, which has formed the basis of financial accounting, is not satisfactory as the basis for forecasting the earning power, solvency, or overall management efficiency of business enterprises. However, the original cost of assets shows how much of the capital which the management has received in trust from the investors and creditors has been invested in such assets. It is the basic concept of financial accounting which controls, under the stewardship of the management, the capital of the investors and creditors paid into the enterprise. The current cost concept is something alien to such financial accounting. Although current cost could be used in combination with acquisition cost, the former cannot supersede the latter.

So far, accounting has generally been divided into financial accounting and management accounting. The former has been characterized as external reporting and the latter as internal reporting. However, this apparently has imposed two exceedingly difficult functions on a single accounting system—financial accounting. Now is the time, it appears, to separate the two principal functions hitherto performed by financial accounting—determination of income available for dividends and the supply of information on the business operations of enterprises—and establish a separate accounting area for each.

Determination of income available for dividends is, after all, a function of accounting for capital maintenance, while the measurement of the business operations of enterprises is a function of accounting for providing the stockholders and creditors with information they need to make decisions on investment or loans. The latter will form accounting for decision-making, together with accounting for supplying information necessary for the management's decision-making, as shown in the chart below:

Accounting for capital maintenance	Accounting for legal capital maintenance
	Accounting for economic capital maintenance
Accounting for decision-making	Accounting for decision-making by investors and creditors
	Accounting for decision-making by management

10

The Classification of Assets in Accounting

A Proposal for the Incorporation of a Cash-Cost Classification to Replace the Current–Fixed Classification on the Balance Sheet

INTRODUCTION

In Japan following the war a new battle raged among scholars here concerning the concept of assets in accounting. At that time I pointed out that, implicit in every one of the theories attempting a unified explanation of asset concepts, was the existence of two separate asset groupings possessing different natures. Of course it was because of the existence of two such asset groupings that the battle over a unified interpretation broke out in the first place, and the existence of these two asset groupings was something very fundamental indeed.

In his paper 'The Cost and Value of Assets', which attempts a unified interpretation of assets from the viewpoint of cost and value, Tetsuzo Ohta (1950: 4) recognizes the two asset groupings as follows:

> In order to advance the theory of asset evaluation German business law scholars once divided assets into 'utilized' items (fixed asset items) and 'marketed' items (merchandise and related assets), and applied separate evaluation standards to each. Their system lacked unity and has long since been abandoned. In contrast to the above system, it is much more reasonable to divide assets into expense items and value items (proposed titles). This is because cash, accounts and notes receivable, etc., all the various itemizations belonging to the so-called cash grouping, in themselves constitute the actual body of cash. Whereas on the other hand, raw materials and supplies, merchandise, and finished goods, property, plant and equipment, etc. are all produced, sold off, and converted into cash by means of business activities. In other words, a dividing line can be drawn with reference to business activities which are the objective of the business.

From *Waseda Business and Economic Studies*, No. 24 (1988), 1–13.

Unsatisfied with merely dividing these two groupings, Ohta delved deeper in pursuit of a coherent, uni-dimensional interpretation and developed the ideas of 'cost' and 'value'.

Katsuji Yamashita (1950, 1951) criticized Ohta's attempts in 'A Critical Examination of Ohta's Theories' and 'The Cash Value of Assets', but even in these papers we find recognition of two asset groupings: Cash (C′) having completed the entire cycle of Cash (C) → Merchandise (M) → (C′); and merchandise (M) still tied up in the C → M part of the cycle. He then attempted a unified explanation from the viewpoint of cash value (1950: 16):

> Ohta's theory stresses the unexpired cost of cash based on the fact that such cash is ultimately used as payment for expenses. But as long as we concern ourselves with the nature of assets on the balance sheet, it goes against fact to disregard the cash value of such money used in making purchases. In this way then, we see within the idea of total asset cash value, cash value as such, existing side by side with cash value already designated as expenses. Land, residual values of property, plant and equipment (except land), accrued revenue, etc., not to mention cash, and marketable securities, etc. belong to the former grouping, while such items as merchandise, finished goods, work in progress, property, plant and equipment (net of residual value) and prepayments for goods or services as yet to be received belong to the latter. There remains the problem of purchased goodwill, but presumably such items will be included in the latter.

The aim of the present paper is to clarify the nature of the two different asset groupings implicit within such theories, and to ask whether a substitute might not be found for the traditional current–fixed classification of assets using a scheme based upon these two asset groupings.

CASH-RELATED ASSETS AND COST-RELATED ASSETS

Ohta intended value as well as cost to represent future usefulness, that is to say expense, and did not intend them to indicate a cashing-in process. In this sense, Yamashita's idea of distinguishing assets and expenses in connection with the M → C′ process did not differ in any fundamental respect, as Kazuo Miyagami (1951) points out in his paper, 'Assets as Recovered-Invested Capital'. The only difference between the two theories is whether assets are viewed in terms of their cost or in terms of their cash value. The former approach is one whereby all assets—those involved in the C → M process as well as the M → C′ process—are uni-dimensionally explained as M. In the latter approach, all assets—those involved in the M → C′ process as well as those involved in the C → M process—are uni-dimensionally explained as C. As a result then, the problem with the first approach is how to explain cash, accounts and notes receivable, etc. in terms of their unexpired cost, and the solution has been to treat them as expense amounts pending the opportunity to be expended. With the latter approach, the problem becomes how to explain inventories, property, plant and equipment, etc. in terms of their cash value, and the solution has been to treat them as items for which no cash payments were made during the accounting period and reduce them to cash.

It is my contention, however, that the two asset groupings implicit in the above, that is to say the asset grouping involved in the $C \rightarrow M$ part of the operating cycle and the asset grouping involved in the $M \rightarrow C'$ part of the operating cycle, are completely different in nature, and if anything, their different natures ought to be stressed. In his paper 'Cash on the Dynamic Balance Sheet', Iwao Iwata (1951) makes clear the fact that the dynamic balance sheet can be derived automatically from a combination of a revenue-expense computation and a receipt-payment computation, and concludes that there is no need to explain various asset items in a single manner, nor in fact can such an explanation be made. Although the point under discussion is different, I question whether it is really necessary to interpret the two asset groupings in a single, unified manner. Suffice it to say that the asset items on the balance sheet are comprised of two essentially different groupings.

It follows that, in order to stress the existence of these two asset groupings, the asset classification on the balance sheet too must be arranged accordingly, and it is my belief that this entails abandoning the traditional classification into current and fixed assets. The reasons for this will be discussed later. First of all I wish to clarify what sort of entities I consider the two asset groupings to be. Assets involved in the $C \rightarrow M$ process I term 'cost-related assets', while assets involved in the $M \rightarrow C'$ process are called 'cash-related assets'. They are understood in the following manner.

Cost-related assets assist in future business activities, and can be regarded as unconsumed expenses to be applied to future period earnings. Because accounting as practised today assumes income measurement on a periodic basis, rather than treating all payments against inventory items and fixed assets as expense during a single operating period, only portions corresponding to revenue for that period are charged as expenses. Remaining amounts are deferred against revenue for later periods. These are cost-related assets. I regard inventory items and prepaid expenses traditionally included under current assets, together with all other non-current assets, as belonging to this grouping.

Cash-related assets include cash and cash equivalent items, together with items collectable as cash in the near future. All are thought of in terms of their cash value. Besides being end-products of a completed business operating cycle, they are intended to be injected back into subsequent operating cycles. Cash-related assets play a supportive role in business activities as a means for making payments. I include all current assets other than inventory and prepaid expenses as belonging to this grouping.

PROBLEMS IN THE NEW ASSET CLASSIFICATION

This then is the way I conceive the classification into cost-related and cash-related assets. There are a few difficulties, however, with such a division. In particular, to which grouping should land, residual values of property, plant and equipment, investment, and deferred charges be assigned?

The reason that land and residual values of property, plant and equipment cause difficulty is that they do not wear out and are not consumed in the manner of other portions of property, plant and equipment, and at the same time are not readily convertible into cash. Yamashita considers these items as having cash value as such, and includes them as part of the $M \rightarrow C'$ process. However, I regard them as belonging to cost-related assets. In most cases, the company will continue to operate so long as purchased land will be used indefinitely in the pursuit of business objectives without wearing out or being consumed, then the acquisition cost of the land becomes a deferred expense against total future revenue. In this case, since the future period, theoretically at any rate, is infinite, what happens is that the actual expense to be charged against revenue in any single accounting period becomes zero. Salvage values on buildings, equipment, and other fixed assets can be thought of in the same manner. Thus at such a time as land and residual values of property, plant and equipment are sold off, original acquisition cost is computed as expense against the amount received for their sale. If the time from when a business is started until the time it is dissolved is taken as a single accounting period, then the total amount of cash collected at the time of dissolution represents the total amount of revenue, and all invested capital is measured as expense against this amount. Sales of land and residual values of property, plant and equipment can be viewed as steps in the dissolution of a business.

The reason invested assets cause difficulty has to do with marketable securities held temporarily as investment of idle funds, and debentures and other bonds and long-term loans held as long-term investment. The former must be sold off in order to convert them into cash. Therefore, in the sense that they require selling, they are easily thought of as assets involved in the $C \rightarrow M$ part of the operating cycle, or, in other words, cost-related assets. The latter, on the other hand, bring in cash at the time of expiration without having to undergo a process of selling, and thus appear as assets belonging to the $M \rightarrow C'$ process, i.e. cash-related assets.

Gilman (1939: 299) divides assets into the three categories of cash, deferred charges to cash, and deferred charges to future income. Debentures, because they have a fixed payment date, are treated as deferred charges to cash, while stock holdings, having no set date of payment, are treated as deferred charges on future income. On the other hand, I regard marketable securities held as temporary investment of idle funds as cash-related assets (M → C′), and long-term invested assets all as cost-related assets (C → M). The rationale for this is as follows.

Marketable securities held as temporary investment of idle funds have as their purpose, not profits from sales, but rather accrual of interest. Because they are limited to securities having a high degree of marketability, selling them is an extremely easy matter, essentially a formal processing of the relevant paperwork. In essence such securities are no different from money in the bank, and therefore may be considered as assets in the M → C′ part of the cycle. Again, I regard revenue as being realized in principle as the acquisition of cash-related assets. In other words, if merchandise is sold and cash-related assets are acquired in payment, then revenue is considered as having been realized in that period. Now when debentures and other bonds and long-term loans are due to be redeemed within the year, then the amount received in redemption is considered as revenue, and the acquisition cost becomes an expense charged against this. In this manner debentures and other bonds and long-term loans held as long-term investment are treated, exactly the same as other long-term invested assets, as belonging to the C → M part of the business operation cycle.

The reason deferred accounts present difficulty has to do with dividend deferments paid to stockholders in the period after the company has been established but before business operations actually begin. Such payments represent prepayments on dividends earned after business operations begin, and cannot be considered as assets. I believe such items should be listed under assets on the balance sheet as part of the capital valuation account, and not as part of either the cash-related or cost-related assets. However, as will be explained later, the cost-related assets can be thought of essentially as items to be eliminated from the amount that was contributed by the stockholders on the balance sheet as uncollected amounts on invested capital, and thus the treatment of such deferred accounts should follow that for cost-related assets.

THE NEED FOR A NEW ASSET CLASSIFICATION (1)

This then represents my views on cost-related and cash-related assets. Why should such a classification be adopted for assets on the balance sheet in place of the traditional classification into current and fixed assets?

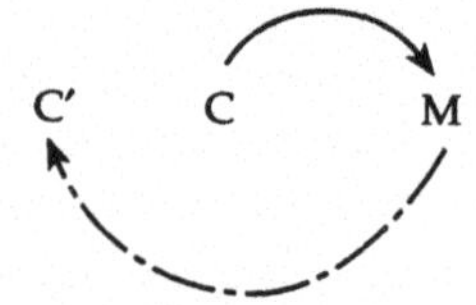

Fig. 10.1. Recovered capital vs. invested capital

The arguments are active (the classification into cash and cost is imperative) and passive (the classification into current and fixed assets could be abandoned without detrimental effect).

As to the main argument why it is imperative to adopt a cash–cost classification, on the balance sheet, cash-related assets are contrasted with the amount that was contributed by the stockholders as recovered capital. Cost-related assets, on the other hand, must be deducted from the amount that was contributed by the stockholders as uncollected portions of invested capital in order to make possible a comparison of recovered capital vs. invested capital (see Fig. 10.1). Thus their fundamental natures are seen as entirely different. Assuming the time a business begins operations until the time it closes operations down as comprising a single accounting period, then all invested capital becomes expense, and assets collected in the very simple form of cash at the end of the accounting period are interpreted as revenue. In this manner, then, the stockholder's equity, indicating invested capital, may be compared on the balance sheet with assets (cash), indicating recovered capital, and the difference between the two is then figured as net income. It becomes possible to view this comparison between invested and recovered capital as a basic function of the balance sheet. Accounting as practised today, however, does not view the time from beginning to closing down of business operations as a single accounting term, but rather chops time up into appropriate divisions designated as accounting periods, and operating results are figured for each such period. For this reason it is necessary to incorporate into income measurement such complex procedures as carrying forward to subsequent periods expenses and revenues not belonging to that period, making the asset configuration depicted at period end a complicated affair indeed, with various manners for indicating liabilities coming into play as well. Not only do we find the idea of treating items converting into cash in subsequent periods as assets, and items requiring payment in cash in subsequent periods as liabilities, but also expenses carried over to following periods have come to be recognized as assets, while revenues deferred to subsequent periods are regarded as liabilities. Even though items converting into cash in following periods may be treated in the same manner as cash and thought of as recovered capital, it is not possible to recognize that expenses carried over to subsequent periods have the same basic nature as recovered capital. Only by carrying out a periodic measurement of income do such expenses come to be recognized as assets on the balance sheet.

In this manner, then, cash-related assets possess the nature of recovered capital, while cost-related assets possess the nature of invested capital. Thus cash-related assets are measured in terms of their cash value and are used in paying liabilities, redeeming capital stock, as well as making dividend payments on profit. Or else such assets are reinvested in the operating cycle. Cost-related assets, on the other hand, are evaluated at invested capital amount, i.e. original cost, and are carried forward and charged against revenues in following periods. Cost-related assets bear a relationship to subsequent period income measurement, and the amounts they are valued at in no way represent cash conversion values. Is it not imperative, then, that we distinguish in some manner between these two asset groupings possessing such entirely different natures? I wonder how many people making use of the balance sheet are actually aware that different headings, indicated by seemingly identical currency values, in fact differ in this respect? This is a source of much of the misunderstanding and confusion. It is our duty to warn of the danger in viewing cash amounts listed on the balance sheet in the same manner as values listed for merchandise and buildings. It is in order to point out the distinction between these two asset groupings that I propose the adoption of a cash–cost classification. Such distinction is not possible under the present current–fixed classification.

In the paper cited above, Miyagami suggests that all assets be viewed as recovered capital. I differ, however, in the respect that such an idea is not extended to include cost-related assets. In the paper 'Income Determination by Means of the Balance Sheet', Yasuichi Sakamoto (1953) explains how cost-related assets should be deducted from invested capital on the creditor side. His view differs, however, in that, concerned with depicting business performance in regard to the internal production process, he includes products, merchandise, and other sale items in what I call the cash-related asset grouping.

A second reason why a cash–cost classification is imperative has to do with the financing of a business. One feature of the present-day accounting structure is that income measurement is carried out period by period on an accrual basis. Proceeds from sales are recorded at the time of sale without waiting for actual receipt of payment, while cost of sales and other expenses are recorded regardless of whether or not there was an actual outlay of cash. For this reason, under the present accounting structure, recorded revenue does not correspond to cash coming in, just as recorded expense does not refer to cash actually paid out, and so the net income arrived at by computation is not related in any sense to the actual amount of cash funds. With accounting conducting its income measurement thus divorced from the inflow and outflow of cash, there appears a period-by-period discrepancy between cash flow and business activity due to an increase in credit transactions and an expansion in the property, plant and equipment used by the business. As a result, it becomes impossible to measure period-by-period business performance in terms of incoming and outgoing cash.

At the same time, however, sales proceeds are collected, material stocks are replenished, and other expenses are paid off, liabilities are made good, etc.; all these things involve cash, and all are vital to the continuation of a business. It makes no difference how large profits might appear on paper: if a business is short of cash and cannot meet payments, then there is nothing to do but fold up shop. Side by side with periodic measurement of income, it is also necessary to compose a detailed financial plan, backed by an appropriate amount of available funds. Moreover, we find taxes paid on money earned as well as cash dividends, all decided on the basis of computed income divorced from actual inflow and outflow of cash. In times of inflation, what appear as increases in income eventually strangle available cash funds. What we must do is strive to increase our understanding of the relationship between business finance and accounting, and more fully co-ordinate the two.

In this sense, then, it is extremely effective to depict the various assets revolving around cash as cash-related assets and manage them distinct from other assets. Only by properly grasping the relationship between business finance and accounting is appropriate management possible. This is the second reason, then, for proposing the adoption of a new cash-cost classification.

THE NEED FOR A NEW ASSET CLASSIFICATION (2)

In the preceding section we considered two active arguments. In spite of anything I might say, however, if the traditional classification into current and fixed assets has greater significance, then my assertions will fail to be convincing. Is there some reason, then, why the current–fixed classification of assets must be preserved? I believe not, and therein lies my passive argument for adoption of a cash–cost classification.

What sort of objectives and what sort of significance does the traditional classification into current assets and fixed assets have? According to

A. A. Fitzgerald and L. A. Schumer (1952: 95–6), the division into current and fixed assets was introduced into the field of accounting from the works of the classical economists Adam Smith, David Ricardo, J. S. Mill, and J. R. McCulloch, and the first time it appeared in financial statements and company law was 1889, after the council called attention to such theories in the case of *Lee* v. *Neuchatel Asphalte Co.* At that time attention was given, in connection with the determination of profits which may be legally dividended, to the distinction between current capital which fulfils its function with regard to production with a single use, and fixed capital which exists in a more permanent form and from which revenues are realized over a longer period of time. From this was derived the claim that losses or decline in value on current capital must be included in computations for the determination of profit, while losses or depreciation on fixed capital legally need not be deducted from income. It is natural to assume, then, that the classification into current and fixed assets first adopted into accounting had significance in regard to such determination of income available for dividends. If the current–fixed assets classification continues to posses only this significance today, there is no discernible reason whatsoever for maintaining such a classification.

This is not to say that one can simply ignore the distinction pointed to at that time between current capital intended for a single use, and fixed capital lasting for much longer use. As W. A. Paton (1945: 6) states, 'The distinction between current cost factors and fixed assets is not a question of duration of investment, but a practical line of cleavage between relatively liquid, rapidly turning resources and facilities representing production factors relatively non-liquid and used throughout a considerable period of time.' To be sure, such a distinction, from the standpoint of economics, appears to be more a distinction between inventory items and fixed assets than between current and fixed assets. The same goal would be achieved just as nicely by my proposed division of cost-related assets into inventory vs. fixed assets.

On the other hand, there are many who contend along with Gilman and other American scholars that the popularization of the present-day classification into current and fixed assets is a result of certain demands from the position of credit analysis. That is to say, the distinction between current and fixed assets was further bolstered by the presumption that it is safer to loan money for buying and selling than it is to loan money for the purchase of fixed assets, because the cycle whereby cash is invested in merchandise, which takes the form of credit and reverts again to cash, is completed in a much shorter period of time than the cycle whereby cash is invested in fixed assets and then reverts back to cash. True, the relationship of current assets to current liabilities is depicted as the current ratio, which has served for a long time as a credit index. The practice of arranging assets according to the order of their cash conversion values, and liabilities in order of the length of time until due date, has become firmly established. It is no exaggeration to say that the requirements of the credit system have entrenched the present fundamental division into current and fixed assets.

But if it is true that the classification into current and fixed assets did derive from the requirements of the credit system, then there is no particular reason why we have to go on making the distinction. The cash value assigned to inventory under current assets by no means represents a cash exchange value; moreover, stable amounts of inventory are generally maintained at all times, which function in very much the manner of fixed assets, and therefore dropping inventory from current assets would give figures all the more advantageous to the aims of credit. Moreover, in an ongoing business where dissolution is not a concern, credit rating ought to be established on the basis of the business's income potential, while knowing this or that about its asset configuration is irrelevant information at best.

For these reasons, then, I believe that not only could the classification into current and fixed assets be discarded without serious effects, but that doing away with such a classification would at the same time remove much of the misunderstanding and confusion it engenders.

CONCLUSION

The above constitutes my concept of the cash–cost classification, together with my reasons for urging its adoption. Can we expect further development of these ideas and eventual adoption as the manner for classifying assets on the balance sheet? Because the current–fixed method of asset classification has become the tradition that it is, such a distinction might conceivably be indicated at the same time on the balance sheet, as long as it does not confuse the cash–cost classification. Current–fixed asset values might be given as footnotes. A three-category classification into cash-related assets, inventory, and fixed assets is another feasible approach.

In the past I have urged the inclusion of a fund statement as part of financial reports. The present paper also derives from the same theoretical approach. While the former suggestion attempts to remedy inadequacies in the existing system of financial reporting, the present suggestion aims more at a revolution in conventional accounting practice. It is no easy task to suggest the adoption of a new classification into cost-related assets and cash-related assets to replace the widely accepted and time-honoured current–fixed asset approach. I only hope the reasoning behind my suggestion is in no way faulty.

REFERENCES

Fitzgerald, A. A., and Schumer, L. A. (1952), *Classification in Accounting* (Melbourne: Butterworth Australia).

Gilman, S. (1939), *Accounting Concepts of Profit* (New York: Ronald Press Co.).

Iwata, I. (1951), 'Dotekitaishohyo no Genkin-Komoku' ('Cash on the Dynamic Balance Sheet'), *Kaikei*, 59/5: 1–17.

Miyagami, K. (1951), 'Kaisyu Tokashihon toshiteno Shisan' ('Assets as Recovered-Invested Capital'), *Kigyokaikei*, 3/12: 1252–7.

Ohta, T. (1950) 'Shisan no Hiyosei to Kachisei' ('The Cost and Value of Assets'), *Kigyokaikei*, 2/8: 632–5.

Paton, W. A. (1945), *Balance Sheet*, ch. 2 of T. W. Leland (ed.), *Contemporary Accounting* (New York: American Institute of Accountants).

Sakamoto, Y. (1953), 'Taishakutaishohyo niyoru Son-eki no Keisan' ('Income Determination by Means of the Balance Sheet'), *Kigyokaikei*, 5/6: 716–23.

Yamashita, K. (1950), 'Ohta Gakusetsu no Ginmi' ('A Critical Examination of Ohta's Theories'), *Kaikei*, 58/4: 15–28.

—— (1951), 'Shisan no Genkinsei' ('The Cash Value of Assets'), *Kaikei*, 60/4: 1–17.

11

The Three Domains of Financial Reporting

Accounting for the Flow of Commodities and the Flow of Money

INTRODUCTION

The various activities of a business induce a flow of commodities and a flow of money. Here flow of commodities refers to the production, consumption, and distribution of social wealth. A business consumes the wealth produced by other business, in turn producing new wealth. The difference between wealth produced and wealth consumed, that is to say the net value of production, is then distributed among those persons contributing to production. Wealth flows into a business through production, and flows out again through consumption and distribution. Opposed to this, the flow of money refers to the income and disbursing of currency, which is the accepted means of exchange. A business exchanges the wealth it produces for currency, which it then uses in payment for wealth purchased from other businesses, and for distribution among persons contributing to production.

In regard to the above my thinking is as follows. The object of business accounting is neither the flow of commodities alone, nor is it the flow of money alone. Rather business accounting must concern itself with the measurement of both the flow of commodities and the flow of money within a business.

ACCOUNTING THE FLOW OF COMMODITIES

Income accounting measures the flow of commodities. Within the framework of income accounting the concept of 'revenue' represents an evaluation of the products a business produces. Revenue is realized at the time

From *Waseda Business and Economic Studies*, No. 25 (1989), 1–11.

of sales. The reason for this is simply that, in general, it is difficult to make an objective evaluation of a business's products at the time of production. Sales is nothing more than a process of evaluating the products of a business. In order for a business to engage in production, it consumes the products of other businesses, and the amount of such consumption is termed 'expense'. The monetary amount left over after deducting the value of outside products consumed from the value of a business's own products equals the value of 'net production'. Net production is distributed among those persons or parties contributing to the productive effort of the business. Wages are paid to workers contributing labour to the productive effort, interest and dividends are paid to creditors and stockholders contributing capital, rent is paid to landowners contributing land, remuneration is paid to managers contributing managerial know-how, and taxes are paid to society in general for what may be considered its indirect and varied contributions to the productive effort of the business.

Income accounting measures this process of production, consumption, and distribution of social wealth engaged in by the business. In the capitalistic economied society of today, however, the productive role played by a business is not the initial motivation. A business is motivated by the capital investor's pursuit of profit. Wages, interest, rent, etc. all represent shares of net production distributed to persons contributing to the productive effort of the business, but such shares are fixed in the form of a contract or agreement between the capital investor and the contributors. In turn the share of net production going to the capital investor is determined as the amount left over after other such shares have been distributed. This means that if wages, interest, rent, and other such payments exceed the value of production of the business, then not only is the capital investor left without a share, but he loses part of the capital belonging to him. Within the amount of net production to be distributed, income accounting views wages, interest, rent, and other such items as expense, while the remainder of the distributed amount comprises the 'profit' category.

Besides serving as units in the social productive function, today's business enterprises also represent the means by which capital investors pursue profits. In spite of the fact that business serves a double function, one must not lose sight of the fundamental nature of income accounting, which is to measure the flow of commodities.

In carrying out its productive effort it often happens that a business acquires outside products before actual consumption. Moreover, production itself requires a bit of time, and products are not necessarily sold off immediately upon completion. This means that social wealth will be stocked within a business to greater or lesser degree. Such social wealth maintained by the company takes the form of inventory, production

TABLE 11.1. *Accounting the flow of commodities*

Revenue = Amount at which the products of a business are evaluated (A)
Expense = Amount of outside products consumed (B) + Amounts distributed to persons contributing to production (C)
Profit = Amount distributed to persons contributing to production (D)

	→ wages	(C) →	labour
	→ interest	(C) →	creditors
Net production (A − B) →	→ rent	(C) →	landowners
	→ taxes	(C) →	society
	→ entrepreneurial remuneration	(D) →	capital investors

Inventory + Production facilities = Purchased but unconsumed outside products + Prepaid shares to persons contributing to production

facilities, etc., and as such represents a reservoir of wealth within the flow of commodities.

Needless to say, present-day income accounting is a periodic affair, with the flow of commodities measured on a period-to-period basis. We see not only outside products acquired for the purpose of conducting the productive effort flowing into the reservoir of wealth, but also wages, interest, rent, and other payments to persons contributing to production. Outflows from this reservoir, on the other hand, are realized at the time the business's own products are sold. For this reason, outside products consumed for the purpose of production, together with wages, interest, rent, and other flows out of the business, can be considered as not having taken place until such time as its own products are sold.

The major points discussed in this section are summarized in Table 11.1.

ACCOUNTING THE FLOW OF MONEY

Cash flow accounting measures the flow of money. Within the framework of cash flow accounting the terms 'receipts' and 'disbursements' are used in referring to amounts of currency flowing in and out of the business. At the present time, however, cash flow accounting is not generally practised. Although net result of currency flow is computed for most businesses, just how such currency flows through the business is usually left unclarified.

Currency flow into a business may be roughly divided into two types: inflow of currency related to the flow of commodities; and inflow of currency having no bearing on the flow of commodities. I refer to the former as 'operating receipts' and the latter as 'financial receipts'. A business receives currency for the sale of its products, and such currency inflow comprises its operating receipts. A business borrows money, or issues stocks or bonds for a price, and the currency that flows in represents one form of financial receipts. Such financial receipts are accompanied by future financial disbursements. Another form of financial receipts includes returns of currency on money lent out. Such financial receipts are based on financial disbursements made in the past.

The flow of currency within a business consists primarily of operational receipts and operational disbursements. In spite of this, however, large amounts of capital must be invested into inventory and facilities so that the business can continue production operation, while at the same time the ever increasing use of credit means that payments on sales of its own products are not easily collectable, and thus the currency flow within many businesses today has come to include a large amount that is financial.

We find a reservoir existing in the flow of currency as well. Currency flowing in does not pass through the business from left to right and out again. Rather currency flows into the currency reservoir within the business, and from there it flows out. Cash and marketable securities possessed by the company represent the balance of this currency reservoir.

The following summarizes the main points in this section:

Operating receipts	⇌	Revenue
Operating disbursements	⇌	Expenses + Distribution of profits
Financial receipts	⇌	Financial disbursements
Receipts − Disbursements	=	Increase or decrease in currency reservoir balance

DISCREPANCIES BETWEEN THE FLOW OF COMMODITIES AND THE FLOW OF MONEY

We have already seen how certain elements in the flow of money are intimately connected with the flow of commodities. These I have termed operating receipts and operating disbursements, and have shown how operating receipts contrast with revenue, while operating disbursements contrast with expenses and distribution of profit.

If product recognition, that is sales, occurred simultaneously with payment of the sales price, if acquisition of outside products occurred simultaneously with payments made for them, and if labour, capital, land, and other contributions to the productive effort occurred simultaneously with their various payments, then the flow of commodities would be expected exactly to match the flow of money. Today, however, it is usual for receipt of payment on product sales to lag far behind. The same holds true for the purchase of outside products. With respect to time, payments are made long after acquisition. Likewise wage, interest, and rent payments, etc. often follow after the actual contribution to the production efforts of the business. In all these instances the flow of commodities precedes the flow of money. Accounts receivable, accounts payable, and accrued expenses all become necessary when the flow of commodities comes before the flow of money. The greater the discrepancy between these two flows, the larger the balances in accounts receivable, accounts payable, and accrued expenses.

Sometimes a business receives payment for its products before they are actually realized. Outside products from other businesses are sometimes paid for before they are actually acquired, while wages, interest, and rent also might be paid out before such contributions to production are actually made. In such cases the flow of money precedes the flow of commodities, giving rise to such things as unearned revenue, advances to suppliers, and prepaid expenses. Here, too, the greater the discrepancy between the flow of commodities and the flow of money, the larger these various balances become.

At present the balance resulting from discrepancies between the flow of commodities and the flow of money is indicated on the balance sheet, together with the balances within these two flows. With the addition of an equity heading indicating the sources of financial receipts, the balance sheet depicts the financial position of the business.

The following summarizes the main points of this section:

Assets = Currency reservoir balance + Commodity reservoir balance + Discrepancy between flow of currency and flow of commodities

Equity = Discrepancy between flow of currency and flow of commodities + Sources of financial receipts

CONCLUSION

Beginning with the assumption that the task of business accounting is to depict the flow of money as well as the flow of commodities, I have demonstrated the existence of three accounting domains: (1) income accounting, measuring the flow of commodities; (2) cash flow accounting, measuring the flow of money; and (3) the balance sheet, incorporating balances from the above two statements together with the various headings resulting from the period-to-period discrepancies between the two flows to arrive at a statement of equity.

In the style of business accounting practised today a statement of receipts and disbursements, or cash flow statement, is generally not prepared. However, if one accepts the existence of the above three accounting domains, then it seems obvious that such a statement should accompany the income statement and balance sheet in reporting the operations and financial position of business. My conclusion, then, is that a cash flow statement is necessary and ought to be included as one of the primary financial statements.

I have long been a proponent of such a style of financial reporting. In previous writings I referred to such a statement as a 'funds statement', intending it in a very broad sense to include a statement of receipts and disbursements or cash flow. However, the term 'funds statement' tends to be interpreted in a rather narrow sense, as a statement indicating the sources and applications of working capital. In order to avoid misunderstanding, I have opted for the term 'cash flow statement'.

One final note. Such notational changes as the transfer from building under construction account to building account, or from unappropriated retained earnings to appropriated retained earnings, have nothing to do with the actual flow of commodities or money and hence have been left out of present considerations.

The following examples are given to help clarify the relationship between the three financial statements.

1. In a case where no discrepancies are seen between the flow of commodities and the flow of money the three statements would appear thus:

Beginning Balance Sheet

Cash	130	Accounts payable	10
Accounts receivable	10	Contributed capital	200
Inventory	20	Retained earnings	50
Property and equipment	100		
	260		260

Income Statement

Beginning inventory	20	Sales	500
Purchases	350	Ending inventory	20
Expenses	50		
Depreciation	20		
Net income	80		
	520		520

Cash Flow Statement

Beginning cash	130	Disbursements for materials	350
Receipts from sales	500	Disbursements for expenses	50
		Purchases of equipment	20
		Ending cash	210
	630		630

Ending Balance Sheet

Cash	210	Accounts payable	10
Accounts receivable	10	Contributed capital	200
Inventory	20	Retained earnings	130
Property and equipment	100		
	340		340

Note in the above case that net income indicated on the income statement exactly matches the difference in cash amounts listed on beginning and ending balance sheets. Also, the two balance sheets show no differences except for cash and retained earnings.

2. When discrepancies exist between the flow of commodities and the flow of money the three statements appear as follows:

Beginning Balance Sheet

Cash	130	Accounts payable	10
Accounts receivable	10	Contributed capital	200
Inventory	20	Retained earnings	50
Property and equipment	100		
	260		260

Income Statement

Beginning inventory	20	Sales	500
Purchases	390	Ending inventory	60
Expenses	50		
Depreciation	20		
Net income	80		
	560		560

Cash Flow Statement

Beginning cash	130	Disbursements for materials	370
Receipts from sales	460	Disbursements for expenses	50
Borrowings	150	Purchases of equipment	300
Capital increase	100	Dividend payments	35
		Ending cash	85
	840		840

Ending Balance Sheet

Cash	85	Accounts payable	30
Accounts receivable	50	Borrowings	150
Inventory	60	Contributed capital	300
Property and equipment	380	Retained earnings	95
	575		575

The relationship between net income on the income statement and beginning and ending cash amounts on the cash flow statement is explained as follows:

Relationship between Earnings and Cash

Net earnings	80	Increase in accounts receivable	40
Depreciation	20	Increase in inventory	40
Increase in accounts payable	20	Purchases of equipment	300
Increase in borrowings	150	Dividend payments	35
Issuance of common stock	100	Increase in cash	Δ45
	370		370

Moreover, differences between beginning and ending balance sheets are explained by comparison of income statement items and cash flow statement items as follows:

Accounts receivable 50 – 10	= Sales 500 – Receipts from sales 460
Inventory 60 – 20	= Purchases 390 – Cost of sales 350
Property and equipment 380 – 100	= Purchases of equipment 300 – Depreciation 20
Accounts payable 30 – 10	= Purchases 390 – Disbursements for materials 370
Borrowings 150 – 0	= Borrowings 150
Contributed capital 300 – 200	= Capital increase 100
Retained earnings 95 – 50	= Net income 80 – Dividend payments 35

12

The Role of Accounting in Industry and Society

INTRODUCTION

Accounting is a form of human activity concerned with the recording and measuring of the economic activities of individuals or organizations as inflow and outflow of money, and disclosing such results to interested parties. Accounting might be done by the property owner himself for the purpose of clarifying increases in his own assets. Another form of accounting involves the use of a household account book to record and balance the income of cash as wages against money paid out for the necessities of daily life. Accounting plays an even more important role, however, when the owner of the assets and the person managing them are not the same. In such cases, accounting, in order to demonstrate managerial responsibility towards the assets the manager was entrusted with, must function to record and compute any increases or decreases in assets, and to disclose such information to the owner. In this sense, then, while the passbook a bank furnishes to its customers for the purpose of recording and computing deposits and withdrawals and indicating current balances is merely another form of accounting, it is essentially different from a household account book. Whereas the decision to keep or not to keep a household account book rests entirely with the individual, the keeping of a passbook is absolutely essential to the idea of banking, and represents an established system in society where people live together as a group.

The functioning of any society involves the exchange of goods and services, which in turn makes use of money as the common medium of exchange. What is important here is that accounting records and measures the economic activities of individuals or groups based upon receipts or payments of such money. When indicating increases or decreases in the number or amount of a single commodity, it is of course perfectly possible to do so by simply counting the number of units involved. In

From *Waseda Business and Economic Studies*, No. 27 (1991), 1–12.

the warehousing industry items are stored and released again on demand, and inventory is kept by recording the number of units taken in and the number of units taken out and computing the number of units remaining in stock. The numbering of units, however, applies only to single commodities, and cannot be used to speak collectively of various different commodities. Accounting, on the other hand, does not stop with merely measuring the inflow and outflow of money. Rather, by measuring in terms of the inflow and outflow of money, accounting makes it possible to measure in a unified manner the whole variety of goods and services in terms of a common yardstick of value. For this reason accounting has been an irreplaceable measuring device for industry, which tosses a whole range of goods and services into the productive process to turn out a whole new range of goods and services. If humans did not have the measuring device of accounting, then most likely industry would never have reached the state of development it has today. Operating in the various areas of agriculture, forestry, fishing, mining, manufacturing, commerce, etc., industry is a form of economic activity which takes materials from nature, adds human energy, and creates or increases their useful value. Industrial development has greatly enriched the economic life of the members of society. It can be said that accounting, by aiding industrial development, has contributed to society. However, recently people are pointing more and more to the adverse affects industry has on society in the form of industrial pollution, etc. Thus when re-evaluating the place of industry in society, it will be extremely meaningful to consider the role that accounting plays, or ought to play, in this relationship.

ACCOUNTING AND THE ACCUMULATION OF INDUSTRIAL CAPITAL

The relationship between industry and society can be approached from many different aspects, but accounting has for the most part treated it as the relationship between those in need of industrial capital and those supplying that need. Industry produces and provides the various goods and services needed by people in society to live, while the capital necessary to industry is supplied in turn by a broad segment of people in society. In the society of today nearly all industry is carried out by stock corporation type enterprises, the reason being simply that this is the most convenient form by which industrial capital can be accumulated from the general populace.

The accumulation of capital in a stock corporation is accomplished by the issuing of stock. Stock represents the legal status of people comprising the stock corporation, that is the stockholders, and is divided into equal fractional parts or shares, each having the same monetary value. Although the value of individual shares may be minuscule, this process makes it possible to collect investments from a large number of people, thereby amassing vast sums of industrial capital.

Within the framework of the stock corporation, the only obligation the shareholder has is to pay for his stock, with no financial responsibility to put out money above the cost of his shares. At present in Japan, the financial responsibility of the shareholder is completed at the time he acquires his shares, and hence he makes no further investment whatsoever. Also within the framework of the stock corporation there is, in principle, complete freedom regarding the transfer of shares, and in cases where stock is bought and sold on the stock exchange, a shareholder may easily dispose of his shares and recover his investment. Such limited shareholder responsibility, together with free transferability, creates a large number of shareholders interested only in the receipt of dividend payments and fluctuations in the value of their stock, and who take no direct part in the actual operation of the company. But it also makes the stock corporation approach to capital accumulation a very simple matter.

Accounting is one of the main pillars supporting the stock corporation system. Because the free transfer of stock is one of the basic principles of this system, the people comprising the body of shareholders are not necessarily always the same. Therefore, it is especially important in the case of stock corporations to decide upon a fiscal year, and then for each and every fiscal year determine the amount of earnings payable as dividends to shareholders, and to make such payments. If earnings for one period are mistakenly computed as earnings for some other period, then shareholders entitled to receive dividend payments for earnings of that period incur an inappropriate loss, while shareholders receiving dividend payments for the other period are recipients of an inappropriate gain. There is no way to compare the magnitude of such problems with the case of privately owned businesses, where earnings for every fiscal period always revert to the same person or persons. Accounting plays a vital role in the computation of earnings for each fiscal period. Because dividends on earnings are such a major concern to stock corporation shareholders, it can easily be said that if accounting did not fulfil its function of appropriately measuring stock corporation earnings for each fiscal period, then capital accumulation by means of the stock corporation would not proceed as smoothly as it does today.

Besides accumulating capital through the issuing of stock, stock corporations also raise capital in the form of loans from banks and other finance agencies. The amount of capital raised in this manner for industrial use has grown in recent years. Also, businesses tend to use more credit when purchasing goods and services essential to their operations from other companies. However, the fact that the responsibility of shareholders is limited means that the assets owned by the company form the sole collateral against capital on loan from creditors. Because shareholders do not bear responsibility for additional outlays of capital, all capital on loan from creditors must be paid back within the limits of the assets owned by the company. Within the framework of the stock corporation, then, the comparison of a company's assets and debts is a vital concern, and it is assumed that the greater the difference between assets and debts, in other words, the greater the company's net assets, the greater the guarantee that it will pay back all capital on loan from creditors. For this reason companies are strictly required by law to decide on a fixed amount of capital, and then maintain net assets at a figure above this amount. If accounting did not fulfil the function of measuring assets and debts and accurately distinguishing between capital stock and surplus, then creditors would fail to be sufficiently protected, and investment in industrial capital in the form of loans would surely not be as widely practised as it is today.

THE SYSTEM OF ACCOUNTING WITHIN SOCIETY

As long as things are viewed from the aspect of industrial capital accumulation, it can be said that the role of accounting within the relationship between industry and society has been to supply investors and creditors with information necessary to the making of decisions regarding investments and loans. In another sense, however, this can be interpreted as saying that accounting operates, through the process of investors and creditors making appropriate decisions, to guide industrial capital in a direction that is most desirable from the standpoint of society. For this reason, the supplying of information relating to the operating performance and financial position of a business by means of accounting has now become standard procedure in today's society.

Responsibility for the management of a stock corporation is placed in the hands of a board of directors chosen at a general shareholders' meeting. In return, the board of directors is required for each fiscal period to report on the operating performance and financial position of the company at the general shareholders' meeting and seek approval. Also it must present a draft proposal for the distribution of net income and seek approval. The Japanese Commercial Code requires that the board of directors include in its report to the regular general shareholders' meeting (1) a balance sheet, (2) an income statement, (3) an operations report, and (4) a proposal regarding the distribution of net income, or the disposition of net losses. Also not long after the above documents have been approved, the balance sheet must be made public. In principle, once the board of directors has received approval on the above items its duties have been discharged. Obviously such documents as the board of directors of a stock corporation submits to the regular general shareholders' meeting or makes public are a product of the accounting process as it records and measures the transactions of the company. Thus accounting performs an extremely vital role in the transmission of information from the board of directors to shareholders, or to creditors, regarding the operating performance and financial position of the company.

Moreover, the Commercial Code makes exceptions regarding the auditing of large companies with capital of 500 million yen or more, or total borrowings of over 20 billion yen, and small companies with capital of 100 million yen or less. The statute providing for such exceptions is the 'statute regarding Commercial Code exceptions pertaining to the auditing, etc., of stock corporations' (Statute No. 22, 1974), generally known as the Auditing Exceptions or Commercial Code Exceptions Statute.

The Auditing Exceptions Statute stipulates that, for large companies, the balance sheet, income statement, operating report, proposal for distribution of net income or disposition of net losses, and their supporting schedules, in addition to being audited by the statute auditors of the company, must also receive an audit by an accounting auditor. The accounting auditor must be agreed upon by a majority of the company's statute auditors and approved at the general shareholders' meeting. Also it is required that the auditor be either a CPA or an audit corporation. It is not always the case that company statute auditors are well trained in accounting auditing. Because of the scale on which they operate and the numbers of shareholders they represent, whether the financial statements of large companies are audited properly or not has a tremendous impact on society. For this reason, then, it is expected that such companies place prime emphasis on their auditing, entrusting it to qualified accounting auditors.

In contrast to this, stock companies with capital of 100 million yen or less are smaller in scale and have a smaller number of shareholders. Their effect on society is not so large, and therefore only those accounting documents presented by the board of directors at the general shareholders' meeting are required to be audited by a statute auditor.

The information function of accounting came to play an increasingly important role with the growing tendency towards the so-called separation between ownership and management in stock corporations. With the progress of science and high-level development of industrial and managerial technologies, industry has been operating on an ever larger scale, while at the same time the economic structure of society has become increasingly complex. Because of this, it was inevitable that the management of stock corporations in most instances be placed in the hands of people specially trained in business management. Such managers are chosen for their superior managerial talents, and are not necessarily required to be shareholders. At the same time, the securities exchange has grown, with widespread circulation of stocks throughout society in the form of investment securities, resulting in the proliferation of shareholders with no concern other than their dividend payments and fluctuations in the value of their stock, i.e. the so-called absentee shareholder. Compared to private concerns where owner and operator are one and the same, the role that accounting plays in such enterprises is inestimably large. For the shareholder not participating directly in management, accounting has become the sole source of information pertaining to the operating performance and financial position of the company in which he has invested.

It is said that a person's ability to act appropriately is determined by the amount and quality of the information available to him. This is true for decisions concerning investments and loans as well. If the person making such decisions has sufficient information regarding the company's operating performance and financial position, then supposedly he will make the appropriate decisions. However, if the information available to him is incomplete or faulty, then there is a great danger that his decisions to invest or lend will be inappropriate, causing him to suffer an incalculable loss. In today's society people basically invest capital at their own individual discretion, in other words, motivated by the desire for profit. If many people were to lose money on investments or loans, then presumably it would become extremely difficult to raise capital in this manner. Thus it can be said that the ability of accounting sufficiently to provide investors and creditors with necessary information is directly related to the ease with which capital can be accumulated, and hence to industrial development and the affluence of society.

For this reason the Securities and Exchange Act stipulates that companies intending to accumulate from a large number of unspecified persons a capital of 500 million yen or more must file beforehand a notification of securities with the Ministry of Finance, while companies having accumulated such an amount of capital in this manner, or companies issuing stock listed on the stock exchange, must file annual securities reports. Such securities notifications and reports are posted and available for public examination at the Ministry of Finance, at the main and major branch offices of the company concerned, and also at the stock exchange for companies listed there. Be it a securities notification or an annual report, an inclusion of the balance sheet, income statement, and other documents relating to financial computation comprise the main body, and it is required that such documents be accompanied by proof of an audit by a CPA or other qualified auditor having no vested interest in the company in question.

ACCOUNTING AND THE PRODUCTIVE CAPACITY OF INDUSTRY

As stated earlier, in today's society nearly all industry is carried out by stock corporation type enterprises. Clearly such companies are born of a profit motive, in which capital owners attempt to manipulate their capital in an advantageous manner. In this sense, then, historically there was very good reason for accounting to depict the relationship between industry and society from the aspect of capital accumulation. On the other hand, however, it is also true that production and distribution in today's society is in fact carried out by the activities of such companies. Here, then, we see the opening by which accounting in recent years has increasingly attempted to approach the relationship between industry and society, from the aspect of industry's productive and distributive function within society.

In today's society it is clear that necessary goods and services are produced by the activities of businesses, and that the distribution of wealth to the people in society takes place through their participation in such production. If the goods and services produced by a company are not necessary to society, then society will not accept them and the business will have to stop their production. Hence that a business continues its operations means that it is producing some sort of goods or services deemed necessary by society.

In the process of producing such goods and services a company consumes raw materials, goods, and services produced by other companies, etc. The difference between the value of the goods and services produced by a company, and the value of the goods and services, etc. that went into their production, is known as added value, and this is distributed among the people participating in production in the form of wages paid to labour, rent paid to the owners of the land and buildings, and interest to people contributing cash capital. Also, the share due society in general is paid as taxes. The final amount left over after all other payments have been made is known as earnings, and is the portion distributed among shareholders. If the amount paid out to other parties is large and earnings are in the red, then not only will the portion going to shareholders be zero, but the capital invested by shareholders could suffer losses as well. Because people living and working together as a social unit use money as the medium of exchange for goods and services, the process of such exchange can be clearly depicted by means of accounting, which records and measures exchanges based on the inflow and outflow of money.

As of yet there is no established procedure by which accounting presents information regarding industrial production and distribution. However, it is obvious that, through the actions of business managers and the government administrative process, this sort of accounting information contributes greatly to the maintenance and expansion of industrial productive capacity, as well as to a more efficient distribution of wealth within society. In the case of large-scale stock corporations, stock is finely divided and there exist no shareholders who actually manage operations, so that a business manager's concern is not so much directed towards the manipulation of ostensible cash capital invested by shareholders as it is towards keeping the business itself in operation. In such businesses, dividend payments are comparable to interest payments on loans, and the status of shareholders is not that much different from that of creditors. The objective that business managers have is nothing other than continued existence of the business itself, together with maintenance and expansion of its productive capacity. Government administration is carried out with the same view in mind. The information accounting provides regarding production and distribution within industry plays a vital role in the decision-making process of business management, as well as in taxation and other government economic policy decisions.

This same type of accounting information is put to effective use when determining rates for public utilities and services. Because operations providing shipping, public transportation, electricity, gas, medical care, and other services essential to the lives of the people in the community tend to be monopolistic in nature, and because they affect such a great number of people, their fees are generally government regulated. Users of such services naturally want the rates kept low. Management too must strive to provide steady and reliable service at low cost by keeping down production costs, etc. At the same time, however, it is equally true that rates must be high enough to cover production costs and ensure a continuing supply of services. For this reason it occasionally becomes necessary for federal or local governments to subsidize such operations from public funds derived from taxes. The information as to whether rates are sufficient to cover production costs is provided by means of accounting. By supplying such information to managers, users, and government agencies, accounting aids in the fixing of appropriate rates and contributes to the welfare of society at large by helping to provide adequate service.

Also consider the role accounting plays in negotiations between labour and management. People contributing to production efforts in the form of labour expect and demand wages that will allow them to live a life of comparative ease and comfort. At the same time, however, it is necessary for business management to ensure compensation, that is to say profits, against capital invested in the productive process. If management ignored the contribution of capital to production and failed to compensate, then capital would desert the company and it would not be able to maintain its productive capacity. Management must concern itself on the one hand with paying wages sufficient to secure a labour force, and on the other hand with guaranteeing the profits needed to accumulate the necessary capital. For this reason it is of the utmost importance that managers know the ability of the company to pay money against wages at the time of group negotiations, and they make use of accounting information regarding production and distribution in industry. During the negotiation process, then, accounting contributes to the preservation of productive capacity and to proper distribution of wealth by providing information necessary to wage settlements.

Recently people have been pointing to the aspects of industry adversely affecting the well-being of society as a whole, and more and more regulations are being passed as the result of citizen complaints and legal actions against industry. Increasing attention is being paid to such problems as measuring the degree of industry's contribution to society, and to the financial burden companies should assume for pollution clean-up, prevention, and compensation. As of the present there is no established procedure for handling these things, but in any respect it is expected that appropriate accounting information will play a decisive role in this area as well. Moreover, accounting is already being employed to measure, not only the economic activity of individual concerns, but the production and distribution process in society as a whole, and applying this information to decisions in government economic policy.

CONCLUSION

In today's society, accounting fulfils the function of recording, measuring, and disclosing information centring on the monetary capital invested in individual enterprises. Because such enterprises represent the arena in which capital owners risk their money for the purpose of realizing profits, it is only natural that the measurement of such profits has become the central concern of accounting. On the other hand, however, in a free economy society, where fair dealing between companies is ensured and competition is completely free, the earnings realized by any individual company represent the strength of society's need for the goods and services it provides, or in other words, the degree of its contribution to society. If there is a large demand for the company's products, then sales will be profitable. But if the demand is small, then sales will not be favourable.

We can turn this around and say that large earnings indicate a great need by society for that company's products, while small earnings indicate a small need. Therefore it can be reasoned that people desiring to make money will invest in profitable businesses, and industrial capital will flow in a way that is advantageous for society as a whole, with the production of necessary goods increasing, and the production of unnecessary items falling off. In this way, then, by providing information necessary to capital owners in the decision-making process, accounting, through the resultant actions of such investors, contributes to an appropriate allocation of capital within society, and by this to a proper tuning of production.

However, this is not the only aspect in the relationship between industry and society to which accounting has application. Accounting has an even greater direct relation to industrial production and distribution within society. Because money, which accounting employs as a yardstick, also serves as the medium of exchange for goods and services in today's society, it follows that the measurements accounting makes of the inflow and outflow of money also depict the process of production and distribution within industry. In fact it would not be amiss to say that what accounting actually measures is not the flow of money itself, but rather the value of goods and services expressed in terms of money, or in other words, increases or decreases in social affluence. Money is nothing more than the medium for representing the values of all the various kinds of goods and services in a single unified fashion. In the case of large-scale stock corporations, which play a prime role in industry today, the basis for managerial action is not solely profits for shareholders, but rather continuing existence of the business itself as a productive economic unit. Because of this, managers desire more that accounting provide them with information relevant to the maintenance of productivity and distribution of wealth in industry. Another important and fundamental task of accounting is to measure the value of goods and services produced by the company, together with the value of the goods and services, etc. that went into their production, and also how the resultant added value is allocated. By making available the results of such computations, it becomes possible, through such managerial actions as planning and control, to effect a more efficient production and distribution of social wealth on the part of industry. Moreover, by providing such information, accounting contributes to the welfare of society at large through appropriate government actions.

In this paper I have examined the relationship between industry and society from the aspect of industrial capital accumulation and from the aspect of industry's productive and distributive function within society, and I have considered the sort of role that accounting plays. We saw that accounting plays a vital role in each of these aspects due to the fact that it employs money as its yardstick. The function of accounting, as mentioned at the beginning of this paper, is to record and measure the economic activities of individuals and organizations, and to disclose such information to interested parties. Through the actions of these people, decided on the basis of such information, accounting ultimately aids industrial development and contributes to the advancement of society.

The conclusions I have drawn about accounting proceed from the premisses (1) that industrial development leads to an improvement in the welfare of society at large, (2) that the introduction of vast amounts of capital is necessary to industrial development, and (3) that capital is fostered by profits. If, however, the first premiss does not find acceptance as such, it will be necessary to revise this reasoning. In order to link industrial development to improvement in the general welfare of society, it is necessary that there be direct controls on the production and distribution process in industry by means of governmental and other social regulations. In this case the ability of accounting to depict the relationship between industry and society from the aspect of industry's productive and distributive function will come to have an even greater relevance.

13

The Accounting Unit of Measure and the Translation of Foreign Currency Transactions

The official foreign exchange rate for the yen was established under the IMF system of exchange rate stabilization in 1949 at 360 yen per dollar. Until 1971 this exchange rate remained stable and Japan was not bothered with accounting problems arising from the translation of foreign currency amounts. In August 1971, when the President of the United States announced the suspension of the convertibility of the dollar for gold, the translation of foreign currency amounts suddenly attracted attention as an important financial accounting problem.

The Japanese Ministry of Finance Business Accounting Deliberation Council first issued an opinion concerning the accounting problems arising from changes in foreign exchange rates in 1968. This opinion described accounting problems that arose following the 1967 devaluation of the British pound. In the two years between 1971 and 1973 the Japanese Business Accounting Deliberation Council issued four opinions on accounting for fluctuations in foreign exchange rates.

The financial statements of foreign branches and subsidiaries are normally stated in foreign currency. In order to combine or consolidate these financial statements with domestic operations, it is thus necessary to translate the amounts stated in foreign currency into the currency of the parent company. At present, in Japan, because it is not customary to disclose consolidated financial statements, translation problems actually occur only concerning foreign branches.

Also, in Japan, when a domestic firm imports or exports goods, in most cases the price is set in terms of US dollars, and payment is made or received in dollars. Therefore, in order for these firms to record in their balance sheet amounts regarding foreign currency and foreign monetary assets and liabilities, translation from the foreign currency is required.

Accordingly, the Business Accounting Deliberation Council opinion has established separate foreign currency translation methods for (1) the

From *Waseda Business and Economic Studies*, No. 15 (1979), 1–9.

financial statements of home offices and branch offices in Japan, and (2) the financial statements of branches abroad. As for the former, the method established states that foreign currency and short-term foreign monetary assets and liabilities are to be reported in yen translated on the basis of the foreign exchange rate prevailing at the balance sheet date. Long-term foreign monetary assets and liabilities are to be reported in yen translated on the basis of the exchange rate prevailing on the day in which the asset or liability was acquired or realized. As for the latter, i.e. the financial statements of branches abroad, the method established permits a choice of two procedures. The first procedure states that foreign currency and foreign monetary assets and liabilities are to be reported in yen according to the same procedure stated in (1) above, which applies to home offices and branch offices in Japan. Inventories, fixed assets, and securities of foreign corporations are to be reported in yen translated on the basis of the exchange rate prevailing on the day in which they were acquired. The second procedure states that all of the amounts stated in the financial statements are to be reported in yen translated on the basis of the exchange rate in effect at the balance sheet date. Finally, in both of these methods, foreign exchange gains or losses are reported in the income statements for the period in which they occur.

Generally speaking, the opinion of the Business Accounting Deliberation Council on this problem has been variable and flexible. While the choice of method of foreign currency translation is left up to each firm, the Council recommends that the method employed be disclosed in a note on the balance sheet.

FOREIGN CURRENCY AS A UNIT OF MEASURE IN FINANCIAL ACCOUNTING

Accounting for fluctuations in foreign exchange rates should be approached, I believe, as a fundamental question of whether or not foreign currency is recognized as an accounting unit of measure. For convenience, I have chosen to call the viewpoint that recognizes both foreign currency and domestic currency as an accounting unit of measure the *foreign currency unit of measure principle*. I have chosen to call the viewpoint that limits the accounting unit of measure to only the domestic currency and does not acknowledge foreign currency as an accounting unit of measure the *foreign currency non-unit of measure principle*. Also, since the former permits the use of foreign currency in parallel with domestic currency as a unit of measure, it may also be called the *plural currency unit of measure principle*. Since the latter implies that the domestic currency is the only accounting unit of measure, it may be called the *single currency unit of measure principle*.

When the economic activities of a firm conducted abroad are rather limited in comparison with the activities at home, in most cases an independent accounting unit is not established to measure the international activities. The foreign currency non-unit of measure principle is typically applied in these circumstances. In other words, even if a transaction is contracted in a foreign currency, from the viewpoint of accounting the transaction is measured in the domestic currency translated at the exchange rate prevailing at the time the transaction was realized. The foreign transaction thus measured is treated exactly the same as a domestic transaction. For example, if a firm acquires land in a foreign country for $100,000, and if the exchange rate at the time of acquisition was 200 yen per dollar, the acquisition price would be recorded as ¥20,000,000. Even if the foreign currency acts as a medium to permit measurement in terms of the domestic currency, the foreign currency does not function as an accounting unit of measure.

Under the foreign currency non-unit of measure principle, changes in the foreign exchange rate are not considered to relate to the unit of measure, but to relate to the attribute to be measured. Therefore a fluctuation in the exchange rate does not directly affect accounting measurement. Of course, accounting measurement has a duty to describe honestly and understandably the nature of transactions and events according to set rules. Thus as a result of a fluctuation in the exchange rate, if there are changes in the value of the assets which the firm holds, or changes in the amount of liabilities which the firm must repay (with these assets), these changes must certainly be measured in the accounting process. It must be noted, here, however, that these types of measurements are fundamentally no different from measurements made when the market price of goods held changes or when default by debtors is expected.

Under the foreign currency non-unit of measure principle, therefore, exchange gains or losses resulting from foreign exchange rate fluctuations are measured according to the exact same accounting principles as applied to the measurement of domestic economic activities. There is absolutely no reason to treat differently the measurement of exchange gains or losses resulting from fluctuations in the exchange rate. For example, in inventory evaluation, where the lower of cost or market rule applies, when the market price of inventory falls below the acquisition cost, revaluation at the market price occurs and a loss is recognized; on the other hand, when the market price of inventory exceeds the acquisition cost, revaluation at the market price does not occur and a gain is not recorded. In the same fashion, we are led to reason that in accounting for fluctuations in foreign exchange rates under the foreign currency non-unit of measure principle, exchange losses are recognized, but exchange gains are not. There is no reason to co-rank exchange gains and exchange losses.

Nevertheless, a firm's economic activities abroad in many cases hold an important share with domestic economic activities. There are even cases where the economic activities of a firm extend over a multitude of countries, so that as far as the regions of activity are concerned, it is impossible to distinguish between the home country and the foreign country. In these cases, the economic activities conducted abroad by branches and subsidiaries are measured in the currency of the country in which they are located. Financial statements are prepared after the results of the measurements made in the currency of each country are translated to domestic currency at the end of the accounting period.

Traditional accounting thought regarding these cases, as appears in the Accounting Research Bulletins of the American Institute of Certified Public Accountants, and in the first method described in the opinion issued by the Japanese Business Accounting Deliberation Council, disclaim foreign currency as an accounting unit of measure. These accounting methods, which require disclosure in terms of the home country's currency of (in the case of the American Institute of Certified Public Accountants) fixed assets, permanent investments, and the capital stock of foreign subsidiaries and branches, and (in the case of the Japanese Business Accounting Deliberation Council), inventory and fixed assets of foreign branches, and the securities of foreign corporations,[1] are clearly a consequence of the view that defines the accounting acquisition cost to be the amount of expenditure as calculated in domestic currency. Accordingly, even though the economic activities conducted by foreign branches and subsidiaries are measured in the currency unit of their respective country, this measurement is apparently only recognized as a temporary calculation. It can be said that the accounting unit of measure is still, as before, the home currency—as such income is calculated in the home currency, and dividends made, apparently, in the home currency.

THE ACCOUNTING MEASUREMENT CONCEPT IN THE INTERNATIONAL AGE

In measuring the international economic activities conducted by branches and subsidiary corporations in terms of the currency unit of the country in which they are located, I believe it to be much more appropriate to employ the foreign currency unit of measure principle, which recognizes measurement in foreign currency as a formal accounting measurement method. One can then consider fluctuations in the foreign exchange rate to relate to the accounting unit of measure.

[1] Translated on the basis of the exchange rate prevailing at the date of their acquisition or their realization.

In accounting there were originally two reasons for using money as a unit of measure. One reason was that money is a common measure of the value of all of the goods and services in an economic society. Another reason was that money is used as a means of payment. The economic activities of firms, which are the object of accounting measurement, involve the production, the consumption, and the distribution of all types of goods and services. Nothing else but money can comprehensively measure the production, the consumption, and the distribution of these goods and services. Also, accounting measurement is based upon the premiss that taxes and dividends will be paid according to the result of that measurement, namely earnings. In today's society, because the distribution of such earnings takes place in the form of money, there is nothing better than money for the accounting unit of measure.

Since foreign currency functions as a common measure for all types of goods and services, and also is used as a means of payment, it is no different than domestic currency. Absolutely no reason exists for disclaiming foreign currency as an accounting unit of measure. For example, when land is acquired abroad for $100,000, from the viewpoint of accounting the acquired cost can be measured as $100,000, and there should be no need to advert to the respective yen amount based on the foreign exchange rate on the date of acquisition.

Under the foreign currency unit of measure principle, measured accounting income is the sum of income earned in domestic currency and income earned in foreign currency. Total measured accounting income of economic activities conducted in all the countries of Japan, the United States, and England is the sum of the income earned in yen, the income earned in dollars, and the income earned in pounds. If there are stockholders spread out among these countries, dividends can be paid to the stockholders of each country in the currency of that country. There is no reason necessarily to presuppose that income will be measured in the domestic currency, or that dividends will be paid in domestic currency. Naturally, the standard of the unit of measure of foreign currency differs from that of the domestic currency. Thus, in order to combine the results measured in terms of the home currency with the results measured in foreign currency, it is necessary to compare the respective standards of the units of measure and convert the results in foreign currency to domestic currency.

The metre, a unit of length, has as its standard the length of a bar, whose cross-section is the shape of an 'X', made of an alloy of platinum and iridium, located in the International Bureau of Weights and Measures in the suburbs of Paris. Similarly, units of length such as the foot or the shaku (Japanese unit, about 0.3 metres) have their own standard of unit of measure. The results of measurements based on these different units can be combined, provided these standards are compared and conversion is executed. For example, if you know that one foot corresponds to 0.3048 metres, you can add a 20-metre length and a 50-foot length and obtain a measurement of 35.24 metres or 115.6 feet. In comparison with these length standards, currency standards used as accounting units of measure are not so precise. Under the foreign currency unit of measure principle, however, we have implicitly acknowledged that the standard for currency, which is the accounting unit of measure, is the purchasing power of that currency at the end of the accounting period. In this way, foreign exchange rates, considered to express the ratio of the relative purchasing powers of the currencies of the various countries, are used as conversion rates to combine the results measured in foreign currency with the results in domestic currency.

Accordingly, under the foreign currency unit of measure principle, all the amounts stated in financial statements measured in a foreign currency should be translated together into the home currency at the foreign exchange rate prevailing at the date of the balance sheet. This is the second method that was given in the opinion issued by the Japanese Business Accounting Deliberation Council. There is no reason to measure, in terms of domestic currency, inventory and the fixed assets of branches abroad, translated at the exchange rate at the time of their acquisition or time of construction. As stated before, under the foreign currency unit of measure principle, fluctuations in the exchange rate are perceived to relate to the unit of measure. Thus any exchange gains or losses resulting from a fluctuation in the exchange rate is considered to be of different nature from an ordinary gain or loss. Since exchange gains or losses arise from a change in the standard of the unit of measure, they should fit in the same category as a gain or loss resulting from a change in the general purchasing power of money. Fig. 13.1 compares accounting measurement under the foreign currency unit of measure principle and under the foreign currency non-unit of measure principle.

SUMMARY

In this article I have discussed accounting problems which arise concerning the measurement of international economic activities when foreign exchange rates fluctuate. I have indicated here that the problem of accounting for fluctuations in the exchange rate can only be solved by approaching the problem from a more fundamental perspective—that is, whether or not to recognize foreign currency as an accounting unit of measure. I have pointed out that accounting up until the present time has consistently relied on measurement in the currency of one country. For the measurement of economic activities conducted world-wide, however, I stated the need to give recognition to foreign currency as a unit

I. Accounting measurement under the foreign currency non-unit of measure principle:

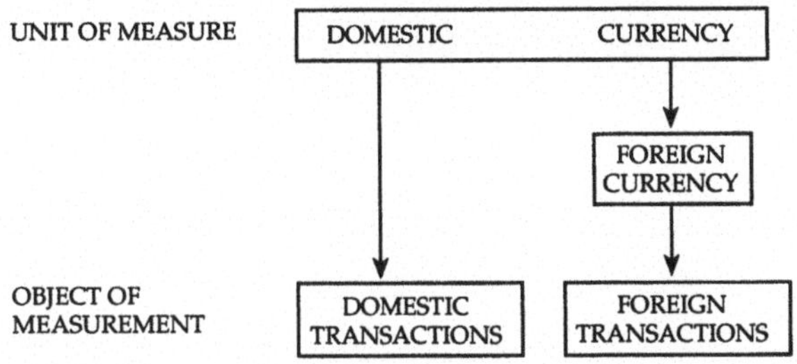

II. Accounting measurement under the foreign currency unit of measure principle:

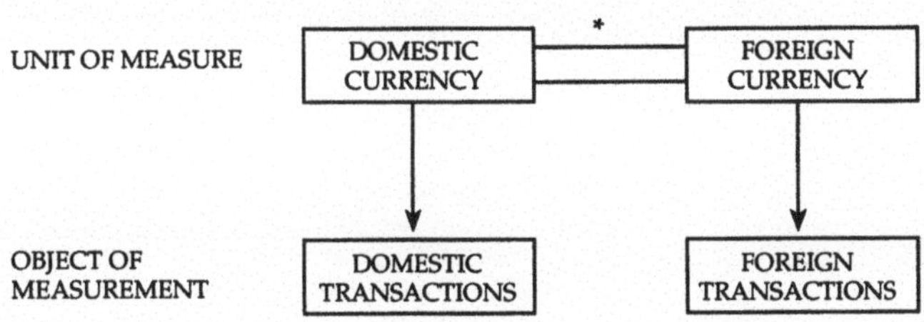

* Translation at the foreign exchange rate on the balance sheet date.

Fig. 13.1. Two methods of accounting foreign currency

of measure and to introduce into accounting the idea that measurement can take place in several currencies. This means that fluctuations in the exchange rate are not considered to relate to the attribute being measured, but to the accounting unit of measure. Thus, according to this way of thinking, all the amounts stated in financial statements measured in foreign currency, regardless of their classification, should be translated together to the domestic currency at the exchange rate prevailing on the balance sheet date. Also, gains or losses resulting from this type of translation, being similar to adjustments to current income made in general price level income statements as a result of changes in the general purchasing power of money, should be distinguished from ordinary gains or losses. In this rapidly developing international economic age, I believe that questions involving accounting for fluctuations in foreign exchange rates must be considered as illustrated here, from the root of the problem.

14

Accounting Standard Selection and its Socio-economic Consequences

Accounting standards represent those resolutions pertaining to measurement and reporting which comprise the basis upon which various financial statements are prepared. Besides indicating the financial position and activities of the business, accounting standards represent an amalgamation of accounting customs and practices recognized over the years as being useful. They indicate the accounting procedures to be followed when preparing financial statements. In a narrow sense, accounting standards refers to practices decided upon by the various agencies responsible for establishing accounting standards, including the Business Accounting Standards Board in Japan, the Financial Accounting Standards Board (FASB) in the United States, the Accounting Standards Board (ASB) in the United Kingdom, and the International Accounting Standards Committee (IASC). In a broader sense, accounting standards might include various regulations pertaining to accounting passed by law. In the very broadest sense of the term, accounting standards include the rules and suggestions put forth by professional accounting organizations, etc.

At one time, funds for financing a business came from the business itself, limiting financial reporting to fulfilling the needs of the person who was both the owner and the manager. That is to say, financial reporting was a private affair. Indeed, making such a report public would only have given an advantage to competitor companies, so such an idea had no place in the thinking of the time. However, an internal source of funds proved insufficient to fulfil the needs of businesses seeking to expand their facilities in response to advances in industrial technology. Consequently, businesses came to rely on external sources for funds.

In Japan, the privately owned industrial conglomerates, known as the Zaibatsu, were forcefully dismembered after the Second World War and the securities exchange was rejuvenated. An economic structure was created whereby industrial capital was amassed from the savings of the general populace, and this contributed greatly to Japan's subsequent economic growth. In this structure, accounting is charged with the responsibility of

From *International Journal of Accounting*, 28/2 (1993), 93–103.

providing information that is necessary to the decision-making process of investors. The actual practice of accounting measurement and disclosure now plays a vital social role. There has been a shift in focus of accounting's function from indicating trustee responsibility to evaluating investment results. As for the various financial statements, the figures they reflect have increased in their accuracy and precision, and the appropriateness in indicating the operating performance and financial position of a business has come to be a major concern.

When accounting information is directed towards a large, unspecified number of general investors, it becomes the target of regulation. The establishment and observance of accounting standards regarding the contents and form of financial reports take on great significance. In Japan, the Securities Exchange and Certified Public Accountants Acts passed in 1948, followed by 'Accounting Standards for Business Enterprises' in 1949, were intended to pave the way for financial reporting regulation. We then see regulation of financial reporting by means of Japan's long-standing Commercial Code, as well as regulation of the financial statements disclosed publicly by companies issuing securities listed on the stock exchange by means of the Securities Exchange Act.

Regulations pertaining to financial reporting are basically of two types: those regulations passed by law or decided upon by an agency responsible for establishing accounting standards (government regulation); and those regulations based upon rules and suggestions made by professional accounting organizations. Regulation of financial reporting in the UK and the US started with professional accounting associations indicating accounting standards to serve as guides for their members actually in accounting practice, and then getting their members to adhere to them. However, it proved to be no easy matter to guarantee the quality of financial reporting by self-regulation on the part of such organizations. At times a company's violation of accounting standards would be overlooked by accountants and incorrect accounting information would be submitted. Every time a case of business fraud appeared, or whenever a major company went bankrupt, it cast doubt on the limits of the non-governmental regulation of financial reporting. In direct response to a public outcry against accounting practices, a gradual strengthening of governmental regulation emerged. In present-day Japan as well, there is a trend towards gradually increased governmental regulation to ensure the quality of financial reporting.

The financial report of a business is prepared by its trustees, or management, and is addressed to its consignees, or shareholders. The information disclosed in the financial statements has a strong bearing, not only on potential shareholders and creditors, but also on employees, consumers, and society as a whole. The fact that the selection of accounting standards pertaining to financial reporting has a variety of consequences for the economic life of society as a whole is yet another reason for the strengthening of government regulation. It is true that, at the time accounting standards are established, flexibility in the choice between accounting approaches is restricted to a certain extent in order to preserve the ability to make meaningful comparisons between one financial report and another.

Accounting standards may be selected for technical as well as political reasons. As far as technical reasons are concerned, selection is basically a problem of recognizing which accounting practices are 'best', and can be settled by seeking the help of accounting theory. From a political point of view, selection becomes a matter of choosing between those parties that will benefit by the selection of a certain practice, and those parties that stand to be hurt. There is a strong potential for political considerations to become woven into the setting of accounting standards. In the legal regulatory process, political pressure from people with vested interests is likely to assume the form of active lobbying. There is no doubt that financial reporting will come to play an even more important role in the relationship between society and economic conditions in which businesses find themselves.

In view of the above, in the present paper I discuss the part that accounting standard selection played in three economic episodes: (1) the rise in domestic petroleum prices, (2) the subway fare increase, and (3) the rapid fall in stock prices that occurred in Japan in the latter half of 1990. These economic episodes force us to re-examine the concept of freedom in the selection of accounting standards.

LAST-IN, FIRST-OUT METHOD AND THE RECENT PETROLEUM PRICE INCREASE

In August 1990 Iraq invaded Kuwait and the price of crude oil rose dramatically. On 3 September the evening newspapers reported that the United Arab Emirates' nationally owned oil company, Abu Dhabi, had informed Japan's oil industry that it was substantially increasing the price on August shipments of crude. According to the report, the price per barrel (158.9 litres) would be \$10.25–\$10.55 higher than for July, with the representative crude, Maban, up \$10.55 (64.1%) to \$27.00. Abu Dhabi also decided to raise the price on August shipments of Arabian light, which is priced in reference to spot purchase prices for other crudes, to \$25.33 per barrel, up \$9.83 over the previous month. These marked the highest prices in four years and eight months (since 1985). Oman, Mexico, and other oil producers followed suit and raised their prices by approximately \$10 per barrel.

Giving this sudden rise in the price of crude as the reason, petroleum suppliers in Japan announced their intentions to raise domestic oil prices beginning in the middle of September. Now even though the price of crude rose in August, oil companies surely must have had reserves of oil purchased before that time. Also, there probably was a supply of oil purchased at pre-August prices still in transit to Japan. So why is it that oil companies were so quick to raise their prices? The oil industry's answer was 'it is because domestic prices are computed on a basis of the last-in, first-out method used to figure the cost of crude'. The Ministry of International Trade and Industry, too, it seems, recognized that, due to the approximately $10 per barrel rise in the price of crude over the July price resulting from Iraq's invasion of Kuwait, the increased cost of oil purchases for August alone nearly equalled the previous year's 170 billion yen normal operating profits for all thirty-one domestic suppliers and refineries together. Thus, they concluded that an increase in domestic petroleum prices was unavoidable.

Strong reaction was voiced by other ministries at a cabinet meeting on 4 September. In reply to the consensus that a 'sudden price increase should be avoided', the Minister of International Trade and Industry promptly announced his intention to work out a solution. It included, among other things, a re-examination of the method used in computing the cost of restocking petroleum supplies or, more specifically, a change from the last-in, first-out method to an average cost method. The oil industry vehemently opposed the plan. Consequently, oil suppliers were allowed to transfer the increase in the cost of oil imports, caused by the situation in the Middle East, to domestic petroleum prices. As of 17 September, the wholesale prices of gasoline, kerosene, and other petroleum products increased 8 yen per litre (approximately 22 cents per gallon).

With the exception of a few companies, oil suppliers had adopted the last-in, first-out method just three years earlier. At that time the yen was getting stronger, the cost of crude was down, and oil suppliers were under attack for not lowering their prices. Their counter to this was that they still had reserves of oil purchased at higher cost, and the average cost had not fallen that much. However, domestic prices proceeded to fall, and for companies figuring gross sales costs by the average cost method, this led to an appreciable reduction in profits. The *Japan Economic News* for 4 April 1987 reported the following:

> In response to the stronger yen, rising oil prices, and other changes in the earning environment, we see a continued attempt by powerful companies to manipulate things by changing accounting standards. By switching over in March to a last-in, first-out method for evaluating inventory, the three big oil suppliers, Nippon Sekiyu, Idemitsu Kosan, and Kyodo Sekiyu, have now placed themselves in a position where it will be easy to push through oil price hikes on the basis of fiscal accounting . . . The aim of these suppliers in making such a switch is to make it easy to push through price increases on domestic prices whenever there is an increase in the price of crude. Even though the previous period was favoured

with a strong yen and low prices for crude, prices at the lower end of the market fell before they could be reflected in cost, and in comparison with Toa Nenryo which employs the last-in, first-out method, and recorded an all-time high in earnings, Nippon Sekiyu's normal operating profits for the period ending March 1987 fell by 20% to 17 billion yen.

Consistency in the application of accounting standards is maintained, while the last-in, first-out method demonstrates its effectiveness as a rationale for raising prices. This is one example where accounting figures influence the decisions of business and government. But viewed socio-economically, it raises the question of whether or not this sort of price hike, linked to fluctuations in the crude oil market, is beneficial. Originally, the last-in, first-out method was devised as a method for eliminating on-the-book profits (paper profits) in a context of galloping inflation. What it does is guard against the erosion of a company's capital through taxation and other assessments against ostensible profits generated by commodity price changes that have no chance of reversing over the long term. But in the above case we see it being used to support a short-term pricing strategy linked to the crude oil market. It will be interesting to see how quickly oil suppliers respond when tensions relax in the Middle East and crude prices drop again.

In any business, the possession of inventory reserves should theoretically act as a cushion to absorb changes in acquisition costs. A constantly fluctuating pricing structure is certainly not desirable. Petroleum price hikes are inevitably reflected in the steel, trucking, and other industries, and the total effect can be massive. This sort of scenario ought to have been foreseen at the time oil suppliers proposed adoption of the last-in, first-out method. It is my belief that more regard should be paid to social and economic consequences whenever a switch of accounting standards is contemplated.

INTEREST PAYMENTS AND THE RECENT SUBWAY FARE INCREASES

On 24 August 1990 the Teito Rapid Transit Authority (RTA) of Japan applied to the Ministry of Transportation for approval of an average 13.3% increase on RTA-operated subway fares. The evening edition of the *Asahi Newspaper* reported: 'the reason given was, costs for new lines, more air-conditioned cars, and increased facilities have gone beyond projected estimates and operating efforts have reached their limits'. The fare increase went into effect in November. Discounting fare adjustments in April, to compensate for the new consumption tax, this marked the first increase in fares in six years.

The figuring of cost plays an important role in the determining of rates for public services. Rates must be sufficient to maintain operations. Article 16 of the Railway Operations Law (4 December 1986, extra edition, Law No. 92) stipulates that fare and rates must receive approval from the Minister of Transportation, and the basis of such approval 'will include compensation for appropriate costs incurred during the course of efficient operation, as well as appropriate profits'. In order to fulfil its function as a major transportation network in an expanding urban area, it is not sufficient for a subway merely to maintain operation of its present lines. It must be continually expanding its lines, and into this is invested vast sums of borrowed capital. Interest payments alone can be substantial, and accounting for such payments presents a problem.

There are two methods in accounting for dealing with the interest payments on money borrowed for construction purposes. Based on the first method, interest is simply charged as an expense to the fiscal period in which it is incurred. The second method includes interest as part of the cost of construction and treats it as future expense when the facility is in use or operation. For ordinary businesses, construction is usually not on such a grand scale as it is for public service operations. Moreover, a clear-cut distinction cannot always be made between capital used for normal operations and capital used for construction, hence interest payments are generally treated by the first method, as current period expenses. For public service enterprises with large amounts of capital invested in facilities under construction, such interest is often accounted for by method two, as part of construction costs to be charged as expenses at a later date. Provisions for such treatment are made in Article 10 of Accounting Standards for Railroads (20 February 1987, extra edition, Ministry of Transportation Ordinance No. 7).

Should interest payments be treated as current period expenses, or should they be counted as construction costs and charged as future expenses? There is really no clear-cut rationale for choosing one approach over the other. Interest on borrowed capital is in one sense a sort of dividend payment on invested capital, and as such ought to be included as a financial expense during the period in which it is incurred. But then, interest on capital necessary for the construction of new tracks is part of construction costs, and logically ought to be borne by fares paid by passengers using the line after it is completed.

This same sort of problem arose in connection with another RTA subway fare increase some ten years ago. Headlines in the *Asahi Newspaper* of 1 June 1978 announced, 'RTA Subways hide profits from fare increase. ¥10 billion manipulated on the books', with the story as follows:

RTA's 1977 financial report was announced on 26 May, showing profits of ¥2.8 billion, but on the 30th it became clear that, in fact, profits of more than ¥10 billion had been hidden through the use of accounting techniques. Interest payments on money borrowed for construction, up until now included as construction costs, and in no way related to income computation, were suddenly entered as expenses on the income statement for 1977, and by such manipulation, ¥10 billion in profits were erased from view. Behind the scenes we see RTA and the Ministry of Transportation employing their cunning to keep the excessive profits realized from last year's sharp subway fare increase from coming to the attention of the public . . . Because RTA has long been operating in the red, interest payments on money borrowed for construction have always been treated separately to keep the revenue–expense deficit from growing too large. They say they switched figures around in hopes that last year's fare increase will bring about a favourable balance in revenues and expenses. But the figure switched around was ¥10.3 billion. As a result, interest payments on the income statement, totalling ¥30.6 billion for 1975 and ¥31 billion for 1976, suddenly jumped to ¥41.9 billion for 1977, with profits disappearing by that amount. Computed according to the accounting method used up until now, what should have been a profit of ¥13.1 billion was consequently whittled down to ¥2.8 billion, which appears as very meagre profits for a year in which substantial fare increases were made.

Entering interest payments on money borrowed for construction purposes as current period expenses rather than as construction costs is clearly a switch in accounting techniques, and not something made from the clear blue sky. Article 4 of Accounting Provisions for Regional Railway stipulates that, 'In keeping company accounts, the same methods shall be applied consistently from period to period, without aberrant changes.' The Ministry of Transportation's comment in regard to this was, 'RTA Subways employed the same accounting method from 1954 to 1977, and from 1977 on they plan to use the new method, so there should be no problem'.

The newspaper also quoted a remark by RTA Subway's vice-president:

It was in no way true that the increase in our fares in step with the financial floundering Metropolitan Subways has led to excessive fares and unexpected profits. Such criticism is way off target. By employing this new accounting technique we now have a sound accounting system. Rather, it can be said that the way our accounting was done up until this time was unsound.

His rationale was that charging interest payments as current period expenses makes for 'sound accounting', and this he rhetorically waved as a banner. There can be no doubt that charging interest payments on capital invested in track under construction as current expenses increases the burden on operations by that amount. But as to whether or not operating difficulties due to such an increased burden can validly be used as an excuse for increasing present fares seems to be a problem that goes beyond accounting theory alone. It would appear there is a need for a more general sort of discussion.

The question as to whether or not interest payments should be entered as costs relating to construction of fixed assets has long been an important point of contention in the field of accounting. In 1912 the Japanese scholar Y. Satoh discussed the pros and cons of this problem in his paper entitled 'Methods of Accounting Interest Payments on Loans'. Tetsuzo Ohta (1968) makes the following observation: 'When it comes to putting accounting into actual practice and you examine the various techniques, you discover there are items remaining for which it is not all that easy to come up with a solution.' Among these, the problem of interest is 'like the bitter tea from used tea leaves', and there is a need to 'remove the dust-covered folder from the filing cabinet' and carefully re-examine this question. He further notes that the argument for treating construction-related interest as a current period expense can only be grounded in conservatism. And this is supposed to give us 'sound accounting'? This whole question is in need of reconsideration.

COST? OR WHICHEVER LESS? THE RECENT DECLINE IN STOCK PRICES

The price of stocks, bonds, and other securities fell sharply in September 1990. 29 September was a Saturday, the 30th a Sunday, so the 28th was the closing day for trading. Under the headline 'Stock Prices Close Below ¥21 thousand', the *Asahi Newspaper* for September 29 reported the following:

> With prices continuing their rapid fall, the Tokyo stock market showed a nearly across-the-board decline, with individual investors rushing to sell off shares because of growing concern for the future brought about by uncertainty over the situation in the Middle East and the increase in the price of oil. For the first time since March 1987, the average price on one portion of shares on the Tokyo Securities Exchange fell below ¥21,000, to close at ¥20,983, down ¥788 from the previous day, and reaching a new record low for this year for the fourth day straight. This marks a 46% decline over the last year's high on 29 December, and surpasses the 44% rate of decline seen during the 1965 securities recession, to become the sharpest decline since the brief period of confusion following the reopening of the Tokyo Securities Exchange after the war in 1949. The volume of trading was 506 million shares.

The question here is: how does a business enter the value of such stocks, bonds, and other securities it possesses on the balance sheet it prepares to indicate its financial position for September? In principle, the Commercial Code adopts a representation on a cost basis, and does not recognize a current or market price representation. However, in situations where the market price falls below acquisition cost, it permits valuation at cost or market price, whichever is less. It is left to the individual business to choose which accounting method it will employ: cost valuation or whichever-less valuation. In this way, then, businesses choosing the cost valuation method simply ignore slight declines in share value. When the decline is very sharp, if there is good reason to expect that prices will recover, then values are still listed at acquisition cost. Businesses choosing the whichever-less method evaluate fallen shares at current market price.

On 26 September 1990, Nippon Telephone and Telegraph (NTT) shares fell to ¥760,000, the lowest since their listing on the Exchange. They recovered slightly on the 27th and closed on the 28th at ¥774,000, a 33% decline over the end of March. The *Japan Economic News* for 28 September reported:

> On the 27th NTT shares reached a temporary record low since their listing on the Exchange. Coming just before the finish of the interim fiscal period ending September, this decline is likely to cause appreciable valuation losses to appear on the interim reports for companies holding NTT stock. Of the four telephone switchboard companies having close affiliation with NTT, Nippon Denki, Hitachi Seisaku Sho, and Fujitsu all employ the whichever less method, and using the 27th closing price, it is expected that together they will figure a valuation loss totalling approximately ¥8 billion. Adding to this the valuation losses for 1988 and 1989 fiscal years brings the September end total to over ¥27 billion . . .

Given the same business operations conducted within the same economic environment, then different current period profits are reported in the financial statements depending on which of the alternate accounting methods is chosen. Businesses employing the whichever-less method record valuation losses whenever the current market price of shares falls below their acquisition cost, resulting in a reduction of current period profits by that amount. Businesses employing the cost basis method do not record valuation losses as long as the decline in market price is not too extreme, or even if it is extreme, as long as there is thought to be a good chance of recovery. With the cost basis method, however, the businesses still must bear such losses, even though they do not appear as a loss on the income statement.

The problem of falling share prices has grave consequences, particularly for the financial community. For the two fiscal years of 1988 and 1989 banks are said to have amassed as much as ¥8.8 trillion in total capital on the domestic and foreign capital markets. They made use of high share prices to gather low interest capital and increased their own proprietary capital, while at the same time off-the-book profits on valuable securities in their possession increased at a yearly rate of 20–30%, and it was expected they would meet the Bank for International Settlements (BIS) regulation concerning the ratio of proprietary capital to total assets. From this we can imagine just how great an effect the plunge in share prices from the beginning of 1990 through September has had. The *Asahi Newspaper* for 22 November summarized the September-end interim reports for twelve metropolitan banks as follows:

Twelve metropolitan banks yesterday announced their interim reports for the period ending in September. Due to the sharp decrease in profit margin caused by rising interest rates and the increasing cost of capital accumulation, and also due to large valuation losses brought on by the recent decline in the market price of stocks and bonds, normal operating profits for these twelve banks are down a whopping 39.4% average over the same period last year. Such a decline in market price is especially damaging to off-the-book profits on stocks. Nearly 60%, or ¥22 trillion, in off-the-book profits for the same period last year were blown away . . . Because of this, the ratio of proprietary capital to total assets has deteriorated, and for nine of these banks has fallen below the 8% level they are required by BIS regulation to achieve by March of 1993.

For the sake of upgrading operations and strengthening the business structure, the finance community has in principle adopted the whichever-less method for evaluating securities. At present, however, many businesses and institutions in fact employ the cost basis method, and for this reason off-the-book losses on bank-held securities resulting from the recent decline in market prices apparently comes to a considerable sum. The *Japan Economic News* for 28 November analyses the interim reports for these banks and reports as follows:

As a result of falling market prices on securities, off the book losses sustained by banks holding such securities suddenly ballooned on their interim financial reports for September. Total off the book losses for metropolitan banks is thought to reach the neighborhood of ¥997 billion, up as much as 38% over March of this year. Off the book losses do not appear in financial computations as such, but if they had been treated as actual losses, then total net deficits for metropolitan banks would have come to more than ¥200 billion, which means that they have been hurt much worse than interim report figures suggest . . . Sumitomo, Tokai and Daiwa employ the whichever less evaluation method. The nine remaining banks employ the cost basis method, and all sustained off the book losses at the interim accounting. From the interim reports of the banks it is surmised that Daiichi Kangyo's off the book losses on securities were greater than ¥271 billion, while those of Mitsubishi and Kyowa were greater than ¥100 billion . . . Supposing that these nine banks had employed the whichever less method, then off the book losses would have been actual valuation losses, forcing the necessity for redemption. A whichever less based computation of net business profits made by simply deducting off the book losses from the net business profits reported for each bank would put six of these banks in the red, with Daiichi Kangyo showing a deficit of ¥182.9 billion.

The above illustrates how the adoption of either the cost basis method or whichever-less method can change the profit figure computed in the financial reports in times when the market price of stocks and securities decreases. But is it really desirable that the selection of different accounting techniques should lead to different profit figures being reported? This is a question that needs further consideration. In particular, adoption of the whichever-less method means that only off-the-book profits are possible when stock and security prices rise, while the cost method means that not only will there be off-the-book profits when stock and security prices are high, but off-the-book losses when prices are low. The mandatory use of the whichever-less method will ensure that a deterioration of operating results, such as those resulting from the recent decline in stock and security prices, will be reported. By applying the cost method, however, one can avoid having such situations reported. Such so-called freedom in the selection of accounting standards leaves us with a major problem in the area of financial information disclosure.

CONCLUSION

Occasionally there exist alternative approaches among the accounting methods which form the basis for the preparation of the various financial statements. In the three recent events described in this paper, we found problems arising from the choice between such alternative accounting methods.

In general, the selection of accounting standards occurs at two levels. At the first level, a business is required by law to follow a specific method in preparing its reports, or conversely, is forbidden from employing a method that is deemed undesirable, or else selection is made by some agency vested with such authority. The accounting provisions contained in the Commercial Code and Accounting Standards for Business Enterprises are typical examples of selection at this level. Decrees or memoranda issued by the supervisory office also belong to this level. Because of the need for economic unification in Japan before and during the Second World War, virtually all accounting standard selection was made at this level. Selection at the second level includes those choices made by individual companies within the accounting standard framework prescribed by legislation or by standard-setting agencies, as well as choices between alternative methods in areas where no standards have been established. At the time it prepares its financial statements, a company must note as an explanation of accounting policy which of the alternative accounting methods it has selected to adopt.

No matter which accounting standard is selected, if it is applied consistently it will give equivalent results over a long period of time. It is also true, however, that for any given fiscal period, the selection of one accounting method in place of another will sometimes lead to profit figures that are smaller or larger than if a different method had been chosen. Companies whose profits are small, or who record deficits and are not able to make dividend payments to shareholders, will not only have a difficult time accumulating funds by the issuing of stock, but will also find it difficult to obtain loans from banks, etc. To prevent such a situation, it sometimes happens that a company will switch accounting standards to give the appearance of more consistent earnings. Switching accounting standards in this manner is certainly different from listing phoney transactions or omitting real ones, listing fictitious assets or debts or failing to list real ones, and the various other types of fraudulent accounting.

Accounting standards have been established so that the financial statement of a business indicates its operating performance and financial position in a manner that is both true and fair. In the past it has been thought that any effects such accounting standard selection might have are neutral. Recently, however, this assumption has come to be questioned. Until now, it was probably true to say that accounting standards have been selected in view of the requirements of businesses alone. But the examples discussed in this paper were all cases of accounting standard selection having a variety of consequences on society and the economy. Cabinet ministers opposing the raising of domestic oil prices tied directly to fluctuations in the price of crude were countered with the argument for 'consistent application of accounting standards'. In the debate over the RTA Subway fare increase, user criticism was countered with 'sound accounting' as a shield. In the third example, the freedom to select accounting standards was used as a device to soften the impact of valuation losses caused by a fall in the price of stocks and securities. Financial statements have a tremendous effect on decisions and actions of the business itself, government, unions, and investors. It would appear the time has come for us to take a new look at the relationship between such freedom to select accounting standards and the consequences such selection might have for society.

There was a time when freedom to select alternative accounting standards was not advocated because of difficulties in attempting to compare and contrast different businesses. This thinking was in vogue when I first began my study of accounting. I remember the confusion at the 7th Japan Accounting Association Convention in 1948—the first such conference to be held since the end of the war. This convention was a gathering of scholars in the accounting field just on the eve of the publication of 'Accounting Standards for Business Enterprises'. Especially instructive was the round-table discussion presided over by Iwao Iwata (1949), centring on the theme 'Improvement and unification of the financial statements'. Freedom in the selection of accounting standards was a new idea then. We were taught the virtues of avoiding government interference in the affairs of a business and of having each individual business choose which accounting standards best fit its situation or needs. The idea of comparing different businesses from the point of view of society was rejected. We learned the importance of the consistent application of accounting standards so that the operating performance and financial position of a business could be observed and compared period by period.

Freedom in the selection of accounting standards was a concept central to financial reporting in a free economic society and was one of the major pillars supporting the prosperity of modern society.

More than forty years have passed since that time, and now I find myself beginning to have doubts regarding the freedom in selection of accounting standards. When pondering the socio-economic consequences of business financial reporting of the type demonstrated in the examples presented in this paper, one cannot help but feel that a certain amount of limitation ought to be placed on the flexibility in the selection of alternative accounting standards.

More than ten years ago Stephen A. Zeff (1978) made the following observation:

> Since the 1960s, the American accounting profession has been aware of the increasing influence of 'outside forces' in the standard-setting process. Two parallel developments have marked this trend. First, individuals and groups that had rarely shown any interest in the setting of accounting standards began to intervene actively and powerfully in the process. Second, these parties began to invoke arguments other than those which have traditionally been employed in accounting discussions. The term 'economic consequences' has been used to describe these novel kinds of arguments.

Accounting reports influence decisions, and actions resulting from such decisions might in turn affect other related persons in a manner that is detrimental. In today's society we have reached a point where accounting standards cannot be established without considering their social and economic consequences.

REFERENCES

Carsberg, Bryan, and Dev, Susan (eds.) (1984), *External Financial Reporting: Essays in Honour of Harold Edey* (London: Prentice Hall International, Inc.).

Iwata, Iwao (1949) (presiding), Roundtable discussion, 'Improvement and Unification of Financial Statements', *Kaikei*, 56/2: 185–216.

Katoh, Morihiro (1990) (translator in charge), *Accounting Principles and Accounting Policy* (Tokyo: Moriyama Shoten).

Ohta, Tetsuzo (1968), 'Concerning the Cost-like Features of Capital Interest', *Sangyo Keiri*, 28/10: 6–11.

Satoh, Y. (1912), 'Methods of Accounting Interest on Borrowed Funds', *Tokyo Keizai Zasshi*, 65 (no. 1634): 284–9.

Solomons, David, *Making Accounting Policy: The Quest for Credibility in Financial Reporting* (Oxford: Oxford University Press, 1986).

Taylor, Peter, and Turley, Stuart (1986), *The Regulation of Accounting* (Oxford: Blackwell).

Zeff, Stephen A. (1978), 'The Rise of Economic Consequences: The Impact of Accounting Reports on Decision Making may be the Most Challenging Accounting Issue of the 1970s', *Journal of Accountancy*, 146/6: 56–63.

15

Socio-economic Environments and the Function of Accounting

Does Accounting have a Larger Role than External Financial Reporting?

STATEMENT OF THE PROBLEM

The thesis of this paper is that different socio-economic environments give rise to varying expectations of the usefulness of accounting. Hence I propose a caution against the recent trend seen in much accounting research and education towards placing heavy emphasis on accounting's function in providing financial information to external users, that is, investors, while often disregarding the fact that other functions exist. By socio-economic environment I mean that environment brought about by business activities, or more specifically, the politico-economic system, the industrial structure, the market for amassing capital, and the level of industrial technology, etc. Moreover, the 'function of accounting' means the role that accounting ought, or is expected, to fulfil. There are at least two cases in which it becomes necessary to consider the function of accounting in relation to the socio-economic environment. The first involves tracing changes in the accounting function from past to present, and then trying to discern the expansion of the accounting function in present-day society in contrast to the new functions which will be expected of future accounting. The second case involves conducting research aimed at the establishment and improvement of practices and systems of international accounting. Of these two, I have decided to place emphasis on the second case, and shall address the subject in this context.

From B. Banerjee (ed.), *Contemporary Issues in Accounting Research* (Calcutta: Indian Accounting Association Research Foundation, 1991), 233–40.

THE EXTERNAL FINANCIAL REPORTING FUNCTION OF ACCOUNTING

One of the factors helping to speed the recovery of Japan's depleted economy after the Second World War and serving as a source for the country's affluence of today is the democratization of securities. Serving as a stimulus for economic reform after the close of the war in 1945, the Allied Command initiated its programme of economic democratization with dismemberment of the huge industrial conglomerates known as the Zaibatsu. In order to do away with the control of the Zaibatsu parent companies over their various subsidiaries, all shares in the possession of the parent companies and their controlling families were required to be turned over to the Holding Company Liquidating Committee, and were then sold off at current value to investors in the private sector by the Securities Regulatory Commission. The aim in dissolving Zaibatsu parent companies and turning over exclusively owned subsidiary stock to the general public was not only to dismember the Zaibatsu empire, which played a leading role in much of the wartime economy through its close ties to the military and governing bureaucracy, but also to recruit many stockholders from the private sector for the purpose of raising much additional industrial capital. This obviously effected a tremendous change in the socio-economic environment at the time.

A Securities and Exchange Act patterned after the American system was enacted in 1947, amended the following year, and put into effect. In 1949 the reopening of the stock exchange, after having been closed for many years, was an important step. Amendments to the Japanese Commercial Code in 1948 and again in 1950 did away with the instalment payment system for stocks, replacing it with a system of authorized shares. As a result of these and other measures such as the recognition of non-par value shares, social institutions underwent great changes.

In addition to institutionalizing the disclosure of financial information to investors, the Securities and Exchange Act also stipulated that financial statements be audited as a means of giving credibility to such information. Because of this, the function of accounting in supplying financial information to investors suddenly came into the limelight. In 1948 the old Registered Public Accountants Act was discarded for a new Certified Public Accountants Act, and the first CPA examination was given in 1949. This year also saw the completion of 'Financial Accounting Standards for Business Enterprises', appearing in the form of an interim report by the Economic Stabilization Board's Investigation Committee on Business Accounting Systems, and this was intended to serve as the standard for preparation of financial statements.

In the preface to 'Financial Accounting Standards for Business Enterprises' it is stated that the standards therein 'represent a condensation of practices generally accepted as being fair and proper from among those developed in the practice of business accounting'. In actual fact, however, the Accounting Standards place major emphasis on depicting the earning power of a business by means of an income computation based on the concept of current operating expenses and revenues, and on providing financial information useful to the investor in the decision-making process. Such ideas were revolutionary in Japanese accounting thought up to that time.

Subsequent to 1948 the trend in Japanese accounting has been further to refine the needs of business financial information oriented towards the investor. In this process we have gleaned many insights from accounting in other developed nations, particularly the United States.

The dissemination of financial information pertaining to a business among its shareholders is absolutely essential whenever such shareholders constitute the principal source for the accumulation of industrial capital. For shareholders, such decisions as whether or not to make new investments or whether to continue with present investments should be made largely on the basis of such financial information. In properly guiding the decision-making process of the investor, business financial information plays an extremely vital role in insuring a healthy development of the securities market. Hence it is generally recognized that investor-oriented disclosure of pertinent financial information, i.e. the external financial reporting function of accounting, is central to the mainstream of accounting thought in major countries around the world, Japan included.

SOME DOUBTS REGARDING THE EXTERNAL FINANCIAL REPORTING FUNCTION

Today the reason that so much emphasis is placed on the external financial reporting function of accounting is due to the importance of industrial capital accumulation from the private sector in relation to the economic development of our modern-day society. And presupposing this is the existence of a sophisticated capital market. Nevertheless, socio-economic conditions in Japan prior to the Second World War did not necessarily demand that accounting should have an important role in disclosing such financial information.

Stock exchanges were first opened in Japan in 1878 at Tokyo and Osaka. In spite of this early date, however, accounting appeared not to concern itself with the providing of financial information to investors until after the Second World War. Japan's first Commercial Code was enacted in 1890, and the section dealing with companies went into effect in 1893. This code underwent revision in 1899, and continues largely down to the code in effect today. The enactment of this code introduced into Japan the so-called 'continental style' of financial reporting whereby a special inventory of assets was prepared along with the balance sheet and income statement. This inventory of assets served as the corner-stone for the Japanese accounting structure. The inventory of assets was a listing in monetary values of movable and immovable properties, securities, and other assets, and had as its goal the clarification of all assets possessed by the company, including its debts. The exact function of the inventory of assets—whether it was supposed to serve as a prelude to preparation of the balance sheet, or whether it was supposed to complement the balance sheet by supplying a quantitative interpretation regarding assets and debts—was not always clear. Nevertheless, Japanese accounting thought at that time, which considered the inventory of assets central to all other financial statements, placed greater useful value on the balance sheet than on the income statement.

Beginning in the 1930s and lasting through the early 1940s there was a movement to standardize the financial statements used to report financial information of businesses. However, such a move was merely an attempt at industrial rationalization aimed at alleviating the effects of the great depression, or else aimed at national unification under war conditions.

The Registered Public Accountant Act was passed in 1927. This created the new professional position of Registered Public Accountant and signified an attempt at improving the whole area of business accounting, but the idea of an audit of financial statements by an independent public certified professional remained undeveloped. Because Japan's vital industries were the exclusive property of the Zaibatsu and the role of the stock exchange as a market for supplying industrial capital was severely limited, the function of accounting to provide financial information to investors was virtually not understood by most people.

Socio-economic environments of this sort are not unique to Japan. More than one hundred nations of the world have not yet developed to a point where their capital markets are capable of supplying sufficient industrial capital. Also, there are the socialist countries where all or a major portion of industrial capital is owned by the state. In the latter countries it does not really make sense to talk about the external financial reporting function of accounting. At the 6th International Conference on Accounting Education in 1987, Agami and Alkafaji (1988: 97) presented a paper in which they stated: 'Accounting systems are products of political, social and economic environments, and they should be adaptive to the ever changing environment. Different countries possess different politico-socio-economic environments, and thus accounting systems in each country should meet the needs of the local environment.' They go on to point out that most nations in the Middle East do not possess sophisticated stock and credit markets, and hence the use for external, investor-oriented financial reporting is rather limited. The same is true for many nations of Asia and Africa.

Professor Jaruga (1988: 373) of Poland in her paper states: 'The functions of accounting correspond to the evolution of the socioeconomic system in the [socialist countries].' According to her analysis, the system of centralized allocation and command management of the national economy with concomitant restrictions on the autonomy of state enterprises caused the control function of accounting to dominate. Subsequent reforms in such countries have been directed towards decentralization and introduction of market systems, stressing micro-efficiency and accountability. The result of this has been an extension of the information function of accounting for decision-making, along with financial management, tax administration, etc. The thing is, however, that in these socialist countries financial reports for state-owned businesses are never made public, and emphasis in business reports and reports concerning allocations is placed on the preparation of figures to be used in the management of the macro-economy. Thus there still seems to be a wide gap between these countries and the socio-economic environment in free-economy nations.

Taking such examples into consideration, then, it seems to me that the importance of the external financial reporting function in accounting is only relative.

CONCLUSION

While I am certainly not denying the importance of the external financial reporting function in accounting, especially in societies such as in developed countries, I do lament the fact that accounting research and education seem to be almost exclusively preoccupied with this function. Recently there has been concern over the gap in what is expected of an audit, that is to say, the difference in what CPAs believe to be the purpose of an audit, and what the ordinary person expects from an audit. For the CPA, an audit of financial statements constitutes an opinion as to whether or not such statements adequately represent the financial position of the firm and the results of its operations in accordance with accepted accounting principles. The uncovering of mistakes and false representations as such are not among the major purposes. The ordinary person making use of such financial statements, on the other hand, expects the discovery and exposure of such errors. Can it not be claimed that such a gap is the result of specialists' preoccupation with the external financial reporting function of accounting?

Accounting has existed since long before capitalist economy societies developed into what they are today. There is no need to go back to the later part of the fifteenth century, the time of Luca Pacioli, when the technique of double-entry bookkeeping first appeared in print. One has merely to consider the conditions that existed when the pioneer publications of modern accounting in Japan, Yukichi Fukuzawa's *Methods of Bookkeeping* and Alexander Allan Shand's *Bank Bookkeeping Methods* appeared, or the conditions in postwar Japan before the appearance of 'Accounting Standards'. What sorts of functions did the socio-economic environments of those periods demand of accounting?

I believe it is time for us to go back to the roots and re-examine the function of accounting. As accounting expands, adapting itself to ever changing socio-economic environments, we must not lose sight of accounting's primary and basic functions. Custodianship and control of resources employed in enterprise activities, providing necessary information to those individuals responsible for day-to-day operations, planning and co-ordinating business activities, these are all functions required of accounting at any period in history and in any socio-economic environment, whether it be that of a developed, developing, or socialist country.

Management accounting has also not received its rightful emphasis in recent years. Johnston and Kaplan (1987: 260) pointed out in their book that the obsolescence of management accounting systems had not occurred overnight, and the systems, the intellectual roots of which can be traced to events sixty to a hundred years ago, worked well for the times in which they were designed. The authors have speculated that the dominance of financial accounting procedures, both in education and in practice, has inhibited the dynamic adjustment of management accounting systems to the realities of the contemporary environment.

In his paper Dickinson (1988: 196) analyses the number of students enrolled in universities in Great Britain from 1980/1 to 1984/5. Although the number of full-time undergraduate accounting students increased during this period, the number of such students coming from overseas decreased slightly. He mentions that the reason for this decline might possibly be that Great Britain is not providing the sort of accounting education required by overseas students. What about accounting education in Japan? Are we providing the sort of accounting education that will be helpful to foreign students after they return home to their own countries?

This question does not pertain exclusively to what is taught to overseas students or to research into matters regarding international accounting. If accounting education at the university or high school levels ignores the fundamental functions of accounting, then it certainly will not fulfil the expectations of society at large. It is my firm opinion that we must once again pay attention to the primary and basic functions of accounting. Financial accounting should continue to be studied and researched, but the other aspects of the accounting process should receive equal attention in our society.

REFERENCES

Agami, Abdel M., and Alkafaji, Yass A. (1988), 'The Accounting Education System in the Middle East', in Someya (1988), 96–104.

Dickinson, John P. (1988), 'Third World Accounting Educational Needs: The Response and Responsibilities', in Someya (1988), 196–204.

Jaruga, Alicja A. (1988), 'Functions of Accounting in Socialist Countries', in Someya (1988), 367–80.

Johnston, H. Thomas, and Kaplan, Robert S. (1987), *Relevance Lost—The Rise and Fall of Management Accounting* (Boston: Harvard Business School Press).

Someya, Kyojiro (1988) (ed.), *Accounting Education and Research to Promote International Understanding* (Westport, Conn.: Quorum Books).

PART III.

CASH FLOW ACCOUNTING

16

The Use of Funds Statements in Japan

THE SCOPE OF OUR STUDY

In July 1959 we conducted a survey of selected Japanese companies under the sponsorship of the Sangyo Keiri Kyokai (The Industrial Management and Accounting Institute) in an attempt to determine how funds statements are used in this country. A total of 563 companies were chosen for the survey, as shown in Table 16.1, from the 601 incorporated companies whose stocks were listed on the Tokyo Stock Exchange on 1 April 1959. Two companies in liquidation and thirty-six banking and insurance companies were excluded. The survey was conducted by mailing a questionnaire to the companies and later sending interviewers for replies. In designing the questionnaire, we considered it most important to make it structurally comparable to those employed in similar surveys in the United States and Canada. However, Japanese companies were in such peculiar circumstances that cash flow statements had to be treated separately from other funds statements. This necessitates caution in comparing the results with those of similar studies conducted in the United States and Canada.

Of the 563 companies chosen for our survey, 308 responded to the questionnaire. Table 16.1 shows the per cent of respondents by size of company. On the whole, the per cent of respondents was rather high. Particularly notable was the fact that it reached as high as 62 per cent in the case of those companies which owned total assets worth ¥10 billion to ¥29.9 billion. The size of each company was determined on the basis of the amount of its total assets reported in its balance sheet as of the closing day in 1958. In the case of companies which closed their accounts twice a year, we used the total assets shown in their balance sheets as of the later closing dates. In Table 16.2 and the following tables, size of company is indicated by A, B, C, D, or E appearing in Table 16.1.

From *Accounting Review*, 39/4 (1964), 983–9.

TABLE 16.1. *Replies to funds statements questionnaire (by size of company)*

Group size of company (total assets)	No. of companies	No. of replies	Per cent replies
A Over ¥30 billion	59	25	42
B ¥10–29.9 billion	111	69	62
C ¥5–9.9 billion	119	66	55
D ¥1–4.9 billion	217	118	53
E Under ¥1 billion	57	30	49
Total	563	308	55

TABLE 16.2. *Responding companies using funds statements (by size of company)*

Group size	No. of companies replying	No. of companies using funds statements	Per cent of respondents using funds statements
A	25	20	80
B	69	55	80
C	66	50	76
D	118	68	58
E	30	17	57
Total	308	210	68

THE PERCENTAGE OF FUNDS STATEMENT USERS

Table 16.2 shows the number and percentage of companies using funds statements. It is clear from the table that a fairly large number of companies were using funds statements and that the use of funds statements increases in proportion to the size of the company. It is quite interesting to see that the percentage of funds statements users is greater among companies of large size.

Table 16.3 shows the use of funds statements as classified by size of company and by availability to interested groups. The table makes it clear that nearly all companies were using their funds statements for managerial purposes. Another, less important, use was to present them to banks. Only a very small number of companies prepared funds statements for reporting to their stockholders. However, it is noteworthy that there are companies, however small in number, which use funds statements in their relations with their stockholders.

TABLE 16.3. *Funds statements—availability to interested groups* (by size of company)

Group size	Management		Stockholders		Bank	
	No.	%	No.	%	No.	%
A	20	100	0	0	8	40
B	55	100	0	0	30	55
C	50	100	0	0	14	28
D	67	99	2	3	21	31
E	16	94	1	6	7	41
Total	208	99	3	1	80	38

TABLE 16.4. *Objectives stated for the inclusion of funds statements in reports to management*

	No.	%
Number of companies preparing funds statements for their managements (including boards of directors)	208	100
Objectives stated:		
(1) To report financial changes not readily seen in either the balance sheet or the profit and loss statement	152	73
(2) To help make financial decisions by company officials and directors (including future planning and capital expenditures)	121	58
(3) To explain the function and use of profit to company officials and directors	76	37
(4) To illustrate the financial strengths and weaknesses of the company	83	40
(5) Miscellaneous	.8	4

PURPOSES OF FUNDS STATEMENTS

Table 16.4 shows several purposes which were considered to be important by the companies preparing funds statements for their managements. The most frequently stated objective of the funds statement as an internal report was to use it as a source of information on certain financial changes. Another use, second in relative importance, was as a basis for financial decisions.

Table 16.5 shows the types of funds statements used for managerial purposes. It makes it clear that a majority of companies using funds statements for managerial purposes were using both the projected and

TABLE 16.5. *Funds statements usage in decision-making (by size of company)*

	Percentage of use					
	A	B	C	D	E	Total
Type of statements used:						
Historical	40	15	40	40	56	35
Projected	10	9	6	8	6	7
Both used	50	76	54	52	38	58

TABLE 16.6. *Funds statements—length of time in use (%)*

Years in use	A	B	C	D	E	Total
1 to 4	15	15	48	46	50	36
5 to 9	55	47	32	31	38	38
10 to 19	15	24	18	18	6	18
20 to 29	10	2	0	2	0	2
30 and over	5	5	0	2	6	3
Not stated	0	7	2	1	0	3
Total	100	100	100	100	100	100

historical funds statements. It is also clear from the table that a majority of companies using either the projected or historical funds statements were using the historical funds statements rather than the projected funds statements.

Table 16.6 shows how long companies had been using the funds statements for managerial purposes. We can see from this table that three-quarters of companies using the funds statements began using it less than ten years ago. It is interesting to note that the largest percentage of large companies had been using it for five to nine years and that of smaller companies for one to four years.

THE CONTENT OF FUNDS STATEMENTS

Table 16.7 shows the number of months or years covered by projected funds statements prepared for managerial purposes. We see from the table that an overwhelming majority of companies made up statements covering six months. It is also clear that in the A group, all companies using the funds statements prepared six-month statements. Further, the table

TABLE 16.7. *Length of fiscal periods of projected funds statements (%)*

	A	B	C	D	E	Total
Monthly	8	6	23	8	0	10
Quarterly	17	13	7	13	0	11
Semi-annually	100	72	83	75	86	79
Annually	34	36	40	28	14	33
2–5 years	17	26	14	13	0	17
Not stated	8	8	7	0	0	2

TABLE 16.8. *Length of fiscal periods of historical funds statements (%)*

	A	B	C	D	E	Total
Monthly	39	24	21	21	13	23
Quarterly	6	8	11	6	7	8
Semi-annually	89	92	89	81	80	85
Annually	12	20	15	18	7	16
2–5 years	6	10	4	2	13	6
Not stated	6	0	4	3	0	3

indicates that a considerably large number of companies prepared two or more statements covering different lengths of time.

Table 16.8 shows the number of months or years covered by historical funds statements prepared for managerial purposes. Here again statements covering six months accounted for an overwhelming majority. However, the second largest percentage here was represented by statements covering one month, as compared with one year or two to five years covered by projected funds statements. A fairly large number of companies were using two or more historical funds statements covering different lengths of time as in the case of projected funds statements.

In many cases, companies using the funds statements for managerial purposes try to relate them to various budgets. Table 16.9 shows the extent to which such an attempt is actually made.

An important problem in the funds statements is how to deal with those expenses which do not accompany any disbursement of funds or those earnings which do not accompany any receipt of funds. Table 16.10 shows what expense and revenue items are treated as non-fund items described above. As might be expected, depreciation accounts for the largest percentage of such items. Although it is permissible to regard the reserves for inventory price decline as a non-fund item, the widespread practice of treating the provision for bad debts as a non-fund item is

TABLE 16.9. *Funds statements—their relationship to various budgets (%)*

	A	B	C	D	E	Total
Related to:						
All budgets	45	53	38	44	35	44
Cash budgets	10	9	28	16	24	13
Capital budgets	25	38	38	18	6	28
Financial budgets	35	42	46	37	41	40
Projected balance sheet	15	20	12	19	0	16
Other budget	0	0	0	7	0	2

TABLE 16.10. *Non-fund items in funds statements (%)*

	A	B	C	D	E	Total
Depreciation	95	91	92	88	88	90
Reserves for inventory price decline	50	64	68	59	65	62
Provision for bad debts	50	69	68	60	59	63
Others	40	40	34	44	41	37

open to question. Such a practice is certainly inappropriate. It betrays a misconception of the relationship between the provision for bad debts and the funds. 'Others' in the table consists mainly of the reserve for retirement allowance.

THE PERCENTAGE OF USERS OF CASH FLOW STATEMENTS

Table 16.11 shows the number and percentage of companies which were using cash flow statements. It is clear from the table that all but two of the companies which answered the questionnaire were using cash flow statements.

The purposes for which cash flow statements were employed are shown in Table 16.12, which makes it clear that all but two of the 306 companies which used such statements were using them for managerial purposes. The table also indicates that a substantial number of companies use cash flow statements in their relations with their banks. In contrast, very few companies employed such statements in their relations with their stockholders.

TABLE 16.11. *Respondent companies using cash flow statements* (by size of company)

Group size	No. of companies replying	No. of companies using cash flow statements	Per cent of respondents using cash flow statements
A	25	25	100
B	69	69	100
C	66	66	100
D	118	116	98
E	30	30	100
Total	308	306	99

TABLE 16.12. *Cash flow statements—availability to interested groups* (by size of company)

Group size	Management		Stockholders		Bank	
	No.	%	No.	%	No.	%
A	25	100	0	0	21	84
B	68	98	1	2	57	83
C	66	100	1	2	55	83
D	115	99	2	2	90	78
E	30	100	1	3	23	77
Total	304	99	5	2	246	80

SPECIFIC MANAGERIAL PURPOSES OF CASH FLOW STATEMENTS

Table 16.13 shows the specific managerial purposes served by cash flow statements and considered most important by companies which issued such statements. The most frequently mentioned purpose was to provide data for the establishment of a cash budget. Following this in relative importance were statements as the bases for various schedules for payment and for making financial decisions. These uses give a clear indication of the nature of the cash flow statements.

Table 16.14 shows the types of cash flow statements used for managerial purposes. It is evident that nearly all companies using the cash flow statements had recourse to both projected and historical cash flow statements.

TABLE 16.13. *Objectives stated for the inclusion of cash flow statements in reports to management*

	No.	Per cent
Number of companies preparing cash flow statements for their management	304	100
Objectives stated:		
(1) To help make financial decisions by company officials and directors (including future planning and capital expenditures)	187	62
(2) To establish cash budgets	254	84
(3) To lay out various schedules for payment	199	65
(4) To lay out schedules for collection of accounts receivable and others	107	35
(5) Miscellaneous	9	3

TABLE 16.14. *Cash flow statements—usage in decision-making* (by size of company)

	Percentage of use					
	A	B	C	D	E	Total
Type of Statements used:						
Historical	0	0	0	2	7	1
Projected	8	4	4	4	0	4
Both used	92	96	96	94	93	95

The table also reveals that a majority of companies using either one or the other of these two types of statements preferred the projected cash flow statements.

Table 16.15 shows how long companies had been using the cash flow statements for managerial purposes. As we see from the table, close to a half of companies using the cash flow statements had adopted it ten to nineteen years before and one-third of the total five to nine years before. On the whole, this type of statement had been in use for a very long time.

THE CONTENT OF CASH FLOW STATEMENTS

Table 16.16 shows the length of time covered by projected cash flow statements used for managerial purposes. We can see from it that the most

TABLE 16.15. *Cash flow statements—length of time in use (%)*

Years in use	A	B	C	D	E	Total
1 to 4	0	3	6	7	0	5
5 to 9	40	21	33	37	43	33
10 to 19	44	46	47	45	40	45
20 to 29	12	7	6	3	7	6
30 and over	4	19	8	6	10	9
Not stated	0	4	0	2	0	2
Total	100	100	100	100	100	100

TABLE 16.16. *Length of fiscal periods of projected cash flow statements (%)*

	A	B	C	D	E	Total
Monthly	56	42	42	31	11	36
Monthly (divided into day, week or ten days)	20	25	14	25	21	22
Quarterly	20	25	11	19	11	18
Semi-annually	28	16	17	16	14	17
Semi-annually (divided into month or three months)	56	61	64	71	75	66
Annually	8	4	9	18	4	7
Annually (divided into month or three months)	16	19	23	14	18	17
3–5 years (divided into years)	8	12	6	5	0	6
Not stated	12	3	8	3	4	5

widely preferred length of time was six months divided into so many months or two three-month periods. It is worthy of note that one-month statements equalled these six-month statements in number. Also notable is the fact that a relatively large number of one-month statements shows cash flow for every day, every week, or every ten days. A large number of companies were using two or more statements covering different lengths of time.

Table 16.17 shows the length of time covered by historical cash flow statements prepared for managerial purposes. Here one-month statements accounted for the greatest majority, slightly exceeding the number of six-month statements showing cash flow for every month or every three months. This finding gives us an idea of the nature of historical cash flow statements. Here again, a very large number of companies were using two or more statements covering different lengths of time.

TABLE 16.17. *Length of fiscal periods of historical cash flow statements (%)*

	A	B	C	D	E	Total
Monthly	57	58	56	67	27	57
Monthly (divided into day, week or ten days)	9	15	13	10	7	11
Semi-annually	30	28	30	19	17	2
Semi-annually (divided into month or three months)	57	49	51	61	54	55
Annually	4	5	8	5	3	5
Annually (divided into month or three months)	4	12	11	10	23	11
2–5 years (divided into years)	4	8	5	1	0	3
Not stated	0	8	0	3	3	3

TABLE 16.18. *How historical cash flow statements are prepared (%)*

	A	B	C	D	E	Total
(1) From accounts kept in general ledger to to record real cash flow	4	0	2	3	3	2
(2) From accounts kept in subsidiary ledger to record real cash flow	0	6	5	11	10	8
(3) From daily cash trial balance or monthly cash trial balance as a separate statement	39	43	25	35	37	35
(4) From documents serving as evidence of receipt and disbursement of cash as a separate statement	61	60	67	63	60	63
(5) Other methods	22	9	8	6	3	8

Table 16.18 shows how companies prepared historical cash flow statements. As we see from it, a majority of companies prepare such statements on the basis of cash receipt and disbursement slips. A particularly remarkable fact here is that some companies, though still small in number, set up cash flow accounts in their general or subsidiary ledgers.

17

A Direct Method for the Preparation of the Cash Flow Statement

INTRODUCTION

There are certain practices in our daily activities which we follow through custom without bothering to understand their real meaning. Of course, such practices were originally introduced for some definite purposes. With the change of times, however, they have either lost their rationale or acquired new meanings never conceived at the beginning. In spite of these developments, we tend to go on in the same old rut as before.

The same may be said of bookkeeping. Needless to say, bookkeeping today is not what it was in the fourteenth or fifteenth century. Ever since it was introduced in the fourteenth or fifteenth century, bookkeeping has developed into its present form to meet the changing needs of business. Indeed, it made remarkable progress during the first half of the twentieth century. Its fundamental structure, designed to serve the dual purpose of determining the income for a given period and showing the financial position at the end of the period, has been considered as something sacred and inviolable and therefore remains unchanged. The fact that financial statements based on bookkeeping invariably consist of an income statement and a balance sheet has apparently caused no surprise or invited no objection.

I should like to suggest a reconsideration of the advisability of limiting the function of bookkeeping to the determination of periodic income and the indication of the financial position at the end of the period. It should not be very hard to see from the accounting structure of bookkeeping that it is comprised of accounting for profit and loss and accounting for cash receipts and disbursements (cash flow). However, bookkeeping today summarizes all cash flow items in a single cash account and shows the balance of this account as a single item in the balance sheet, while details of profit and loss are recorded in the numerous accounts concerned and listed in the income statement. Now what is the reason underlying this

From *Waseda Business and Economic Studies*, No. 1 (1965), 1–17.

difference in treatment between profit and loss accounting and cash flow accounting?

PROFIT AND LOSS APPROACH

To illustrate that profit and loss accounting and cash flow accounting are both sides of the coin called bookkeeping, assume that these business transactions have been completed for the month of December 19xx:

(*a*) E. Sato started business with a ¥500,000 cash investment.
(*b*) Purchased office furniture for ¥300,000 in cash.
(*c*) Purchased merchandise on account, ¥800,000.
(*d*) Sold merchandise for cash, ¥450,000.
(*e*) Purchased merchandise for cash, ¥250,000.
(*f*) Borrowed ¥500,000 from bank.
(*g*) Paid account payable, ¥700,000.
(*h*) Sold merchandise on account, ¥900,000.
(*i*) Collected account receivable, ¥600,000.
(*j*) Paid bank loan, ¥200,000.
(*k*) Paid ¥150,000 for salaries, 60,000 for rent, and ¥40,000 for miscellaneous expenses. Salaries payable amounted to ¥100,000.
(*l*) Purchased government bonds in cash, ¥100,000.
(*m*) Estimated depreciation on office furniture, ¥50,000.
(*n*) Merchandise inventory at the end of the period, ¥250,000.

If a profit and loss method of bookkeeping is used to record the above transactions, the procedure is precisely the one that is generally followed in bookkeeping today. Here is how the above transactions are journalized, entered in accounts, and listed in a trial balance by the profit and loss method of bookkeeping:

(*a*) Cash	¥500,000	
E. Sato, capital		¥500,000
(*b*) Equipment	300,000	
Cash		300,000
(*c*) Purchases	800,000	
Accounts payable		800,000
(*d*) Cash	450,000	
Sales		450,000
(*e*) Purchases	250,000	
Cash		250,000
(*f*) Cash	500,000	
Notes payable		500,000
(*g*) Accounts payable	700,000	
Cash		700,000

(*h*)	Accounts receivable	900,000	
	Sales		900,000
(*i*)	Cash	600,000	
	Accounts receivable		600,000
(*j*)	Notes payable	200,000	
	Cash		200,000
(*k*)	Salary expense	150,000	
	Rent expense	60,000	
	Miscellaneous expenses	40,000	
	Cash		250,000
	Salary expense	100,000	
	Accrued salaries payable		100,000
(*l*)	Government securities	100,000	
	Cash		100,000
(*m*)	Depreciation of equipment	50,000	
	Equipment		50,000
(*n*)	Merchandise inventory	250,000	
	Purchases		250,000

Cash

(*a*)	500,000	(*b*)	300,000
(*d*)	450,000	(*e*)	250,000
(*f*)	500,000	(*g*)	700,000
(*i*)	600,000	(*j*)	200,000
		(*k*)	250,000
		(*l*)	100,000

Accounts receivable

(*h*)	900,000	(*i*)	600,000

Merchandise inventory

(*n*)	250,000		

Government securities

(*l*)	100,000		

Equipment

(*b*)	300,000	(*m*)	50,000

Accounts payable

(*g*)	700,000	(*c*)	800,000

Accrued salaries payable

		(*k*)	100,000

Notes payable

(*j*)	200,000	(*f*)	500,000

E. Sato, capital

		(*a*)	500,000

Sales

		(*d*)	450,000
		(*h*)	900,000

Purchases

(*c*)	800,000	(*n*)	250,000
(*e*)	250,000		

Salary expense

(*k*)	150,000		
(*k*)	100,000		

Rent expense

(*k*)	60,000		

Miscellaneous expenses

(*k*)	40,000		

Depreciation of equipment

(*m*)	50,000		

Trial Balance
31 December 19xx

	Debits	Credits
Cash	¥250,000	
Accounts receivable	300,000	
Merchandise inventory	250,000	
Government securities	100,000	
Equipment	250,000	
Accounts payable		¥100,000
Accrued salaries payable		100,000
Notes payable		300,000
E. Sato, capital		500,000
Sales		1,350,000
Purchases	800,000	
Salary expense	250,000	
Rent expense	60,000	
Miscellaneous expenses	40,000	
Depreciation of equipment	50,000	
	¥2,350,000	¥2,350,000

It has long been our practice to prepare an income statement and a balance sheet from these records. In this procedure, the profit and loss accounts are closed by the journal entries shown below. No further elaboration is needed here since this bookkeeping procedure is widely used and understood by accountants. It should be pointed out, however, that this procedure, which calls for entry of all cash flow items in a single cash account, has the obvious disadvantage of not being able to show details of the cash flow.

(*o*) Profit and loss summary	¥1,200,000	
Purchases		¥800,000
Salary expense		250,000
Rent expense		60,000
Miscellaneous expenses		40,000
Depreciation of equipment		50,000
(*p*) Sales	1,350,000	
Profit and loss summary		1,350,000
(*q*) Profit and loss summary	150,000	
E. Sato, capital		150,000

CASH FLOW APPROACH

If the cash flow approach of bookkeeping is employed for business transactions, the results obtained will be quite different from those produced by the profit and loss approach illustrated above. The cash flow approach, applied to the foregoing business transactions, brings about the following results:

(*a*) Cash	¥500,000	
E. Sato, capital		¥500,000
(*b*) Equipment	300,000	
Disbursements—fixed assets purchased		300,000
(*c*) Profit and Loss	800,000	
Accounts payable		800,000
(*d*) Receipts—Cash sales	450,000	
Profit and loss		450,000
(*e*) Profit and loss	250,000	
Disbursements—Cash purchases		250,000
(*f*) Receipts—Notes payable	500,000	
Notes payable		500,000
(*g*) Accounts payable	700,000	
Disbursements—Accounts payable		700,000
(*h*) Accounts receivable	900,000	
Profit and loss		900,000
(*i*) Receipts—Accounts receivable	600,000	
Accounts receivable		600,000
(*j*) Notes Payable	200,000	
Disbursements—Notes payable		200,000
(*k*) Profit and Loss	250,000	
Disbursements—Current expenses		250,000
Profit and Loss	100,000	
Accrued salaries payable		100,000
(*l*) Government securities	100,000	
Disbursements—Government securities		100,000
(*m*) Profit and loss	50,000	
Equipment		50,000
(*n*) Merchandise inventory	250,000	
Profit and loss		250,000

Cash

(*a*)	500,000		

Accounts receivable

(*h*)	900,000	(*i*)	600,000

Merchandise inventory

(*n*)	250,000		

Government securities

(*l*)	100,000		

Equipment

(*b*)	300,000	(*m*)	50,000

Accounts payable

(*g*)	700,000	(*c*)	800,000

Accrued salaries payable

		(*k*)	100,000

Notes payable

(*j*)	200,000	(*f*)	500,000

E. Sato, capital

		(*a*)	500,000

Profit and loss

(*c*)	800,000	(*d*)	450,000
(*e*)	250,000	(*h*)	900,000
(*k*)	250,000	(*n*)	250,000
(*k*)	100,000		
(*m*)	50,000		

Receipts—Cash sales

(*d*)	450,000		

Receipts—Accounts receivable

(*i*)	600,000		

Receipts—Notes payable

(*f*)	500,000		

Disbursements—Cash purchases

		(*e*)	250,000

Disbursements—Accounts payable

		(*g*)	700,000

Disbursements—Current expenses

		(*k*)	250,000

Disbursements—Government securities

		(*l*)	100,000

Disbursements—Fixed assets purchased

		(*b*)	300,000

Disbursements—Notes payable

		(*j*)	200,000

Trial Balance
31 December 19xx

	Debits	Credits
Cash	¥500,000	
Accounts receivable	300,000	
Merchandise inventory	250,000	
Government securities	100,000	
Equipment	250,000	
Accounts payable		¥100,000
Accrued salaries payable		100,000
Notes payable		300,000
E. Sato, capital		500,000
Profit and loss		150,000
Receipts—Cash sales	450,000	
Receipts—Accounts receivable	600,000	
Receipts—Notes payable	500,000	
Disbursements—Cash purchases		250,000
Disbursements—Accounts payable		700,000
Disbursements—Current expenses		250,000
Disbursements—Government securities		100,000
Disbursements—Fixed assets purchased		300,000
Disbursements—Notes payable		200,000
	¥2,950,000	¥2,950,000

Here, sales and various other profit and loss accounts are not set up; all profit and loss transactions are entered in a single profit and loss account. On the other hand, a number of accounts are set up to record different cash flow transactions. This does not differ, in principle, from the procedure followed in entering all profit and loss transactions in sales and other related profit and loss accounts. Therefore, the cash flow records provide the basis for the preparation of a cash flow statement and a balance sheet. Like the profit and loss accounts, the cash flow accounts are closed as shown below. Obviously, the cash flow approach produces a detailed cash flow statement, although it has the admitted disadvantage of not being able to show the details of profit and loss items.

(*o*) Disbursements—Cash purchases	¥250,000	
Disbursements—Accounts payable	700,000	
Disbursements—Current expenses	250,000	
Disbursements—Government securities	100,000	
Disbursements—Fixed assets purchased	300,000	
Disbursements—Notes payable	200,000	
Receipts and disbursements summary		¥1,800,000

(*p*) Receipts and disbursements summary	¥1,550,000	
Receipts—Cash sales		¥450,000
Receipts—Accounts receivable		600,000
Receipts—Notes payable		500,000
(*q*) Receipts and disbursements summary	250,000	
Cash		250,000
(*r*) Profit and loss	150,000	
E. Sato, capital		150,000

INTEGRATION OF BOTH APPROACHES

Of the two approaches outlined above, one is widely accepted throughout the world while the other is virtually ignored. As far as the accounting structure is concerned, however, there is no difference when chosing between these two approaches. Technically, there is no reason whatsoever to believe that the profit and loss approach is indisputably superior to the cash flow approach.

Nevertheless, the fact remains that the profiit and loss approach is preferred in practically all cases. There must be some reason deeper than the problem of accounting techniques. It may be that bookkeeping is supposed to meet the demand of investors who want increasing returns on their investments—or demands motivated by a desire to examine the amount of income to determine whether or not their investments are successful. The importance of profit and loss accounting in bookkeeping has not lessened in the least. On the contrary, it has increased remarkably, as suggested by the application of the profit and loss concept to an area of social significance—i.e. the measurement of productivity. Under the circumstances, I have no intention of rejecting bookkeeping as it is widely accepted today.

However, something should be done about cash flow accounting. The development of bookkeeping primarily as a tool for income determination has forced cash flow accounting to play second fiddle to income determination. Of course, this is not without reason. When firms needed relatively few fixed assets and could easily convert them into cash, there was little need for detailed cash flow accounting because in such cases profit and loss were closely related to cash flow.

Modern business, however, is being operated in a different world. The remarkably increase in the use of credit and advanced production techniques which require huge fixed capacity have created a glaring discrepancy between profit and loss accounts on the one hand and cash flow on the other. Therefore it is necessary to give serious consideration to cash flow accounting as distinct from profit and loss accounting. The keenly felt need for improved bookkeeping procedures is evidenced by the now widespread business practice of preparing cash flow statements from balance sheets and income statements in order to determine the flow of funds. In this connection, I should like to emphasize the value of the cash flow approach.

If a new procedure integrating the profit and loss and cash flow approaches is applied to the previously described illustrative business transactions, both profit and loss and cash flow accounting can be combined within a single accounting system. The results can be shown in a statement of accounts consisting of an income statement, a cash flow statement, and a balance sheet, as presented below:

(*a*)	Cash	¥500,000	
	E. Sato, capital		¥500,000
(*b*)	Equipment	300,000	
	Disbursements—Fixed assets purchased		300,000
(*c*)	Purchases	800,000	
	Accounts payable		800,000
(*d*)	Receipts—Cash sales	450,000	
	Sales		450,000
(*e*)	Purchases	250,000	
	Disbursement—Cash purchases		250,000
(*f*)	Receipts—Notes payable	500,000	
	Notes payable		500,000
(*g*)	Accounts payable	700,000	
	Disbursements—Accounts payable		700,000
(*h*)	Accounts receivable	900,000	
	Sales		900,000
(*i*)	Receipts—Accounts receivable	600,000	
	Accounts receivable		600,000
(*j*)	Notes payable	200,000	
	Disbursements—Notes payable		200,000
(*k*)	Salary Expense	150,000	
	Rent Expense	60,000	
	Miscellaneous expenses	40,000	
	Disbursements—Current expenses		250,000
	Salary Expense	100,000	
	Accrued salaries payable		100,000
(*l*)	Government securities	100,000	
	Disbursements—Government securities		100,000
(*m*)	Depreciation of equipment	50,000	
	Equipment		50,000
(*n*)	Merchandise inventory	250,000	
	Purchases		250,000

(*o*) Profit and loss summary	¥1,200,000	
Purchases		¥800,000
Salary expense		250,000
Rent expense		60,000
Miscellaneous expenses		40,000
Depreciation of equipment		50,000
(*p*) Sales	1,350,000	
Profit and loss summary		1,350,000
(*q*) Profit and loss summary	150,000	
E. Sato, capital		150,000
(*r*) Receipts and disbursements summary	1,550,000	
Receipts—Cash sales		450,000
Receipts—Accounts receivable		600,000
Receipts—Notes payable		500,000
(*s*) Disbursements—Cash purchases	250,000	
Disbursements—Accounts payable	700,000	
Disbursements—Current expenses	250,000	
Disbursements—Government securities	100,000	
Disbursements—Fixed assets purchased	300,000	
Disbursements—Notes payable	200,000	
Receipts and disbursements summary		1,800,000
(*t*) Receipts and disbursements summary	250,000	
Cash		250,000

A. Income Accounts:

Sales

To P & L	1,350,000	(*d*)	450,000
		(*h*)	900,000
	1,350,000		1,350,000

Purchases

(*c*)	800,000	(*n*)	250,000
(*e*)	250,000	To P & L	800,000
	1,050,000		1,050,000

Salary expense

(*k*)	150,000	To P & L	250,000
(*k*)	100,000		
	250,000		250,000

Rent expense

(*k*)	60,000	To P & L	60,000

Miscellaneous expenses

(*k*)	40,000	To P & L	40,000

Depreciation of equipment

(*m*)	50,000	To P & L	50,000

Profit and loss summary

Purchases	800,000	Sales	1,350,000
Salary expense	250,000		
Rent expense	60,000		
Miscellaneous expenses	40,000		
Depreciation	50,000		
Net income	150,000		
	1,350,000		1,350,000

B. Cash Flow Accounts:

Receipts—Cash sales

(*d*)	450,000	To R & D	450,000

Receipts—Accounts receivable

(*i*)	600,000	To R & D	600,000

Receipts—Notes payable

(*f*)	500,000	To R & D	500,000

Disbursements—Cash purchases

To R & D	250,000	(*e*)	250,000

Disbursements—Accounts payable

To R & D	700,000	(*g*)	700,000

Disbursements—Current expenses

To R & D	250,000	(*k*)	250,000

Disbursements—Government securities

To R & D	100,000	(*l*)	100,000

Disbursements—Fixed assets purchased

To R & D	300,000	(*b*)	300,000

Disbursements—Notes payable

To R & D	200,000	(*j*)	200,000

Receipts and disbursements summary

Cash sales	450,000	Cash purchases	250,000
Accounts receivable	600,000	Accounts payable	700,000
Notes payable	500,000	Current expenses	250,000
To Cash	250,000	Government securities	100,000
		Fixed assets purchased	300,000
		Notes payable	200,000
	1,800,000		1,800,000

C. Balance Sheet Accounts:

Cash

(*a*)	500,000	R & D summary	250,000
		Balance	250,000
	500,000		500,000

Accounts receivable

(*h*)	900,000	(*i*)	600,000
		Balance	300,000
	900,000		900,000

Government securities

(*l*)	100,000	Balance	100,000

Merchandise inventory

(*n*)	250,000	Balance	250,000

Equipment

(*b*)	300,000	(*m*)	50,000
		Balance	250,000
	300,000		300,000

Accounts payable

(*g*)	700,000	(*c*)	800,000
Balance	100,000		
	800,000		800,000

Accrued salaries payable

Balance	100,000	(*k*)	100,000

Notes payable

(*j*)	200,000	(*f*)	500,000
Balance	300,000		
	500,000		500,000

E. Sato, capital

Balance	650,000	(*a*)	500,000
		Net income	150,000
	650,000		650,000

D. Financial Statements

Tokyo Supply Company
Income Statement
Month of December 19xx

Sales		¥1,350,000
Cost of goods sold		800,000
Gross margin on sales		¥550,000
Expenses:		
Salaries	¥250,000	
Rent	60,000	
Depreciation of equipment	50,000	
Other expenses	40,000	400,000
Net income		¥150,000

Tokyo Supply Company
Cash Flow Statement
Month of December 19xx

Cash balance, 1 December 19xx		¥500,000
Receipts:		
Cash sales	¥450,000	
Accounts receivable	600,000	
Notes payable	500,000	1,550,000
Total cash to be accounted for		¥2,050,000
Disbursements:		
Cash purchases	¥250,000	
Accounts payable	700,000	
Current expenses	250,000	
Government securities	100,000	
Fixed assets purchased	300,000	
Notes payable	200,000	1,800,000
Cash balance, 31 December 19xx		¥250,000

Tokyo Supply Company
Balance Sheet
31 December 19xx

Assets	
Cash	¥250,000
Accounts receivable	300,000
Government securities	100,000
Merchandise	250,000
Equipment	250,000
	¥1,150,000

Liabilities and Proprietorship	
Liabilities:	
Accounts payable	¥100,000
Accrued salaries payable	100,000
Notes payable	300,000
	¥500,000
Proprietorship:	
E. Sato, capital	650,000
	¥1,150,000

CONCLUSION

The history of bookkeeping furnishes no evidence that a comparison of the profit and loss and cash flow approaches unequivocally established the former's superiority to the latter. In the course of its development into what it is today, bookkeeping has never faced the need for improved cash flow accounting. This is why it has developed exclusively along the line of profit and loss accounting. The cash flow approach is solely a product of logic which has emerged from theoretical studies. It still remains a concept yet to be applied in actual practice.

Nevertheless, economic development today is such that the need for cash flow accounting is making itself felt with growing intensity. In view of this new situation, I doubt the advisability of leaving bookkeeping as it is now. In summary, a method has been suggested for integrating the profit and loss and cash flow approaches. The proposed improvement of bookkeeping would not involve any serious technical problem. Now is the time, I believe, to abandon conventional practices for modernized bookkeeping procedures.

18

The Development of Funds Flow Accounting

Funds flow accounting is the accounting that clarifies the sources from which enterprises raise funds and the purposes to which they apply the funds. As the problems of income accounting are embodied in the income statement, so problems of funds accounting are crystallized in the funds statement. Therefore, the development of funds flow accounting is that of the funds statement.

The funds statement shows the sources from which an enterprise raised funds and how the funds were applied within a certain period of time. Generally, the funds statement is prepared to sum up the financial and investment activities of an enterprise and to disclose the changes in its financial position.

This kind of statement is variously called an Application of Funds Statement, a Source and Application of Funds Statement, a Funds Statement, or a Funds Flow Statement. Recently, the Accounting Principles Board of the USA recommended the term *Statement of Changes in Financial Position* in its written *Opinion No. 19*. Following this Opinion, the *International Accounting Standard No. 7* adopted the same term. Thus the term *Statement of Changes in Financial Position* is widely used today.

The purpose of this paper is to trace the development of the funds statement and clarify some of the points of dispute in the recent funds statement literature. Although the preparation and disclosure of the funds statement is stipulated today by the International Accounting Standard, and is becoming internationally recognized, most of the history of the funds statement is found in the accounting practices of the USA. The funds statement was born in American accounting practices of the late nineteenth century and its use has continued over the past hundred years. Therefore this paper first follows the development of the funds statement in the USA and then assesses its impact on the international scene. This development can be divided into three stages:

From M. J. R. Gaffikin (ed.), *Contemporary Accounting Thought; Essays in Honour of Raymond J. Chambers* (Sydney: Prentice Hall of Australia, 1984), 115–24.

(1) Origin of the funds statement (1863 to 1910s)
(2) Development of the funds statement (1920s to 1950s)
(3) Public recognition and internationalization of the funds statement (1960s to the present)

ORIGIN OF THE FUNDS STATEMENT

The terms and tools we use in our daily lives and businesses today did not appear all of a sudden; they were gradually moulded into their present forms. The funds statement is no exception.

In discussing the development of the funds statement, I once began my argument (Someya 1956: 37) with the *Where got, where gone statement*, found in William Morse Cole's *Accounts, their Construction and Interpretation* (1908). In this book Cole states, 'Such a table as that which we have been constructing was practically unknown in published reports until about five years ago; each year since that time one or more railroads have added something of this sort to their exhibits, usually under such a title as "Summary of Financial Transactions for the Year"' (p. 132). It is obvious that such a summary table was used in the business world of early twentieth century America.

The *Where got, where gone statement* was devised to show clearly the changes in a comparative balance sheet; a decrease in a resource and an increase in a liability between two points in time were entered in the source 'where got' column, and an increase in a resource and a decrease in a liability were entered in the application 'where gone' column. Cole further explains as follows:

> It is evident, in the first place, that an increase in a resource account indicates that something has been spent to acquire that increased resource. Similarly, a decrease in a liability account indicates the same sort of thing, for the liability must have been paid off, and therefore something has been spent. Conversely, a decrease in a resource account indicates that something has been taken from this account during the year and spent elsewhere; or, what amounts to the same thing, this decrease is part of an exchange of one asset for another. Similarly, again, an increase in a liability account indicates that the firm has borrowed some sort of property and hence it by so much has had means to spend. (pp. 127–8)

Cole says that by preparing a *Where got, where gone statement*, we will know from what sources all incomes are drawn and to what purposes all expenditures are applied. Although the *Where got, where gone statement* simply divided the increased and decreased sums of money of each account on comparative balance sheets into sources and applications, one can recognize in it the origin of the funds statement.

Nevertheless, Cole only illustrated one of the supplementary financial statements used at the time. On the other hand, L. S. Rosen and Don T.

DeCoster (1969: 125) revealed the existence of the following statements before Cole's *Accounts* (1908) was published. These were 'funds' statements (1) that accounted for changes in cash, (2) that summarized the changes in each balance sheet account including details of increases or decreases in 'income' accounts and 'retained earnings', (3) that reported the causes of changes in current assets, and (4) that reported the causes of changes in working capital. Rosen and DeCoster pointed out the following examples:

> 1) In 1863, The Northern Central Railroad issued a '... summary of the financial transactions of the Company ...'. It listed the January 1 cash balance and three principal 'receipts' in one column, and the December 31 cash balance plus the main outlays for expenses and assets in another column. The Assam Company in England prepared a similar report for the year ending March 31, 1862. It accounted for the changes in cash in the bank, cash on hand, and stamps. The American Bell Telephone Company included a 'Cash Statement' in its annual report for the year ending February 28, 1881. The statement differed from the above reports in that a sub-total existed for 'operating expenses'. This idea of separating annually-recurring items from infrequent financial outlays has continued into present practice.
>
> 2) The Missouri Pacific Railway Company and its subsidiary, St. Louis, Iron Mountain & Southern Railway, prepared their reports called 'Statement showing Resources and their Application during the Year 1893'. They had two parts, called 'Resources' and 'Application of Resources'. The four headings listed under 'Resources' were: Net Earnings, as per Income Account, Miscellaneous Credits to Income Account, Increase in Liabilities During Year 1893, and Decrease in Assets During Year 1893. Three similar headings were listed under 'Application of Resources'. The statements were thus *classified* listings of the changes during the period in all balance sheet accounts.
>
> 3) In 1902, United States Steel Corporation and Subsidiary Companies issued a 'Summary of Financial Operations of All Properties ... Showing the Net Resources for the Year and Disposition Thereof'. The two main parts of this report showed a listing of the changes in the individual current asset account categories, less accounts payable, and a schedule portraying the major causes of the increase in current assets. A noteworthy feature of the report is that it started with net income and 'added back' such items as depreciation. This procedure is still followed by most corporations today.
>
> 4) The report was changed slightly for the 'year ending December 31, 1903'. Instead of balancing to current assets, the statement was reconciled to current assets less current liabilities. A separate part of the report showed the changes in each of what are now called 'working capital' accounts. (Rosen and DeCoster 1969: 125–6; their emphasis)

Both Cole's *Where got, where gone statement* and the four kinds of 'funds' statements revealed by Rosen and DeCoster were devised to give financial activity information not disclosed by income statements and balance sheets. In other words, these statements were made to give financial activity information that income statements and balance sheets cannot provide.

We now know that these early 'funds' statements were the origins of the major features of today's funds statements.

However, the people at that time did not have fixed ideas about what financial information could be obtained through these statements and, therefore, they were uncertain about which of the foregoing financial statements was to be generally adopted. This situation lasted until the 1910s.

DEVELOPMENT OF THE FUNDS STATEMENT

In the 1920s one form of funds statement rapidly came to dominate, the funds statement of H. A. Finney.

Finney was in charge of the Students' Department of *The Journal of Accountancy* and gave the answers to the CPA examination of May 1921, prepared by the American Institute of Accountants, in *The Journal's* July 1921 issue. One question was to prepare a statement of resources and their application, using the balance sheet and some other data. Finney's solution (1921) comprised three statements: (*a*) Comparative balance sheet with columns of Decrease and Increase, (*b*) Statement of application of funds, and (*c*) Schedule of working capital and deferred charges.

In Finney's statement of application of funds, the total funds provided by (1) net profits before providing for depreciation and bad debts, (2) issue of bonds, and (3) sale of investment in stocks and sale of machinery were equal to the total funds applied to (1) purchase of fixed assets, (2) payment of dividends, and (3) increase in working capital and deferred charges (details exhibited in Schedule of working capital and deferred charges). The term 'funds' that we generally use today was first used in this statement.

The structure of Finney's statement of application of funds was in the balanced form of debit and credit. That is to say, Finney's statement was almost the same as that of The United States Steel Corporation, prepared in 1903, except that the changes in working capital were listed as one item of funds source or application and the total funds provided were equal to the total funds applied. Since Finney often published solutions to similar CPA examination questions for *The Journal*, he greatly influenced many accountants, and his form of funds statement came into wide use.

Finney did not define the term 'fund' in preparing his funds statement. In a reply to a Mr Esquerré who pointed out and criticized Finney's obscure use of the term in *The Journal of Accountancy* (1925), Finney (1925: 507) simply said that 'the term "funds" suggested something more than cash'. It took several years before Finney's funds statement was improved in form to disclose the cause of changes in working capital. This kind of improved funds statement was gaining the main position in the field. Rosen and DeCoster (1969: 130) describe the trend as follows: 'The "funds" statement which shows the causes of a change in working capital gained greater and greater acceptance, especially among academicians, in the twenty-five years to 1950.'

Nevertheless, in this period there was much criticism about the funds statement disclosing the causes of changes in working capital. It was difficult for the layman to understand that 'funds available from operations' were indicated as net profits for the current period plus expense items which did not involve the flow of funds, such as depreciation, to disclose the changes in financial positions which involved the changes in working capital in the funds statement. Therefore, W. A. Paton (1938) and others suggested that the funds statement list the details of such profit and loss items as amount of sales, cost of sales, and changes in working capital as the source and application of funds. M. Moonitz (1943) and others suggested that the funds statement indicate that inventories were not funds but an item of application of funds, such as fixed asset, and that the idea of funds was limited to working capital that does not include inventories. Therefore, the increase or decrease of inventories was listed in the source or application of funds. E. B. Day (1951) and others prepared a funds statement that limited the idea of funds to cash, to show that not the amount of sales nor the amount of goods laid in but the cash receipts and disbursements were disclosed as the source and application of funds.

Among these works the significant criticism was that important financial activities, which did not involve working capital changes, were not listed in the funds statement, which only indicated a change in financial positions involving working capital changes. When one acquires fixed assets by issuing stocks or one converts bonds into stocks, there will be no changes in working capital. Therefore such financial activities are not listed in the funds statement, which focuses on a change in working capital. As a solution to such criticism, L. Goldberg (1951) and others classified accountable events into two categories: external transactions and internal operations; they suggested listing the former, 'dealings between an undertaking and other persons', in the statement of funds. It followed that such a funds statement listed important financial activities that did not involve a change in working capital.

The funds statement was almost completed in its basic framework in the 1920s. Today's funds statement follows this basic framework in concept and format. On the other hand, many revised opinions were presented in the decades up to the 1950s. Although these opinions were not widely adopted, they foresaw the problems we encounter in using the funds statement in today's society and indicated how to cope with these problems. By the 1960s, when the funds statement was publicly recognized and internationalized, use of its terms and forms became very flexible. In order to understand this fact, we have to refer to the disputes and opinions on the funds statement presented from the 1920s to the 1950s.

PUBLIC RECOGNITION AND INTERNATIONALIZATION OF THE FUNDS STATEMENT

Since the 1960s the funds statement has gradually been recognized publicly as one of *the* financial statements, and it has played a great international role. The American Institute of Certified Public Accountants finished its research on the funds statement in 1961 (Mason 1961) and issued 'The Statement of Source and Application of Funds', *Opinions of the Accounting Principles Board No. 3*, in 1963. This is the first formal opinion concerning the funds statement by a major institute of accountants and it states:

> The board believes that a statement of source and application of funds should be presented as supplementary information in financial reports. The inclusion of such information is not mandatory, and it is optional as to whether it should be covered in the report of the independent accountant. (para. 8)

Although the inclusion of funds statements in annual financial reports to stockholders was not made mandatory in *Opinion No. 3*, major stock exchanges supported the inclusion and the business world also accepted it. As a result, the number of companies that included funds statements in their annual reports to stockholders greatly increased. According to Rosen and DeCoster's research on a group of 100 corporations randomly selected from *Fortune*'s 1964 list of the largest US companies, 'in 1962, only 39 companies provided a "funds" statement, whereas by 1965 and 1967 the figures were 83 and 89, respectively' (1969: 133).

As the usefulness of information concerning the source and application of funds was widely recognized, the Accounting Principles Board examined whether the presentation of such a funds statement was necessary in supplementing income statements and balance sheets. The Board also examined the standards to be followed in preparing a funds statement and issued 'Reporting Changes in Financial Position', *APB Opinion No. 19*.

APB Opinion No. 19 demanded that profit enterprises disclose the statements that summarize the changes in financial position:

> The Board concludes that information concerning the financing and investing activities of a business enterprise and the changes in its financial position for a period is essential for financial statement users, particularly owners and creditors, in making economic decisions. When financial statements purporting to present both financial position (balance sheet) and results of operations (statement of income and retained earnings) are issued, a statement summarizing changes in financial position should also be presented as a basic financial statement for each period for which an income statement is presented. These conclusions apply to all profit-oriented business entities, whether or not the reporting entity normally classifies its assets and liabilities as current and noncurrent. (para. 7)

In this *Opinion*, the Board concluded that 'the statement summarizing changes in financial position should be based on a broad concept embracing all changes in financial position' (para. 8), and recommended that the title of this statement should be *Statement of Changes in Financial Position.*

Following this, the AICPA's committee on Auditing Procedure issued 'Reporting on the Statement of Changes in Financial Position', *Statement on Auditing Procedure No. 50,* and revised the short form of the independent auditor's report as follows:

We have examined the balance sheet of X Company as of December 31, 19– and the related statements of income and retained earnings and changes in financial position for the year then ended. Our examination was made in accordance with generally accepted auditing standards, and accordingly included such tests of the accounting records and such other auditing procedures as we considered necessary in the circumstances.

In our opinion, the aforementioned financial statements present fairly the financial position of X Company at December 31, 19–, and the results of its operations and the changes in its financial position for the year then ended, in conformity with generally accepted accounting principles applied on a basis consistent with that of the preceding year. (para. 31)

The decade of the 1970s was the period of internationalization of accounting. The funds statement, developed in the USA, was also taken up internationally. In 1973 the Accountants International Study Group, organized by the accountants' groups of Canada, England, and America, issued a report after researching the funds statement practices of these three countries. The funds statement practice of Canada is similar to that of the USA. In the United Kingdom, though a little behind in its development compared with the other two countries, the Institute of Chartered Accountants in England and Wales issued 'Statements of Source and Application of Funds', *Statement of Standard Accounting Practice No. 10,* in 1975, and the funds statement has been recognized as one of the necessary financial statements.

After a few years, 'Statement of Changes in Financial Position', *International Accounting Standard 7,* was born. *International Accounting Standard 7* was approved by the International Accounting Standard Committee in 1977 and issued in October of the same year. *International Accounting Standard 7* adopts the title 'Statement of Changes in Financial Position' and stipulates that the statement should be prepared as one of the financial statements.

A statement of changes in financial position should be included as an integral part of the financial statements. The statement of changes in financial position should be presented for each period for which the income statement is presented. (para. 20)

Funds provided from or used in the operations of an enterprise should be presented in the statement of changes in financial position separately from other sources or uses of funds. Unusual items which are not part of the ordinary activities of the enterprises should be separately disclosed in the statement. (para. 21)

Each enterprise or group of enterprises should adopt the form of presentation for the statement of changes in financial position which is most informative in the circumstances. (para. 22)

CONCLUDING REMARKS

As I have already observed, the funds statement has a history of a hundred years. Still, the statement of funds is young and immature compared with the income statement and the balance sheet. The major concepts and formats of the income statement and the balance sheet are already standardized to a great extent. On the other hand, the concept of 'funds' and the format used in the funds statement are vaguely defined and considerable flexibility is permitted.

For example, although I*nternational Accounting Standard 7* stipulates that the enterprise 'should adopt the form of presentation for the statement of changes in financial position which is most informative in the circumstances', it does not specify what form is to be used. As for the concept of funds, the *International Accounting Standard 7* demands that the term 'funds' to be used in a 'Statement of Changes in Financial Position' be specified in meaning, but it does not fully define what concept of funds is to be used.

For purposes of this Statement, the term 'funds' generally refers to cash, to cash and cash equivalents, or to working capital. In a statement of changes in financial position the particular use of the term is not clear. (para. 4)

The explanation may be that the purpose of preparing a funds statement is still not clear, while it is generally accepted that an income statement supplies information on the operating results of an enterprise and a balance sheet supplies information on its financial position. Although an income statement and a balance sheet supply important financial information about an enterprise, these two statements alone cannot provide all the financial information we need. That is why a funds statement, which supplies the financial information undisclosed by either the income statement or the balance sheet, has been developed.

Nevertheless, it seems that people needed much more financial information than that indicated on an income statement and a balance sheet. From among the various statements devised between the late nineteenth century and the 1910s to convey various information, the funds statement that discloses a change in working capital developed rapidly. The reason for this development was that people wanted information in a solid form about any change in the liquidity of an enterprise. After the 1960s, when the funds statement was publicly recognized, the recommended title was *Statement of Changes in Financial Position*. This indicates that people expect to get all the information concerning changes in financial position.

It is true that in the funds statement showing only the causes of a change in working capital, only a change in the financial position involving a change in working capital is disclosed. Such a funds statement does not disclose important information concerning the financial activities which do not involve a change in working capital. That is why a new approach was devised. In order to disclose all financial activities, the concept of funds was extended and thus a new statement of funds was drawn up. This shift in emphasis can be seen in the title 'Statements of Changes in Financial Position', recommended by the AICPA's *Accounting Principles Board's Opinion No. 19* and adopted by *International Accounting Standard 7*.

In criticizing the shift in emphasis after the 1920s from the funds statement which shows broadly a change in financial position to that which indicates the causes of a change in working capital, Goldberg (1951: 485) once asserted that 'the "shift in emphasis" has been in the wrong direction and that the earlier concepts were more cogent, more satisfying and more rational'.

In this sense, the shift in emphasis from supplying information concerning a change in liquidity to supplying information concerning a change in financial position, shown in *APB's Opinion No. 19* and *IAS 7*, is most welcome.

There are, however, many kinds of financial information that cannot be disclosed by income statements or balance sheets. And it seems unreasonable to impose responsibility to disclose such other information on funds statements alone. If the statement put emphasis on one factor, the other factors would be neglected. And if too much or too varied information were listed in one statement, such a statement would be messy and confusing. Thus, there are many unavoidable problems to be solved in funds statements.

REFERENCES

Accountants International Study Group (1973), *The Funds Statement—Current Practices in Canada, the United Kingdom and the United States* (March).

American Institute of Certified Public Accountants, Accounting Principles Board (1963), 'The Statement of Sources and Application of Funds', *Accounting Principles Board Opinion No. 3*.

American Institute of Certified Public Accountants, Accounting Principles Board (1971), 'Reporting Changes in Financial Position', *Accounting Principles Board Opinion No. 19*.

American Institute of Certified Public Accountants, Committee on Auditing Procedure (1971), 'Reporting on the Statement of Changes in Financial Position', *Statement on Auditing Procedure No. 50.*

Cole, W. M. (1908), *Accounts, their Construction and Interpretation* (New York: Houghton Mifflin; rev. and enlarged, 1915).

Day, E. B. (1951), 'Cash-Balance Approach to Funds Statement Promotes Clarity in Financial Reports', *Journal of Accountancy*, 91 (Apr.), 600–3.

Finney, H. A. (1921), 'Students' Department, Examination in Accounting Theory and Practice, Part I, May 18, 1921 with Solution', *Journal of Accountancy*, 32 (July), 64–7.

—— (1925), 'Statement of Application of Funds, A Reply to Mr. Esquerré (Students' Department)', *Journal of Accountancy*, 39 (June), 497–511.

Goldberg, L. (1951), 'The Funds Statement Reconsidered', *Accounting Review*, 26 (Oct.), 485–91.

Institute of Chartered Accountants in England and Wales (1975), 'Statements of Source and Application of Funds', *Statement of Standard Accounting Practice No. 10* (Institute of Chartered Accountants in England and Wales).

International Accounting Standards Committee (1977), 'Statement of Changes in Financial Position', *International Accounting Standard No. 7.*

Mason, P. (1961), '"Cash Flow" Analysis and the Funds Statement', *Accounting Research Study No. 2* (American Institute of Certified Public Accountants).

Moonitz, M. (1943), 'Inventories and the Statement of Funds', *Accounting Review*, 18 (July), 262–8.

Paton, W. A. (1938), *Essentials of Accounting* (New York: Macmillan).

Rosen, L. S., and DeCoster, D. T. (1969), '"Funds" Statement: A Historical Perspective', *Accounting Review*, 44 (Jan.), 124–36.

Someya, K. (1956), *Shikinkaikeiron* ('Funds Flow Accounting') (Tokyo: Chuokeizaisha).

19

The Development of Funds Flow Accounting in Japan

FUNDS FLOW ACCOUNTING COMES INTO PROMINENCE

The end of the war in 1945 found the Japanese economy burnt out. Most factories and other production facilities had been consumed in the flames of war. The conscription of human and material resources exclusively for war production had been going on for so long that, even in those factories escaping actual destruction, the potential for making even a conservative new beginning was minimal. People had lost their houses and clothing in the blaze. But to this was added the needs of the large number of returning soldiers and civilians who had been living abroad before the war. The shortage of housing and clothing was drastic. The production of goods and services was far less than demand and post-war Japan was engulfed in a wave of inflation.

Under these conditions businesses had to invest large amounts of capital in factories, machinery, and other facilities in order to restore productivity. Moreover, as business picked up, inflation increased rapidly. Because of this inflation, the cash value of inventory stock increased drastically, further increasing the need for large amounts of capital. In spite of this, the capital market remained weak and capital accumulation in these businesses did not always proceed as desired. Many businesses incurred significant debt to financing agencies.

It was during this period that expressions such as 'all in the books, nothing in the hand' and 'the profitable road to bankruptcy' became bywords. In the midst of such inflation a business could easily sell its products at a profit, but parts and raw materials could only be restocked at a cost greater than previous cost. Sales continued to rise sharply, yet managers, without exception, were plagued by a constant shortage of money with which to pay their bills. While profit and loss accounting showed them with large profits on paper, in actual fact businesses had no cash funds available, and many of them were forced into bankruptcy

From *Waseda Business and Economic Studies*, No. 23 (1987), 1–12.

because they were unable to meet payment deadlines. The inability to raise funds, in spite of large profits on the books, meant difficulty in amassing capital for expansion or even to meet the escalating value of inventory.

In recent business accounting theory, with its shift from cash basis accounting to accrual basis accounting, the tendency has been to remove funds flow accounting as an object of research and view it as a problem for the businessman himself. However, the shortage of funds for taxes and other disbursements despite large profits recognized in the books, besides being a constant source of worry for managers at the time, was also seen by accounting scholars as a challenge. Therefore in order to discover the reasons for such a situation and to devise some means for countering it, scholars unremittingly poured their efforts into this field of investigation. The leader in this crusade was Tetsuzo Ohta.

Ohta (1949) viewed the inadequacy of funds despite tremendous profits as a natural feature of inflation, and accounted for it by saying that businesses were in fact not realizing profit. He pointed out how normal business accounting, which serves so effectively as a guide for operations in times of normal economy, gives a false picture in times of inflation, and hence he argued for the need for funds flow accounting. The imaginary profits born of inflation are poorly handled by stable price accounting. A funds flow accounting would demonstrate this, and also reveal the true cause for the money shortage, knowledge of which is essential for adequate managerial planning.

The mistake in thinking that just because there is a profit there must also be a corresponding surplus of cash cannot be explained away simply as an error committed by persons unknowledgeable in the ways of accounting. The purpose of accounting is to explain fully and completely, and any inadequacy in the explanation suggests that accounting itself is worthless or of little use. Ohta insisted that, at the very least, an effort should be made to find out upon which points funds flow accounting and income flow accounting agree, and upon which points they differ. In this way he set the foundation for further investigation into the theory of funds flow accounting.

STATEMENT OF SOURCE AND APPLICATION OF FUNDS

Investigation of funds flow accounting theory in the ten years following the war centred around the statement of source and application of funds or funds flow statement, variously known in the literature as statement of application of funds, or simply funds statement. The statement of source and application of funds was originally prepared as a tool in analysing comparative balance sheets, but because of the way in which it classifies monetary increases and decreases in the various categories of the comparative balance sheet according to the source of the fund and how it is used, it gained recognition as an indicator of the financial activity of a business not otherwise displayed by the income statement and balance sheet. Kaichiro Bamba (1949) got things underway by calling attention to the fact that a statement of source and application of funds is included among the supplementary statements attached to annual shareholder reports for American companies. He explained the development and preparation procedures of the statement of source and application of funds in America, and its effectiveness in making more accessible to interested persons information regarding changes in a company's ability to make payments, or liquidity.

Different trains of investigation were subsequently taken up by Kyojiro Someya, Kaichiro Nishino, Manji Nakamura, Toshiro Otsuka, and others. Someya (1951), in addition to contrasting the statement of source and application of funds of R. B. Kester with its predecessor, the 'where got, where gone' statement, and clarifying the various features of the modern funds statement, also suggested that this statement be included along with the income statement and balance sheet among financial statements as a means of accounting for funds flow. Nishino (1950) explained the preparation of the source and application of funds statement according to R. A. Foulke (1950) and J. N. Meyer (1952), and also pointed out the importance of the method whereby the various categories of the income statement are used to explain the relationship between funds flow and net profit for that period.

Nakamura's examination (1951) of the statement of source and application of funds proceeded from Kester's development (1946) of financial analysis theory. According to Nakamura's view, a statement of funds exists solely as a tool for business management, and not because of any value it might have for labour, for shareholders, or for public officials, etc., and he insisted that the social application of such a statement be a topic for future research. Moreover, while regarding the statement of source and application of funds as one aspect of working capital accounting, he also turned his attention to other funds flow accounting developments in England such as the double account system and P. Taggart's (1934) two-part balance sheet. Otsuka (1953) pointed out that the source and application of funds statement contains valuable information not found in the balance sheet or income statements and, based on the fund theory of W. J. Vatter (1947), regarded it as a new system for financial reporting. But, he maintained, as long as the statement of source and application of funds continues to be prepared from the balance sheet and income statement, then this funds-based system of accounting will remain in a position secondary to the more traditional style of financial reporting, unable to escape its framework or come out from under its influence. Otsuka suggested that if the statement of source and application of funds were assigned a position as a separate financial statement, or if it had at its source a new and independent system of funds flow accounting, then it would make possible the development of a more progressive form of financial reporting.

TWO THEORIES OF FUNDS FLOW ACCOUNTING

During this period funds statement research proceeded on the basis of accounting literature from America. The statement of source and application of funds was considered as something prepared from, and secondary to, the balance sheet, income, and other financial statements. Although a number of funds concepts were discussed, the general tendency was to view this statement as a tool limited to describing the financial activity of a business through representation of its working capital. For this reason, the attempt to account for discrepancies between income and actual funds available by means of the source and application of funds statement came under heavy attack, mainly from people with business experience. Jikichi Fujimaki (1953) pointed out that, while the statement of source and application of funds has relevancy to the broad concept of operating funds, it bears little relation to the narrow definition of funds as cash on hand. He divided transactions into cash transactions involving the receipt and payment of cash, and accounting transactions not involving an actual flow of cash. Cash transactions were further classified as profit and loss or income transactions and exchange transactions. Using such a bookkeeping system for cash available, he proposed directly to identify the relationship between profit and loss accounting and the in-flow and out-flow of cash.

The relevance of funds flow accounting to business lies, not in the preparation of a statement of source and application of funds secondary to the balance sheet, income, and other financial statements, but rather in a new and independent system of funds flow accounting. In a paper published in 1955 (Someya 1955) I recognized two accounting domains, profit and loss accounting and receipt and payment accounting. Determination of profit and loss leads to the income statement, while computation of receipts and payments leads to the statement of source and application of funds. I proposed a system of accounting whereby both of these computations are incorporated into the balance sheet. The source and application of funds statement was considered as a broad concept including a statement of receipts and payments. The funds concepts were employed in this statement elastically, with cash on hand at the centre, and ranging from cash or equivalent asset in the narrowest sense to net working capital in the broadest.

In my book *Shikin Kaikeiron* ('Funds Flow Accounting') (1956), I attempted to establish the domain of funds flow accounting using the accounting domain pertaining to cash type assets, and founded upon the two asset concepts of cash type assets (monetary assets) and expense type assets (non-monetary assets). My expansion of the idea of funds to encompass all working capital, including inventory assets, came under heavy attack by Shozo Ichimura (1960). Ichimura claimed that there are shortcomings in a theory of funds flow accounting centred around cash on hand. The idea of funds as capital within the framework of cash type and expense type assets is itself an important problem for consideration. Contained within such criticism we see a groping towards another type of funds flow accounting, based more upon the fund theory of accounting of W. J. Vatter (1947).

MOVEMENT BALANCE SHEET

One feature of funds flow accounting research in the last half of the 1950s and first half of the 1960s is that people began paying attention to the movement balance sheet (*Bewegungsbilanz*) developed in Germany. Germany too, having experienced a drastic shortage of funds after the war, was beset by the same sort of economic conditions that gave rise to funds flow accounting in Japan. The movement balance sheet, as a means for indicating the origin and employment of funds, was first proposed by W. Bauer in 1926, appeared as a money-based balance sheet in the works of E. Walb (1948), and is said to have been picked up and completed by H. Ruchti (1955) after the war.

The first person to introduce the development of this movement balance sheet into Japan was Kiyoshi Kurosawa (1958). According to his interpretation, the money-based balance sheet of Walb, more properly designated as a funds balance sheet, is nothing more than a grafting of American accounting concepts of funds statements onto a dynamic balance sheet. A movement balance sheet which merely contrasts the flow of funds with the present condition of funds does not advance one step beyond the concepts of the source and application of funds statement. He viewed the development of Ruchti's movement balance sheet as a development away from cash dynamics to fund dynamics. Kurosawa clarified two features regarding Ruchti's movement balance sheet: (1) all business operations involving monetary flows are serially recorded by means of a three-part computation involving capital, disbursements, and investments; gross and net movement balance sheets are prepared by periodic and comprehensive adjustment of these entries; (2) the balance sheet and income statements comprising the financial report are then prepared from these movement balance sheets.

Subsequent investigation of the German movement balance sheet was undertaken by Ryuji Takeda (1962). Takeda understood the special feature of German funds flow accounting to be that a source and application of funds statement is not prepared secondarily to other financial statements, but rather that the flow of funds can be acknowledged and identified directly from the accounting structure itself. He stressed the usefulness of W. Thoms's (1957) functional computation accounting. Moreover, besides showing that the development of movement balance sheet theory in the years following the Second World War had its impetus in social conditions in Germany, whereby increases in internal reserves had to be undertaken at the same time that profits were being used to compensate for the large-scale capital losses incurred as a result of the war, Takeda pictured the development of the movement balance sheet as a synthesis of three trends:

(1) development of the technical aspects of money-based balance sheet theory presaged in the works of Bauer and Walb;
(2) the development of a funds dynamics theory which attempts to resolve funds problems together with problems of income, as an offshoot of an income dynamics theory;
(3) an attempt to employ the movement balance sheet as a tool in management planning. Takeda's book *Taishakutaishohyo Shikinron* ('Balance Sheet Fund Theory') (1962) is noteworthy as a systematic and exhaustive treatment of the development of German funds flow accounting.

INTEREST IN FUNDS FLOW MANAGEMENT

Clearly the mainstream of funds flow accounting research following the Second World War has been an attempt to remedy the deficiencies in the traditional system of financial reporting, which was fashioned around the central concept of profit determination, and to develop a more adequate system of reporting. At the same time it is also true that investigations into funds flow accounting forged ahead in connection with funds flow management. Funds serve as oil to the cogs of operations management. Just the right amount of funds must be applied at just the proper time in order for a business to run smoothly. Not enough funds could halt operations, while a surplus of funds could lower capital effectiveness.

Anticipating the amount of funds needed for sales, production, equipment, and other facility investments, the entire range of operation activities, and then arranging that these funds get applied when and where they should be is indeed the essence of business management.

Research into the area of funds flow management has been conducted by Eiichi Furukawa (1955) in connection with financial management, and by Kazuhito Kunihiro (1955) in connection with funds statement development. Furukawa divides financial management of a business into two types, narrow and broad. The objective of management in the narrow sense of the term is to maintain the ability to meet payments, which is done through the collection and disbursement of cash and preservation of a favourable reserve as a difference between the two. In the broad sense of the term, management objectives involve increasing the profitability of a business, which proceeds through all phases of accumulation and application of capital requisite to the proper conduct of all operations within the business. Moreover, Furukawa views the profit or depreciation value indicated by profit planning as self-financing, and points to their important relationship to funds flow planning. Besides clarifying the relationship between funds flow planning and profit planning, he also divides the content of funds flow planning into working fund planning and fixed fund planning.

Kunihiro considered funds flow accounting to be the notational computation of ready cash in the narrow sense of receipts and payments. While both financial reporting and operations management are important as objectives, he was especially concerned with management, and insisted that funds flow planning be such that it fully served a funds management function. In order to accomplish this he sought to unify profit and funds management into a single whole and developed a series of unique funds statements, including an increase or decrease in funds statement, a combined profit and loss/receipt and disbursement statement, a combined profit and funds statement, and a funds flow statement. In his funds flow statement he indicates all receipts and payments as three sections of the working fund, the basic fund, and the financing fund.

The National Association of Accountants published its Research Report No. 38, 'Cash Flow Analysis for Managerial Control', in 1961. This report surveyed the methods used to collect and report financial data considered necessary for the financial management of cash assets. It has had an important influence on financial management research in this country. Published in 1965, R. K. Jaedicke and R. T. Sprouse's extremely popular work, *Accounting Flows: Income, Funds and Cash*, examines the fundamental concepts, principles, and procedures of accounting essential to the financial management of business, based upon the three flow concepts of cash flow, funds flow, and income flow. This book was introduced into Japan by Tamba and Takamatsu.

FROM SOURCE AND APPLICATION OF FUNDS STATEMENT TO CHANGES IN FINANCIAL POSITION STATEMENT

The American Institute of Certified Public Accountants' widely acclaimed Research Report No. 2, '"Cash Flow" Analysis and the Funds Statement', appeared in 1961, followed by APB Opinion No. 3, 'The Statement of Source and Application of Funds', in 1963. These were the first public statements to appear by leading accounting organizations regarding the statement of source and application of funds. H. R. Anton's *Accounting for the Flow of Funds* (1962), which presents a comprehensive examination of funds flow analysis, also came out at this time.

In APB Opinion No. 3 it was stated that a source and application of funds statement should be included among supplementary reports attached to the financial reports of businesses, but no provisions were made for making such disclosure mandatory. However, APB Opinion No. 19, 'Reporting Changes in Financial Position', appearing in 1971, stipulates that companies must include a statement summarizing changes in their financial situation. This statement is to be based on broad principles encompassing any and all fluctuations, and the name tentatively given to this statement was Statement of Changes in Financial Position. As a result, the statement of changes in financial position came to be included, along with the various other financial statements, in the annual reports of American businesses, and the audit examination by a CPA extends to this statement as well. Such practice came into the international limelight in 1977 with the appearance of the International Accounting Standards Committee's IAS No. 7, 'Statement of Changes in Financial Position'.

The idea of funds flow accounting became more and more appealing in the inflationary economy following the Second World War as the gap between profit, as measured by profit and loss accounting, and actual money available for payments widened. The more rampant inflation became, the more obvious were the deficiencies of an accounting based on profit and loss determination. Funds flow accounting began to appear as a means of salvation, and it was for this reason that funds flow accounting theory, centring on the concept of ready cash, was developed. Eventually, however, the economy got back on its feet again, capital accumulated, and things began operating at full steam. In addition there was a gradual shift in interest towards investment and capital-building activities so important to any business. The establishment of a financial reporting system which includes a statement of changes in financial position prepared in accordance with broad funds concepts clearly reflects these changes in the economic environment.

In Japan, too, there was a blossoming of research in connection with the adoption of the statements of source and application of funds and changes in financial position, revolving around the APB Opinions and IASC statements. From 1955 on through the 1980s a great many people became involved in such investigations.

RECENT TRENDS

A survey of the most recent investigations into funds flow accounting theory reveals two trends: (1) study of new funds flow accounting developments in other countries, and (2) a re-evaluation of the fundamental concepts of funds flow accounting. In the first category we see investigation of K. Käfer's funds flow accounting theory (1967) by Shoji Yasuhira and others (1974, 1976), which straddles the fence between the American source and application of funds statement and the German movement balance sheet. The Japan Accounting Association Study Group led by Kiyoshi Ogawa is examining trends in major countries interested in business financial disclosure, in particular the United States, Canada, England, and West Germany, and attempts to address the fundamental questions of funds flow accounting. It is essential to keep up to date with research trends in other countries.

Research in the second category includes examination of the English double account system, the fund theory of accounting of Vatter, Walb's money-based balance sheet, etc. The exact domain of funds flow accounting has not yet been defined. What remains to be done is to review the bases upon which funds flow accounting is founded, together with the socio-economic conditions which gave birth to it.

REFERENCES

American Institute of Certified Public Accountants (1963), 'The Statement of Source and Application of Funds', *Accounting Principles Board Opinion No. 3* (New York: AICPA).

—— (1971), 'Reporting Changes in Financial Position' *Accounting Principles Board Opinion No. 19* (New York: AICPA).

Anton, Hector R. (1962), *Accounting for the Flow of Funds* (New York: Houghton Mifflin).

Bamba, Kaichiro (1949), 'Shikin-unyohyo to sono Riyo' ('Funds Statement and its Uses'), *Kigyokaikei*, 1/6: 35–8; 1/7: 8–13.

Bauer, Walter (1926), 'Die Bewegungsbilanz und ihre Anwendbarkeit, insbesondere als Konzernbilanz', *Zeitschrift für Handelswirtschaftliche Forschung*, Jahrg. 20, Heft 11: 285–544.

Foulke, Roy A. (1950), *Practical Financial Statement Analysis* (2nd edn., New York: McGraw-Hill), 469–87.

Fujimaki, Jikichi (1953), 'Son-eki Keisan to Shikinshushi tono Kankei Haaku' ('Profit and Loss Calulation in its Relation to Funds Received and Disbursed'), *Kaikei*, 64/5: 819–27.

Furukawa, Eiichi (1955), *Zaimukanri* ('Financial Management') (Tokyo: Ganshodo Shoten).

Ichimura, Shozo (1960), 'Wagakuni ni okeru Shikin Kaikeiron no Tenkai to sono Mondaiten' ('Fund Theory of Accounting as Accepted and Developed in Japan'), *Kaikei*, 77/6: 826–41.

International Accounting Standards Committee (1977), 'Statement of Changes in Financial Position', *International Accounting Standard No. 7*.

Jaedicke, Robert K., and Sprouse, Robert T. (1965), *Accounting Flows: Income, Funds and Cash* (Englewood Cliffs, NJ: Prentice-Hall).

Käfer, Karl (1967), *Kapitalflussrechnungen: Funds Statement, Liquiditätsnachweis, Bewegungsbilanz als dritte Jahresrechnung der Unternehmung* (Zurich: Verlag des Schweizerischen Kaufmännischen Vereins).

—— (1974), *Praxis der Kapitalflussrechnung: Aufstellung und Auswertung, Aufgaben und Lösungen* (Zurich: Verlag des Schweizerischen Kaufmännischen Vereins).

Kester, R. B. (1946), *Advanced Accounting with Practice Problems* (4th edn., New York: Ronald Press Co.), 660–75.

Kunihiro, Kazuhito (1955), 'Shikin-Kaikei no Arikata' ('What Funds Flow Accounting should be'), *Sangyokeiri*, 15/8: 24–31.

Kurosawa, Kiyoshi (1958), *Shikin Kaikei no Riron* ('Theory of Funds Flow Accounting') (Tokyo: Moriyama Shoten).

Mason, Perry (1961), '"Cash Flow" Analysis and Funds Statement', *Accounting Research Study No. 2* (New York: AICPA).

Meyer, John N. (1952), *Financial Statement Analysis: Principles and Technique* (2nd edn., New York: Prentice-Hall).

National Association of Accountants (1961), 'Cash Flow Analysis for Managerial Control', *Research Study No. 38* (New York: NAA).

Nakamura, Manji (1951), 'Kester Zaimubunsekiron no Tenkai' ('Development of Financial Analysis by R. B. Kester'), *Shodaironsyu*, No. 6: 77–109.

Nishino, Kaichiro (1950), 'Sikin-unyohyo no Tsukurikata' ('Method for the Preparation of Funds Statement'), *Zeikeitsushin*, 5/12: 19–29.

Ogawa, Kiyoshi, *et al.* (1983), *Gendai Shikinkaikei no Dohko* ('Recent Trends in Funds Flow Accounting') (Tokyo: Kunimoto Shobo).

Ohta, Tetsuzo (1949), 'Kanezumari to Kanaguri Kaikei' ('Cash Shortage and Cash Availability Accounting'), *Kigyokaikei*, 1/2: 57–9.

Otsuka, Toshiro (1953), 'Zaimuhokoku ni okeru Shikinhyo no Chii oyobi sono Hatten' ('The Role of Funds Statement and its Development in Financial Reporting'), *Kaikei*, 64/1: 65–79.

Ruchti, Hans (1955), 'Erfolgsermittlung und Bewegungsbilanz', *Zeitschrift für handelswirtschaftliche Forschung*, NF, Jahrg. 7, Heft 11: 499–520.

RKW (1961), *Liquiditätsrechnung im Dienste der Unternehmungsführung*, ed. Arbeitskreis Liquidität des Bundesausschusses (Wiesbaden: Betriebswirtschaft BBW).

Someya, Kyojiro (1951), 'Kester no Shikin-unyohyo to Cole no Where-got-where-gone-hyo' ('The Statement of Source and Application of Funds of R. B. Kester and the Where got, Where gone Statement of W. M. Cole'), *Kaikei*, 59/3: 18–34.
—— (1955), 'Shikinkaikei Ryoiki no Ninshiki' ('Recognition of the Domain of Funds Flow Accounting'), *Sangyokeiri*, 15/8: 32–8.
—— (1956), *Sikin Kaikeiron* ('Funds Flow Accounting') (Tokyo: Chuokeizaisha).
—— (1977), *An Introduction to Flow of Funds Accounting* (Tokyo: Institute for Research in Business Administration, Waseda University).
Taggart, P. (1934), *Profits and Balance Sheet Adjustments* (London: Gee & Co., Ltd.).
Takamatsu, Kazuo (1972), 'Kaikei ni okeru Mittsu no Furo Gainen' ('Three Flow Concepts of Accounting'), *Kaikei*, 101/1: 40–51.
Takeda, Ryuji (1962), *Taishakutaishohyo Shikinron* ('Balance Sheet Fund Theory') (Tokyo: Doubunkan).
Tamba, Yasutaro (1967), 'Sikin-Furo-Bunseki to sono Zaimukanri jono Juyosei' ('Funds Flow Analysis and its Role in Financial Management'), *Sangyokeiri*, 27/12: 6–14.
Thoms, Walter (1957), *Inhalt und Form der funktionalen Kontorechnung* (Berlin: Herne).
Vatter, W. J. (1947), *The Fund Theory of Accounting and its Implications for Financial Reports* (Chicago: University of Chicago Press).
Walb, E. (1948), *Finanzwirtschaftliche Bilanz* (Duisburg: H. E. Visser).
Yasuhira, Shoji, *et al.* (1974, 1976), *Kapitalflussrechnungen, Funds Statement, Liquiditätsnachweis und Bewegungsbilanz als dritte Jahresrechnung der Unternehmung von Karl Käfer* (The Japanese Translation Edition; 2 vols., Tokyo: Chikura Shobo).

20

The Use of Funds Statements and Cash Flow Statements in Japan

INTRODUCTION

In July of 1959, supported by the Sangyo Keiri Kyokai (The Industrial Management and Accounting Institute), I conducted a survey on the use of funds statements and cash flow statements among major companies in Japan. The results of that survey appeared in Japanese in the Institute's publication, *Sangyo Keiri*.

Prior to this, Hector R. Anton, in affiliation with the Business Survey Department at the University of Washington, had conducted a survey on the use of funds statements in companies throughout the United States and Canada, with his results appearing in the October 1954 issue of *Accounting Review*. In order to faciliate comparison between those findings and my own, I formulated questions along the lines established by Professor Anton. My results subsequently appeared in the October 1964 issue of *Accounting Review*.[1]

A quarter century has gone by now, so would it not be of some interest to find out just how funds and cash flow statement practices have changed during this time? To this end, I proposed to undertake the same survey once again. The survey was conducted in February of 1985, as follows.

Companies Surveyed: Excluding 108 banks, investment agencies, and insurance agencies, 924 companies were selected from the 1,032 companies listed in Section One of the Tokyo Stock Exchange as of 21 January 1985.

Survey Methods: Questionnaires were mailed on 22 January 1985 in care of the heads of the accounting departments of the selected companies, with a request that they be returned by 20 February 1985. All but a few questions could be answered by circling the letter of the correct response, with more than one answer allowed for each question.

There were nineteen questions in all, divided into three categories: (1) Company Status, (2) Funds Statement, (3) Cash Flow Statement. Also included were the following definitions for funds and cash flow statements:

From *Waseda Business and Economic Studies*, No. 28 (1992), 1–14.

[1] Reprinted above, Ch. 16

TABLE 20.1. *Responding companies according to size*

Size (capital stocks)		No. of companies	% of total
A	Over ¥20 billion	73	16.7
B	¥10–19.9 billion	66	15.1
C	¥5–9.9 billion	101	23.1
D	¥2.5–4.9 billion	113	25.9
E	Under ¥2.5 billion	84	19.2
Total		437	100.0

Funds Statement: an accounting statement which records current period income, depreciation, the issuing of company stocks and bonds, money from long term loans, etc. as sources of funds, and fixed asset investments, redemption of company bonds, repayment of long-term loans, etc. as uses of funds, and which relates to working capital (i.e. the difference between current assets and current liabilities).

Cash Flow Statement: an accounting statement which records items of cash receipts and cash payments, and relates to the balance of cash.

In the present survey, 437 companies returned their completed questionnaires, representing 47.2% of the 924 companies surveyed. In the 1959 survey the response rate was 308 out of 563, or 55%; however, at that time members of the survey team paid visits to companies in the Tokyo and Osaka areas to request return of the questionnaire, in addition to the request for compliance mailed along with the questionnaire. 47.2% is a reasonable compliance rate, and 437 respondents is a very satisfactory number for accomplishing the objectives of the present survey.

Table 20.1 shows the number of responding companies classified according to size. In the present survey the size of each company was determined on the basis of the amount of its capital stocks shown in its balance sheet as of the closing day in 1984. There was no uneven distribution among responding companies. In the tables that follow, company size is indicated by the letters A, B, C, D, and E, as defined in Table 20.1.

USE OF THE FUNDS STATEMENT

Table 20.2 indicates the number and percentage of companies making use of funds statements among the 437 respondents. Except for smaller companies with capital of less than 2.5 billion showing 83.3%, over 90% of the companies in each category made use of funds statements, with a total average of 92.4%. In the previous survey the total average of funds statements users was 68%. Thus it is clearly evident that, over the past

TABLE 20.2. *Number and percentage of companies using funds statements*

Size	No. of respondents	No. of users	%
A	73	68	93.2
B	66	63	95.5
C	101	96	95.0
D	113	107	94.7
E	84	70	83.3
Total	437	404	92.4

TABLE 20.3. *Funds statements: intended parties*

Group size	Management		Stockholders		Banks		Foreign investors	
	No.	%	No.	%	No.	%	No.	%
A	67	98.5	2	2.9	32	47.1	21	30.9
B	62	98.4	2	3.2	32	50.8	6	9.5
C	95	99.0	0	0	38	39.6	6	6.3
D	104	97.2	1	0.9	37	34.6	3	2.8
E	70	100.0	1	1.4	32	45.7	0	0
Total	398	98.5	6	1.5	171	42.3	36	8.9

quarter century, the use of funds statements has become almost standard practice in business operations.

Table 20.3 indicates the sort of purposes funds statements are used for, classified according to the parties for whom they are intended. It can be seen that nearly all companies make use of funds statements for managerial purposes. In contrast, only a small number of companies include a funds statement in the financial report made to stockholders. An average of 42.3% of the companies presented funds statements to banks and other creditors, a slight increase over the previous survey. Finally, the practice of including funds statements in financial reports intended for foreign investors, a question added to the present survey, was found to be quite common among the larger companies.

THE FUNDS STATEMENT FOR MANAGERIAL PURPOSES

Table 20.4 indicates which uses are considered most important by companies employing funds statements for managerial purposes. The most

TABLE 20.4. *Intended uses for managerial funds statements*

	No.	%
Companies employing funds statements for managerial purposes	398	100
Intended use:		
(1) For clarifying financial changes not readily discernible in the balance sheet and income statement	369	92.7
(2) To aid company officials when making decisions regarding financial matters (including capital expenditures and other future planning)	190	47.7
(3) To help clarify profit calculation and profit use (including dividends) to company officials	87	21.9
(4) To illustrate financial strengths and weaknesses of the company	129	32.4
(5) Other	4	1.0

TABLE 20.5. *Use of estimated and historical funds statements*

	Percentage of use					
	A	B	C	D	E	Total
(1) Estimated funds statements only	6.0	1.6	1.0	1.0	1.4	2.0
(2) Historical funds statements only	4.5	8.1	9.5	21.1	24.3	14.1
(3) Both types used	89.5	90.3	89.5	77.9	74.3	83.9

frequently reported use of internally intended funds statements is for indicating financial changes. This is followed by use in the decision-making process regarding financial matters.

Table 20.5 illustrates the use of estimated and actual funds statements for managerial purposes. As can be seen, more than 83% of the companies employ both types of statements. In the previous survey this figure was 57%. Such an increase indicates how widespread the use of funds statements for managerial purposes has become, and how greatly they have come to be valued.

Table 20.6 indicates the number of years that have passed since the company first began using funds statements for managerial purposes. We see that 40% of the companies have twenty years' or more experience using such statements, while three quarters of the companies have ten years or more. On the previous survey, three-quarters of the companies

TABLE 20.6. *Funds statements: number of years in use (%)*

Years in use	A	B	C	D	E	Total
1–4	0	0	0	4.8	0	1.3
5–9	1.5	9.7	7.4	19.2	18.6	11.8
10–19	19.4	30.6	40.0	34.6	47.1	34.9
20–29	20.9	24.2	27.4	20.2	18.6	22.4
30 or more	43.3	24.2	17.9	6.7	7.1	18.3
No information	14.9	11.3	7.4	14.4	8.6	11.3

TABLE 20.7. *Projected time period for estimated funds statements (%)*

Time period	A	B	C	D	E	Total
1 month	4.7	5.3	5.8	8.5	5.7	6.1
3 months	7.8	3.5	4.7	4.9	5.7	5.3
6 months	70.3	71.9	69.8	68.3	71.7	70.2
1 year	56.3	56.1	55.8	59.8	43.4	55.0
2–5 years	29.7	22.8	18.6	14.6	9.4	19.0
Other	3.1	0	1.2	0	0	0.9

had been using funds statements for less than ten years. This is a good example of the changing times.

Table 20.7 shows the time periods projected in estimated funds statements used for managerial purposes. From it we see that nearly all companies prepare either 6-month or 1-year statements, or both. It should be noted, however, that one company in five prepares long-term estimated funds statements with a projected period of 2–5 years. This is particularly true for large companies with capital stocks of ¥20 billion or more, where the ratio is nearly one company in three.

Table 20.8 shows the period of time covered by historical funds statements intended for managerial purposes. Here too we find that a majority of the companies prepare either 6-month or 1-year statements, or both.

Companies preparing funds statements for managerial purposes relate such statements to the various types of budgets. Table 20.9 indicates the extent to which this is done. Many companies use such statements as they relate to all budgets; however, we can see that the relationship to the financial (capital raising) budget is also deemed to be of importance.

An important part of the funds statement is the treatment of non-fund items, that is to say, items not accompanied by an actual receipt or disbursement of funds. Table 20.10 indicates which items are treated as non-fund items. Nearly all companies include depreciation. This is followed

TABLE 20.8. *Time period covered by historical funds statements (%)*

Time period	A	B	C	D	E	Total
1 month	14.3	9.8	17.0	20.4	14.5	15.9
3 months	7.9	4.9	4.3	2.9	2.9	4.4
6 months	79.4	65.6	77.7	79.6	76.8	76.4
1 year	68.3	59.0	50.0	48.5	40.6	52.3
2–5 years	1.6	4.9	4.3	3.9	4.3	3.8
Other	4.8	0	3.2	1.0	0	1.8

TABLE 20.9. *Relationship of funds statements to the various types of budgets (%)*

	A	B	C	D	E	Total
All budgets	55.9	54.0	53.1	45.8	47.1	50.7
Cash budgets	11.8	9.5	6.3	6.5	8.6	8.2
Capital budget	22.1	15.9	18.8	24.3	21.4	20.8
Financial budget	54.4	55.6	50.0	46.7	47.1	50.2
Estimated balance sheet	16.2	19.0	13.5	13.1	20.0	15.8
Other	0	0	10.0	1.9	1.4	1.0

TABLE 20.10. *Non-fund items included in the funds statement (%)*

	A	B	C	D	E	Total
Depreciation	92.6	98.4	95.8	92.5	90.0	93.8
Reserve for price fluctuation	48.5	34.9	43.8	31.8	20.0	35.9
Reserve for uncollectable debts	58.8	52.4	70.8	57.0	48.6	58.4
Retirement fund	72.1	66.7	69.8	49.5	57.1	62.1
Other	20.6	4.8	3.1	9.3	10.0	9.2

by retirement funds, reserve for uncollectable debts, and reserve for price fluctuation, in that order.

USE OF THE CASH FLOW STATEMENT

Table 20.11 shows the number and percentage of companies making use of cash flow statements. Of the 437 companies that returned their questionnaires, we see that all but one prepare and use such statements. Unlike the balance sheet and income statement, the preparation of a cash flow statement is not required by law. However, such statements have become indispensable to the operations of each and every company.

TABLE 20.11. *Number and percentage of companies using cash flow statements*

Size	No. of respondents	No. of users	%
A	73	73	100
B	66	66	100
C	101	100	99
D	113	113	100
E	84	84	100
Total	437	436	99.7

TABLE 20.12. *Cash flow statements: intended parties*

Group size	Management		Stockholders		Securities reports		Banks	
	No.	%	No.	%	No.	%	No.	%
A	70	95.9	0	0	51	69.9	35	47.9
B	66	100	0	0	33	50.0	29	43.9
C	100	100	1	1.0	52	52.0	44	44.0
D	111	98.2	0	0	53	46.9	54	47.8
E	84	100	1	1.2	43	51.2	41	48.8
Total	431	98.8	2	0.4	232	53.2	203	46.6

Table 20.12 indicates the various purposes for which cash flow statements are used, classified according to the parties for whom they are intended. Of the 436 companies using such statements, 431 do so for managerial purposes.

Many companies also use cash flow statements in their relations with their banks. In contrast, almost no companies use such statements in their relations with stockholders. Over half the companies, however, replied that they employ cash flow statements when indicating the cash flow situation in their annual securities reports filed with the Ministry of Finance.

Table 20.13 indicates which intended uses are thought to be most important by companies using cash flow statements for managerial purposes. Use in planning the cash budget is most predominant, followed by use in establishing payment schedules, and use in the drafting of plans regarding finance. Use of cash flow statements in determining target dates for collection of receivable accounts dropped from 35% in the previous survey to roughly 11% in the present, but other than this, results remain pretty much the same. All in all, the nature of the cash flow statement is clearly illustrated.

TABLE 20.13. *Intended uses for managerial cash flow statements*

	No.	%
Companies employing cash flow statements for managerial purposes	431	100
Intended use:		
(1) For company officials in making decisions regarding financial matters (including capital expenditures and other future planning)	201	46.6
(2) In planning the cash budget	387	89.8
(3) In planning various types of payment schedules	218	50.6
(4) In determining target dates for collection of accounts receivable, etc.	47	10.9
(5) Other	10	2.3

TABLE 20.14. *Use of estimated and historical cash flow statements*

	Percentage of use					
	A	B	C	D	E	Total
(1) Statements of estimated cash flows only	0	3.0	2.0	2.7	0	1.6
(2) Statements of actual cash flows only	0	1.5	0	3.6	1.2	1.4
(3) Both types used	100	95.5	98.0	93.7	98.8	97.0

Table 20.14 illustrates the use of estimated and historical cash flow statements for managerial purposes. As is obvious, nearly all companies make use of both types of statements. This is particularly true for large companies with capital stocks of ¥20 billion or more.

Table 20.15 shows the number of years that have passed since the company began using cash flow statements for managerial purposes. We see that over 60% of the companies have used such statements for twenty years or more, indicating that cash flow statements have generally been in use longer than funds statements, as illustrated in Table 20.6.

Table 20.16 illustrates the time periods projected in estimated cash flow statements used for managerial purposes. As can be seen, over half the companies make use of 6-month statements divided into months or quarters. Also one company in three employs 1-month statements. While the use of 1-year estimated cash flow statements divided into months or quarters is still quite high, it is interesting to note that long-term statements covering 2–5 years are not so widely used.

TABLE 20.15. *Cash flow statements: number of years in use (%)*

Years in use	A	B	C	D	E	Total
1–4	0	0	1.0	0	0	0.2
5–9	0	0	1.0	4.5	2.4	1.9
10–19	14.3	19.7	22.0	25.2	35.7	23.9
20–29	17.1	24.4	28.0	26.1	29.8	25.5
30 or more	57.1	43.9	39.0	27.0	23.8	36.7
No information	11.4	12.1	9.0	17.1	8.3	11.8

TABLE 20.16. *Projected time period for estimated cash flow statements (%)*

Time period	A	B	C	D	E	Total
1 month	34.3	26.2	32.0	31.8	26.5	30.4
1 month (divided into days, weeks, or beginning-middle-end)	20.0	24.6	13.0	20.6	16.9	18.6
3 months	20.0	12.3	13.0	16.8	19.3	16.2
6 months	11.4	9.2	18.0	20.6	15.7	15.8
6 months (divided into months or quarters)	52.9	52.3	55.0	49.5	42.2	50.4
1 year	12.9	10.8	12.0	12.2	8.4	11.3
1 year (divided into months or quarters)	24.3	29.2	30.0	11.2	16.9	21.6
2–5 years (divided into years)	7.1	7.7	4.0	5.6	4.8	5.6
Other	1.4	1.5	2.0	0.9	1.2	1.4

Table 20.17 illustrates the time period covered by historical cash flow statements. From it we see that 6-month statements divided into months or quarters and 1-month statements are the most frequently used, and their use is nearly the same. In comparison with the previous survey, the use of 1-year actual cash flow statements divided into months or quarters rose from 11% to 29%. That is to say, at present nearly one company in three prepares and uses such 1-year statements.

Table 20.18 shows the methods used in preparing historical cash flow statements. From it we see that two companies out of three prepare them as separate statements based on cash receipts and cash payments slips. The second most popular method is to prepare separate statements based on daily or monthly tabulations of cash flows. However, we also note a slight, though definite, increase over the previous survey in companies establishing accounts in the general or subsidiary ledgers for the purpose of keeping track of actual cash flows. This is especially true for companies

TABLE 20.17. *Time period covered by historical cash flow statements (%)*

Time period	A	B	C	D	E	Total
1 month	52.9	48.4	49.0	54.6	40.5	49.3
1 month (divided into days, weeks, or beginning-middle-end)	7.1	7.8	8.2	8.3	9.5	8.3
6 months	11.4	4.7	9.2	10.2	8.3	9.0
6 months (divided into months or quarters)	55.7	43.8	52.0	47.2	47.6	49.3
1 year	8.6	6.3	6.1	6.5	4.8	6.4
1 year (divided into months or quarters)	28.6	42.2	30.6	27.8	19.0	29.0
2–5 years (divided into years)	0	4.7	1.0	1.9	2.4	1.9
Other	1.4	4.7	2.0	0.9	0	1.7

TABLE 20.18. *Methods used in preparing historical cash flow statements (%)*

	A	B	C	D	E	Total
(1) Account for keeping track of actual cash flows established in general ledger	8.6	10.9	8.2	5.6	3.6	7.1
(2) Account for keeping track of actual cash flows established in subsidiary ledger	11.4	10.9	4.1	5.6	4.8	6.8
(3) Prepared as a separate statement based on daily or monthly tabulations of cash flows	22.9	17.2	27.6	23.1	25.0	23.6
(4) Prepared as a separate statement from cash receipts and payments slips	61.4	68.8	65.3	69.4	66.7	66.5
(5) Other methods	12.9	9.4	11.2	11.1	9.5	10.8

having capital of ¥10 billion or more, where one company in five uses one or the other of these approaches.

DISCUSSION

The present survey is an attempt to discover what sorts of changes have occurred in the practices of various companies regarding funds and cash flow statements since the previous survey, conducted in July of 1959. For this reason, questions asked in the present survey were nearly identical with those in the previous one. The most significant changes revealed by the present survey are as follows:

1. Of the companies returning their questionnaires, 68% replied that they made use of funds statements at the time of the first survey. In the present survey this figure had grown to 92%.

2. Of the responding companies, 57% replied that they made joint use of both estimated and actual funds statements, while in the present survey this figure had increased to 83%.

3. In the previous survey, three-quarters of the companies had made use of funds statements for less than ten years, while in the present survey three-quarters of the companies had more than ten years' experience with such statements.

4. The most frequently used statements of estimated and actual funds were those covering a period of six months, a finding that was the same for both surveys. The present survey revealed, however, that the use of one-year estimated and actual funds statements had increased noticeably.

5. The most frequently used statements of estimated and actual cash flows were those covering periods of six months or one month, the same as for the previous survey. The present study did reveal, however, a noticeable increase in the use of one-year cash flow statements, paralleling the increase seen for funds statements.

6. The most commonly used method for preparing statements of actual cash flows was as separate statements based on cash receipts and payments slips, a finding that did not differ from the previous survey. However, the present survey also revealed a slight, but definite, increase in the number of companies that established accounts for keeping track of cash flows, either in the general ledger or in subsidiary ledgers.

The period between the 1959 survey and the present has seen great changes in the economic environment surrounding these companies. There have been changes in the laws affecting the accounting structure as well. The Commercial Code, in particular, has undergone revision to allow for interim dividend payments, with the result that most companies have now switched from six-month to one-year accounting periods. This fact has had no small impact on the time period for which funds and cash flow statements are prepared.

In spite of the above, however, the present survey seems to indicate that the changes in practices that it reveals have, in fact, become firmly established in actual use, both for funds, and for cash flow statements.

In closing, I wish to express my sincerest gratitude to the persons and companies participating in the present survey. Without such co-operation, studies of any sort run the risk of turning out empty and meaningless results. I hope to continue investigation of funds and cash flow statements based on the present work.

21

How Accounting Department Heads of Major Japanese Companies View Cash Flow Statements

In 1971 the Accounting Principles Board of the American Institute of Certified Public Accountants published Opinion No. 19 (APB 19), 'Reporting Changes in Financial Position', which required all companies to prepare a statement summarizing changes in financial position, and to include it as part of their annual report, together with the income statement and balance sheet. Based on very broad concepts embracing all changes in financial position, the statement quickly gained acceptance in the United States, and even came to receive a CPA audit. Such practice came into the international limelight in 1977 with the publication of International Accounting Standards No. 7 (IAS 7), 'Statement of Changes in Financial Position'.

In 1987 the Financial Accounting Standards Board of the Financial Accounting Foundation published Statement of Financial Accounting Standards No. 95 (SFAS 95), 'Statement of Cash Flows', which supersedes APB 19, and requires disclosure of a statement of cash flows as part of the financial report, in place of a statement of changes in financial position. SFAS 95 became effective for annual financial statements for fiscal years ending after 15 July 1988. Such a development in the United States, long enjoying a position of leadership in accounting theory and practice around the world, cannot help but have great impact on accounting theory and practice in other nations.

In the explanatory notes to IAS 7 it is noted, 'the title "statement of changes in financial position" is used throughout this statement; in some countries "Statement of Source and Application of Funds", or a similar title, is used'. The following explanation is also given: 'For purposes of this statement, the term "funds" generally refers to cash, to cash and cash equivalents, or to working capital. In a statement of changes in financial position the particular use of the term is made clear' (para. 4).

The noteworthy feature of SFAS 95 is that by requiring disclosure of

From *Waseda Business and Economic Studies*, No. 29 (1993), 1–14.

a statement of cash flows in place of a statement of changes in financial position, it eliminates the ambiguities connected with the term 'funds', and indicates a certain trend. As is stated,

> A statement of cash flows shall explain the change during the period in cash and cash equivalents. The statement shall use descriptive terms such as 'cash' or 'cash and cash equivalents' rather than ambiguous terms such as 'funds'. The total amounts of cash and cash equivalents at the beginning and end of the period shown in the statement of cash flows shall be the same amounts as similarly titled line items or subtotals shown in the statements of financial position (balance sheet) as of those dates. (para. 7)

As the world rushes ahead towards the realization of a world economy, there is ever increasing pressure to adjust the accounting standards of the various individual nations to an international standard. Any deviation from such an international standard could very well become the cause of friction between nations. In this light, Japan too should seriously begin considering the inclusion of some sort of flow statement, be it a funds statement, a statement of changes in financial position, or a statement of cash flows, as part of a business's financial report.

STUDY PURPOSE AND METHOD

The present survey was conducted for the purpose of finding out what sort of knowledge accounting department heads of major Japanese businesses have regarding the statement of cash flows.

Companies Surveyed

The study group consisted of the 1,222 companies listed in Section 1 of the Tokyo Stock Exchange as of 1 October 1991.

Survey Method

Questionnaires were mailed out at the beginning of October 1991 in care of the accounting department heads of the above companies, together with the request that they be returned by the end of November. All questions were multiple choice. For some questions more than one answer was permitted.

Furthermore, in order to clarify just what is meant by the term 'statement of cash flows', and to illustrate the direct and indirect methods for reporting cash flows from operating activities, the two cash flow statement examples found in Appendix C of SFAS 95 were included along with the questionnaire.

TABLE 21.1. *Number of responding companies according to size*

Company size (total assets)	Number responding	Total responders (%)
¥1 trillion or more	56	14.3
¥500–999.9 billion	40	10.2
¥100–499.9 billion	142	36.3
¥50–99.9 billion	76	19.5
Less than 50 billion	77	19.7
Total	391	100.0

391 of the 1,222 companies surveyed returned their completed questionnaires, for a response rate of 32%. Table 21.1 shows the number of responding companies according to size of operations, as determined by the figure for total assets given on the latest balance sheet for each of the companies.

PURPOSE OF STATEMENT OF CASH FLOWS

SFAS 95 states that the purpose of a statement of cash flows is to provide relevant information regarding cash receipts and cash payments of an enterprise during a given period (para. 4). Such information, when used with related disclosures and information from the other financial statements, should help investors, creditors, and other interested parties in making the following judgements (para. 5):

(*a*) Assessment of the enterprise's ability to generated positive future net cash flows
(*b*) Assessment of the enterprise's ability to meet obligations, its ability to pay dividends, and its needs for external financing
(*c*) Assessment of the reasons for differences between net income and associated cash receipts and payments
(*d*) Assessment of the effects of both cash and non-cash investing and financing transactions on the financial position of the business for the period

In the event that the practice of including a statement of cash flows among the financial statements made public is adopted by Japan sometime in the future, for what sorts of purposes can it be expected to be helpful? The answer to this question is shown in Table 21.2. As we see, 'assessment of the enterprise's ability to meet obligations, its ability to pay dividends, and its needs for external financing' had the greatest response, followed by 'assessment of the effect of both cash and non-cash investing and financing transactions on the financial position of the business for that period'.

TABLE 21.2. *Purpose of statement of cash flows*

Response item	No. responding	%
Assessment of the enterprise's ability to generate positive future net cash flows	65	16.6
Assessment of the enterprise's ability to meet obligations, its ability to pay dividends, and its need for external financing	155	39.6
Assessment of the reasons of differences between net income and associated cash receipts and payments	48	12.3
Assessment of the effect of both cash and non-cash investing and financing transactions on the financial position of the business for that period	114	29.2
No Answer	9	2.3
Total	391	100.0

A so-called funds statement was used in the United States since the latter part of the nineteenth century as a means for disclosing information pertaining to the financial activities of a business. Such a statement was highly regarded as an indicator of the source and allocation of funds, and increasingly more and more companies came to include it in their annual reports along with the income statement and balance sheet. This was replaced in 1971 by the statement of changes in financial position, which was further replaced in 1987 by the statement of cash flows.

Japan was greatly influenced by such American accounting practices after the close of the Second World War, and much attention was given to funds flow statements. Although not included as part of the publicly disclosed financial report as such, the preparation and use of such statements came to be quite popular in actual business practice.

In most cases the object of computation, that is to say 'funds', is defined as net working capital, represented as the difference after current liabilities are deducted from current assets. This term retains a great amount of flexibility, however. Sometimes it might be used to mean cash, and at other times to indicate the difference after current liabilities are deducted from current assets, except inventory.

Contrary to this, SFAS 95 does away with such ambiguities connected with the term 'funds', defining the statement of cash flows as a statement whose purpose is to provide information about cash receipts and cash payments during a period, thereby focusing on cash, or cash and cash equivalents (para. 7).

As used in this context, the term 'cash equivalents' refers to short-term, highly liquid investments that are (*a*) readily convertible to determined

TABLE 21.3. *A statement of cash flows as the statement of choice for providing information about the financial activities of business*

Response item	No. responding	%
Agree	283	72.4
Not agree	106	27.1
No answer	2	0.5
Total	391	100.0

TABLE 21.4. *Alternative fund concepts*

Funds defined as	No. responding	%
Cash only	26	24.5
Cash and marketable securities	56	52.8
Current assets – inventory – current liabilities	6	5.7
Working capital (= current assets – current liabilities)	11	10.4
Other	6	5.7
No answer	1	0.9
Total	106	100.0

amounts of cash, and (*b*) so near maturity that there is virtually no risk of changes in value due to changes in interest rates. Generally speaking, only investments having maturities of three months or less fit this definition. Examples of cash equivalents given in SFAS 95 include short-term Treasury bills, commercial paper, etc.

Assuming that sometime in the future Japan does decide to adopt the practice of including among the other publicly disclosed financial statements a statement providing information about the financial activities of a business, would a statement of cash flows of this type be, in fact, the proper statement to choose?

The answer to this question is shown in Table 21.3, with nearly three-quarters of the responding companies expressing agreement, and one-quarter not agreeing. Table 21.4 indicates what other opinions are held concerning the definition of funds by the 106 companies not agreeing with the idea of having a statement of cash flows focus on cash, or cash and cash equivalents. As we see, over half these companies prefer the definition 'cash and marketable securities', with second place going to 'cash only'. Another possibility expressed was that, in order to prepare a statement of cash flows in a manner appropriate to the circumstances of the particular business, individual enterprises should be allowed to

TABLE 21.5. *Preferred method for indicating cash flows*

Response item	No. responding	%
Gross method	225	57.5
Net method	37	9.5
Gross method, with net method permitted for certain items	122	31.2
No answer	7	1.8
Total	391	100.0

select which definition of cash and cash equivalents they prefer under a given set of conditions, and then indicate their selection in a footnote.

FORM AND CONTENT OF THE STATEMENT OF CASH FLOWS

There are two methods for indicating cash flow during a period: the gross method, whereby cash receipts and cash payments are entered as gross amounts; and the net method, whereby related cash receipts and cash payments are cancelled out and only net amounts are entered. Although SFAS 95 states that it is generally more useful to indicate cash receipts and cash payments as gross amounts, it does admit the indication of net amounts for certain items (para. 11). If and when Japan does decide to adopt the practice of including a statement of cash flows, which of these methods should be used, the gross, or the net?

Table 21.5 shows which of these methods was preferred for indicating cash flow. Over half the companies expressed a preference for the gross method; nevertheless, nearly one company in three preferred a gross method with net amounts permitted for certain items. Table 21.6 indicates for which items the net method was thought useful. As can be seen, the most popular item was 'money procured or paid back on short-term loans', followed by 'increases or decreases in investment securities'. Other items suggested included changes in short-term operating funds such as increases or decreases in marketable securities or short-term loans, as well as increases or decreases due to advances, prepaid expenses, deposit payments, and warranties, etc.

SFAS 95 stipulates that a statement of cash flows shall classify cash receipts and cash payments as to whether they result from investing, financing, or operating activities. Investing activities include making and collecting loans, as well as acquiring and disposing of debt or equity instruments, tangible fixed productive assets, etc. Financing activities

TABLE 21.6. *Items to be indicated as net amounts*

Response item	No. responding	%
Cash flows from operating activities	19	9.8
Increases or decreases in tangible fixed assets	8	4.2
Increases or decreases in investment securities	40	20.7
Money procured or paid back on long-term loans and corporate bonds	26	13.5
Money procured or paid back on short-term loans	82	42.5
Other	17	8.8
No answer	1	0.5
Total	193	100.0

TABLE 21.7. *Three-way classification of cash flows*

Response item	No. responding	%
Accept	330	84.4
Not accept	57	14.6
No answer	4	1.0
Total	391	100.0

include amassing capital from shareholders, as well as returning it, the paying of shareholder dividends, and the borrowing and repaying of money. Operating activities include producing and selling goods, providing services, together with all other transactions not defined as investing or financing activities. In general, operating activities include those transactions having a bearing on the determination of net income.

If and at such time as Japan decides to adopt the practice of including a statement of cash flows, will this three-way classification of cash receipts and cash payments, whether resulting from investing, financing, or operating activities, find acceptance?

Table 21.7 indicates the response to this question. As we see, nearly all companies expressed acceptance of such a classification. Table 21.8 indicates the reason for non-acceptance. Most companies answered that a two-way classification into operating activities and other activities would be preferable, while only a few companies replied that there is no particular need for classifying receipts and payments of funds in this manner. Among the companies answering 'other', the opinion was expressed that a three-way division should be made into ordinary or current activities, investing and lending activities, and fund-procuring activities. Also, there

TABLE 21.8. *Reason for not accepting a three-way classification of cash flow*

Response item	No. responding	%
There is no particular need for such classification	13	22.8
A two-way classification into operating activities and other activities is preferable	41	71.9
Other	3	5.3
Total	57	100.0

TABLE 21.9. *Method for indicating cash flow from operating activities*

Response item	No. responding	%
Direct method	142	36.3
Indirect method	156	39.9
Either	85	21.7
No answer	8	2.1
Total	391	100.0

was the suggestion that operating and investing activities are very closely related, and the category to which loans, for instance, are delegated depends on the company. Therefore, say that, even though a three-way classification is adopted, it might be preferable to allow individual companies a certain amount of freedom in choosing which items belong to which categories, depending on the priorities of the company in question. Which choices are made could then be explained in a footnote, etc.

When reporting cash flows resulting from operating activities in the statement of cash flows, SFAS 95 recommends indicating gross cash receipts and gross cash payments for the various major headings, with their difference representing the net cash flow from operating activities (para. 27). This is known as the direct method of entry. At the same time, however, SFAS 95 also recognizes an alternative indirect method, whereby depreciation and other income items not involving receipts or payments of cash are removed from net income to give net cash flow (para. 28). If and when the use of a statement of cash flows is adopted in Japan, which of these two methods is preferable for indicating cash flow from operating activities?

The response to this question is shown in Table 21.9. Here we see that companies preferring the indirect method numbered slightly more than those preferring the direct method. Among those answering 'either method', some preferred the direct method, with the indirect method

TABLE 21.10. *Reporting non-cash investing and financing transactions*

Response item	No. responding	%
Necessary	258	66.0
Not necessary	128	32.7
No answer	5	1.3
Total	391	100.0

reserved for certain items, and vice versa, while still other companies said that both methods should be employed.

SFAS 95 also recognizes certain types of investing and financing activities which have an effect on assets and liabilities, but do not involve cash receipts or cash payments during the period. Information pertaining to such non-cash transaction—the conversion of debt to equity, for example—is to be reported in related disclosures. In the event that a statement of cash flows is eventually adopted in Japan, will it be necessary to report such non-cash transactions in this manner?

The response to this question is shown in Table 21.10, where approximately two-thirds of the companies deemed such reporting necessary, and the remaining one-third said it was unnecessary.

DISCUSSION

The present survey was conducted in an attempt to discover what attitudes the heads of accounting departments of major Japanese companies have regarding a statement of cash flows as a means for disclosing information pertaining to the financial activities of an enterprise. What we surveyed was their knowledge concerning such statements.

The practice of including some sort of statement depicting the funds or cash flows of a business as part of financial statements along with the income statement and balance sheet in annual reports was pioneered in the United States. An important step in this development was the 1987 publication of SFAS 95, 'Statement of Cash Flows', which stipulates the disclosure of a statement of cash flows in place of the previously reported statement of changes in financial position. Today such reporting represents the trend, not only in the USA, but internationally as well.

With the continued rapid emergence of a world economy, there is a pressing need for some sort of adjustment in the accounting standards of the various nations. At some time in the future Japan too will almost surely find it necessary to adopt the practice of including a statement of

TABLE 21.11. *Should a statement of cash flows attain the status of a major financial statement?*

Response item	No. responding	%
Support	231	59.1
Oppose	158	40.4
No answer	2	0.5
Total	391	100.0

TABLE 21.12. *Reason for opposing major financial statement status*

Response item	No. responding	%
Financial information is sufficiently disseminated by the income statement and balance sheet. There is no need for a statement of cash flows	12	7.4
Information regarding receipts and payments of cash is essential, but not enough to warrant inclusion as a major financial statement. Appended disclosure is adequate	105	64.4
A lot of work is involved in the preparation of a cash flow statement, and its value to investors and creditors does not always outweigh the cost of preparation	37	22.7
Other	6	3.7
No answer	3	1.8
Total	163	100.0

cash flows as part of the financial statements. The questions in the present survey were constructed with just such a development in mind.

The present practice in Japan is to indicate a statement of cash flows in the annual securities report, which is filed with the Ministry of Finance. Will the practice of including some sort of statement depicting the cash flows of a business within the financial report itself, and on an equal footing with the income statement and balance sheet, find acceptance among Japanese companies?

The answer to this question is shown in Table 21.11, with nearly 60% of the responding companies supporting such a move, but over 40% opposing it. The reasons for opposing it are shown in Table 21.12. Well over half of the opposing companies indicated that, while such information is essential, appended disclosure is adequate. Nearly one-quarter of the respondents remarked that the cost and effort involved in preparing such a statement outweigh any benefits that might be obtained.

In addition to the above, the following problems were also pointed out:

1. Because of the complex manner in which operational and financing activities are entangled in the receipt and payment of cash, a high level of specialized knowledge is necessary properly to interpret information from a schedule of cash receipts and payments. For example, a deficit in operating receipts and payments does not in every case indicate a deterioration of the company's financial position. In fact, it might be the result of improvement. Since general investors could easily misinterpret such information, it should be limited to appended schedules intended for specialists.

2. About the only parties making use of cash flow statements are institutional investors and financing institutions, and not the general public. They cannot, therefore, in actual fact be considered necessary. Even if the reporting of such information were to become mandatory, it would be necessary to establish formats for different types of enterprises.

3. In the case of the banking industry, the classification of cash is not always as clear as it is in most other business enterprises, and there is a question as to just what information is actually transmitted by the presently employed statement of cash flows.

4. A statement of cash flows is important, but whether it should be included as part of financial statements on an equal footing as the income statement and balance sheet can only be discussed from the viewpoint of cost vs. benefit, taking into consideration the work-load of the company, its auditing schedule, etc. If the company conducts a large number of transactions, then this can only be done by using a computer and making a very detailed analysis.

5. Since a statement of cash flows is already included in the annual securities report, then whether or not it is included in the audited financial report would make no difference at all in the amount of information going to shareholders. As things stand, I do not actively object to submitting such a statement as part of the financial report, but I can find no reason for agreeing to this either.

For over forty years now, I have argued that some sort of flow of funds statement should be provided as part of the financial report, without ever insisting that this be a statement of cash flows. The present study surveyed the heads of accounting departments, and the views expressed therein represent the opinions of those persons directly involved in the preparation and disclosure of financial reports. From the results of the study, I was forced to recognize the need for developing much more convincing arguments before such proposals for including a statement of cash flows in the financial report will find general acceptance in Japan. It might be interesting some day to survey the views held by, say, certified public accountants.

Moreover, the opinion was also expressed that, in this age of subsidiaries, affiliations, and other types of conglomerate groupings, what is needed is a shift in emphasis from thorough disclosure of individual companies to complete and adequate disclosure for such groups as a whole. Individual financial reports could easily be misleading for investors. This same idea would hold true for statements of cash flows as well.

In conclusion I should like to express sincere appreciation to the many people who co-operated in the present survey. Their thoughtful responses to sometimes very irritating questions will certainly prove invaluable to my continued investigation in this area. In fact, I consider it my duty to produce meaningful results.

INDEX

The manufacturer's authorised representative in the EU for product
safety is Oxford University Press España S.A. of El Parque Empresarial
San Fernando de Henares, Avenida de Castilla, 2 - 28830 Madrid
(www.oup.es/en or product.safety@oup.com). OUP España S.A. also acts
as importer into Spain of products made by the manufacturer.
Printed and bound by CPI Group (UK) Ltd, Croydon, CR0 4YY
14/09/2026
02216286-0002